O HOLY MOUNTAIN!

O HOLY MOUNTAIN!

Journal of a Retreat on Mount Athos

M. BASIL PENNINGTON, O.C.S.O.

Michael Glazier, Inc.
Wilmington, Delaware

First paperback edition published 1984 by Michael Glazier, Inc.,
1723 Delaware Avenue, Wilmington, Delaware 19806

ISBN: 0-385-13530-0 (cloth); 0-89453-382-7 (paperback)
Library of Congress Catalog Card Number: 83-83054
Copyright © 1978 and 1984 by Cistercian Abbey of Spencer, Inc.

Grateful acknowledgement is made to the following for permission
to use previously copyrighted material:
Cistercian Publications, *William of Saint Thierry: Golden Epistle*.
Reprinted by permission of the publisher.

Scripture texts used in this work are taken from the NEW AMERICAN
BIBLE, copyright © 1970, by the Confraternity of Christian Doctrine,
Washington, D.C., are used by permission of copyright owner. All
rights reserved.

To
Archimandrite Aimilianos
and his sons,
with gratitude

CONTENTS

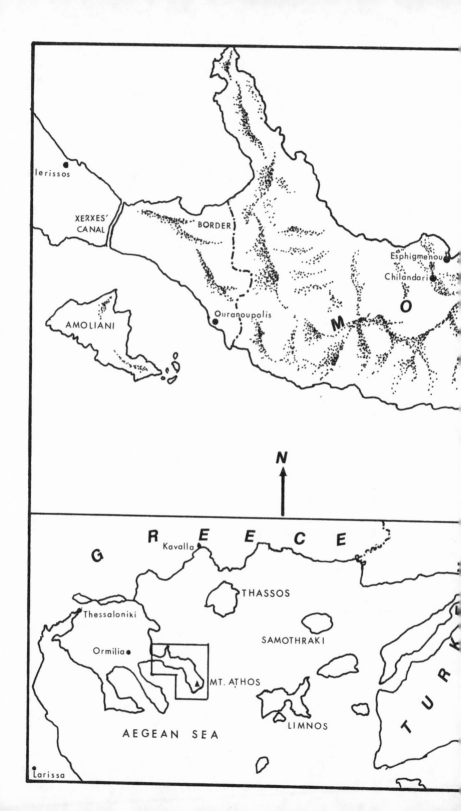

THE MONASTIC REPUBLIC
OF MOUNT ATHOS

0 ——————— KM ——————— 10
0 ——————— MILES ——————— 6

● Orthodox monasteries
■ Western monastery
▲ Sketes ● Towns

AEGEAN

SEA

N

...ographou

Vatopedi

Konstamonitou

Docheiariou

Ptopheti
Iliou

Ag.
Andreou

Karyes

Pantokratoros

Stavronikita

Iviron

Xenophontos

Koutloumousiou

Philotheou

Ag.
Panteleimonos
(Rossiko)

Xeropotamou

Karakallou

Daphni

T

I

Simonos Petras

H

Morphonou

SUMMIT
2033 METERS
(6670 FT.)

Megisti
Lavra

Grigoriou

O

S

Dionysiou

Prodromou

Ag. Pavlou

New Skete

Ag. Anna

Kavsokalyvia

Karoulia

Katounakia

BEFORE

❧❀❧

❧ I don't know in what century the Swiss invented the cuckoo clock, but this distracting little item, along with the printed books that filled the high bookcases and the few photographs on the walls, was the only indication that we were not witnessing a scene from the twelfth or fourteenth century. Archimandrite Aimilianos sat in the corner behind a small table with a rich covering, as is the practice of prelates in the Byzantine world. His attire, the simple black robe of the monk, the heavy leather belt, the black skouphos—does it take its origin from the fez? It looks quite like it—in itself gave no indication that this was the Hegumen, the superior of the monastery, but his whole bearing spoke of dignity. And the calm of his well-rounded face and his limpid eyes spoke of something more—an ever-present Vision of Peace, a ray of the Taboric Light.

Across from the prelate, on a wicker settee, sat another monk in a somewhat different habit—one in the know would recognize it as the humble gray robe of the twelfth-century Cistercian. That monk was myself. The scene was in the corner reception room of the hegumenate of the medieval Athonite Monastery of Simonos Petras. The Archimandrite had just said: "It is unheard of. Never before has a Catholic monk stayed so long on the Holy Mountain." But love was to transcend history in this historic place, so bound by the traditions and customs of history. And thus began my retreat, one which I certainly had not intended to be a historical landmark or even a significant ecumenical event, but which perhaps in God's designs will prove to be that.

It may seem strange to some, the idea of a Trappist monk going on retreat. Isn't his whole life a retreat? It is in a way. He does ordinarily go apart and stay apart. But strictly speaking, a retreat is a temporary thing—a stepping back for the moment, in order to be able to step forward with renewed vigor to fuller accomplishment. Every person—no matter what be his course in life—needs retreats, whether they be quiet moments of daily meditation and reflection or longer periods of withdrawal. And the monk is no exception. It is true, he would ordinarily find this time of retreat within his own monastery, in the heart of his monastic community, or perhaps in a hermitage in the woods behind the abbey. But there are exceptions to every rule. And this particular monk was convinced that at this particular moment in his life's journey the Lord wanted him to go a bit farther apart for his retreat, and his Father Abbot confirmed this discernment.

When I was a young religious I was one day working with a group of monks landscaping our newly constructed retreat house. As we were easing an eighteen-foot maple into the hole prepared for it, it suddenly lunged forward. And there was Brother B., arms and legs waving excitedly, the tree resting squarely on his tummy. At this point he came forth with one of those classical statements: "This wasn't in the postulants' guide!" I have always retained that "word" as something of a résumé of my life as a monk.

Although I was in the middle of the first row below the balcony of Saint Peter's, in 1958, when the new Pontiff stepped out, I shared the common difficulty of getting that roly-poly little pastor in white to focus in the spot that so long had been occupied by the lean ascetic figure of Pius XII. Certainly as I bowed my head to receive his first papal blessing, I had no suspicion how much Pope John was to affect the course of my own life—as well as that of the rest of the human family.

Three months later I joined the mob that crammed the street cars going to Saint Paul's-Outside-the-Walls. We weren't even beginning to get used to this Pope who moved about so freely—a lover of tradition, of history, an incarnation, as it were, of them, and yet so free of them. Oh, how he enjoyed the papal pomp, this childlike pastor! He went up and down the nave and all four aisles of the great basilica on his portable throne, surrounded by the ostrich fans and the arcs of powerful lights, the silver trumpets vying with the shouts of the wildly enthusiastic crowd: *Viva il Papa!* And then he entered the monastery next door, dropped all the fine trimmings, and joined the monks in a cup of coffee. Again, as the Holy Father spoke of a vision —of a synod, a council, a new code of Canon Law—I had no glimmer of what this might mean for me and for all my brothers and sisters across the face of the earth.

The Synod came and went, not much of a ripple on the face of the sea of time—just as had been predicted. Then came the Council. And again—one of those things not in the postulants' guide—I found myself in the Square as the river of white miters flowed into Saint

Peter's. Like so many others in Rome at that time, I was caught in its current, one of many quasi *periti* (experts). It was exciting—yes! It was demanding—yes! It was hopeful—yes! It was heartbreaking—yes, yes! How could we ever bring home to our brothers or even live out in our own lives what the Spirit gave us in those days? We had to try—and pay the price.

One thing led to another. Code was to follow Council. I soon had a couple of degrees in Canon Law. But the new Code for this Church that was happily becoming aware of the fact that it is a people of every tribe and tongue and nation—and must be that and rejoice in it and respect it—her new Code could only be very generic, trace out only the broadest and most fundamental lines of community structure and life. The particular laws of national conferences and religious institutes and monastic federations would be more significant. And so we began those journeys to meetings at home and abroad to prepare the new laws—the section for monks in the new Code, the constitutions for our own Order.

But law must follow life, not make life conform to it. Renewal must begin in the hearts and spirits of persons and communities. For us this meant getting in touch with our Cistercian Fathers. We have to get to know them, their times, their wisdom, if we are to live out of their fullness in today's world. And so soon I was engaged in an immense translation project, in a new publishing house, in international symposia, in a center for studies.

The years were full and busy. And there were other dimensions, above all the ecumenical: discovering the richness of contemplative and monastic life among our Anglican brothers and sisters, exploring our common roots with our Orthodox brethren; and beyond the ecumenical—discovering a communality with the ancient monastic traditions of the Far East.

I have always believed that the Church is the whole of the People of God and that every baptized Christian should exercise fully his responsible part in the daily program, leaving those called to special ministries free to fulfill them in holiness. So in 1973 I was happy to turn over the responsibilities for the translation project, the publications, the meetings, the conferences, and the symposia to the capable people at the newly established Institute for Cistercian Studies and go off to Europe to the Orthodox-Cistercian Symposium at Oxford University. This rich and enriching sharing proved to be the first step toward my retreat on Mount Athos. After the symposium I went East to return the visits of our Orthodox confreres and paid my first visit to the Holy Mountain. It was a fairly short visit, though longer than those ordinarily allowed. I was deeply impressed. In fact, my soul was marked, I am sure, indelibly.

In a way I think we can say Mount Athos is the monk's native land. Certainly, it is the only *monastic* republic existing in the world today. And it boasts of being the oldest existing republic. Over ten centuries ago the first Synod was formed. And still today the Holy Mountain is ruled by the Synod, consisting of the representatives of the twenty autonomous monasteries: Megisti Lavra, Aghiou Pavlou, Dionysiou, Grigoriou, Simonos Petras, Xeropotamou, Aghios Panteleimonos, Xenophontos, Docheiariou, Konstamonitou, Zographou, Chilandari, Esphigmenou, Vatopedi, Pantokratoros, Iviron, Stavronikita, Koutloumousiou, Philotheou, and Karakallou; you will meet most of these names again in the course of the journal. The Synod in its turn chooses a Council of four men, one of whom, the Protos, is the head of the Holy Government. In practice, it is the Secretary of the Iera Kinotis (Holy Community) who handles most of the daily affairs. There is a Greek governor resident on the Holy Mountain and a small contingent of soldiers, but they are supposed to concern themselves only with external affairs. Spiritually, Mount Athos is directly under the Patriarch of Constantinople.

Besides the twenty monasteries, and dependent upon them, are a variety of other types of monastic establishments. A kellion is a small, relatively independent community under the guidance of a Gerontas (Elder, or Spiritual Father). It has its own liturgical life and order of Services (Offices) and usually supports itself by crafts and its garden and orchard. The name "skete" is used to denote various types of monastic communities. Some of the Russian sketes (Aghiou Andreou [Saint Andrew's], Propheti Iliou [Prophet Elijah's]) and the Romanian Skete (Prodromou [the Forerunner's, i.e. Saint John the Baptist's]) were quite large—larger than many of the monasteries—yet the Greeks did not want to give them the status of monastery in order to keep secure control of the Mountain. (There are seventeen Greek monasteries, one Russian [Aghios Panteleimonos, or Saint Panteleimon], one Bulgarian [Zographou], and one Serbian [Chilandari]. Each monastery has one vote in the Iera Kinotis.) So they were left with the rank of sketes. "Skete" usually means a very small household of two or three to six or so monks (today it sometimes means one) or a cluster of such households like Kavsokalyvia or Aghia Anna. And then there are the many hermitages where monks seek a life of the fullest possible solitude. One is very slow to encroach upon this. In all there were about fourteen hundred monks living on the Holy Mountain at the time of my retreat. This is perhaps three hundred more than I found in 1973.

The hermit and the monk in the skete will usually have his rule of life—his canon—blessed by his Spiritual Father, although there is a basic general rule for the skete providing especially for those who live in a colony of households. These would maintain a common church —a kyriakon—where they would gather on Sundays and feasts and a guesthouse—a kanonikon. On most days they would hold Services— or Offices, as we call them in the West—in their own house-chapel, perhaps have Liturgy if one member is a priest, but the Services would be simpler than those in the monastery, and "prayer on the rope"—the repetition of the Jesus Prayer ("Lord Jesus Christ, Son of the Living God, have mercy on me") counted on the knots of the prayer cord, the komvoschinion—might replace some of them altogether.

In the monasteries, the Services hold a central place. This is not to say that the Hegumen may not exempt particular monks from many or even all the Services so that they can prolong their prayer in the cell or complete the necessary work of the monastery—cooking, baking, gardening, maintenance, hospitality, study, icon painting, etc. The content (psalms, hymns, canticles, troparia [antiphons and responsories], readings) and structure of the Services are very similar to that in the West, the division being determined by the common tradition. But the brothers on the Mountain tend to celebrate several Services at the same time. The Midnight Service (vigils, or Matins), Orthros (Lauds), and the First Hour (Prime) are celebrated in the early morning, sometimes with the addition of the Third and Sixth Hours (Tierce and Sext). The Ninth Hour (None) is celebrated before Vespers in the evening, and Apodeipnon (Compline) at sunset. In fervent communities, Liturgy (Mass) is offered daily after the First or Sixth Hour, though on fast days (usually Monday, Wednesday, and Friday) it is not celebrated in the main church, the katholikon, but in one of the small chapels about the monastery. In addition, on the fast days before the meal (there is only one community

meal on fast days, though a little something left over from lunch
may be taken by the individual monk in the evening) the Paraklisis,
or Service of Comfort (in the sense of strengthening), is sung. In the
evening before Apodeipnon the monks will pray the long and very
beautiful Acathist Hymn in honor of the Holy Virgin Mother of
God.

The monks' day begins—at Saint Benedict legislates for the monks
of the West—at the seventh hour of the night, an hour or so after
midnight. But on Mount Athos it is more literally that, for on the
Holy Mountain they follow Byzantine time. Twelve o'clock is when
the sun goes down. (But, perhaps as a witness to the freedom that
ever prevails among monks, one monastery—Iviron—computes its
time from sunrise. This, though, has its practicality, for they are on
the eastern side of the Mountain.) Some monasteries do change
their clocks each day; others, only every month or so. Each monastery has its own time. (In my journal I ordinarily used Greek civil
time as being a sort of standard time.) And the Mountain has its
own calendar, too. Though all the rest of the Orthodox world—except the Greek Schismatic Church and the zealot Russian Church-
Outside-of-Russia—has accepted the calendar reform of Pope Gregory XIII, on Mount Athos they still follow the Julian calendar.
This calendar is now thirteen days behind the Gregorian. Hence, you
will notice a shifting of dates in my journal and references to the
West celebrating different feasts.

When they first rise, the monks on the Mountain have a period of
prayer in the cell, more frequently with a particular canon (a rule de-
termining what prayer they will say—so many komvoschinions and
so many metania [prostrations]) from their Spiritual Father. They
will then gather for the Midnight Service in the liti (the outer part
of the katholikon, the narthex). This is followed by Orthros, the
First Hour, and Liturgy in the katholikon. On an ordinary day these
might last four or five hours. Then the monks return to their cells for
rest, prayer, or study, or they may have work to do. Each one's schedule is worked out with the Gerontas. The Third and Sixth Hours or
the Paraklisis precedes the meal, which comes around midmorning.
The siesta is not as common as one would have expected. Work is in
order after lunch, though it might be preceded by some time of
relaxation. The Ninth Hour (in the liti these lesser Hours serve as a
sort of preparation for the principal Hours in the katholikon) and

Vespers come two or three hours before sunset and are followed by a
meal on nonfast days.

On the eve of great feasts and Sundays (though there are many exceptions) Little Vespers is celebrated (a half hour instead of an hour
or more) and there is no Apodeipnon. About an hour after sunset
the Agripnia—the All-Night Vigil—begins, which includes Great
Vespers and Orthros, possibly special processions and the blessing of
water, and goes on to Liturgy and a festive meal. The whole might
be a twelve- or fourteen-hour nonstop Service, though more usually it
runs only eight or nine hours and may have a break before Liturgy.

The program I have described is that of the cenobium. There are
basically two types of monasteries: cenobitic and idiorrhythmic. In
the former the monks live a shared life, eat in a common refectory,
and obey a Hegumen whom they have elected for life. In the renewed monasteries the Hegumen is usually also the Gerontas, or Spiritual Father, of the community, but not always. According to the
typicon (constitution) of Mount Athos, he must be a priest. Monks
in idiorrhythmic monasteries have relative independence. Each receives an allowance from the common income of the monastery and
can add to it (and might well need to) by his own labors. He is subject in some ways to his chosen Spiritual Father. The monks might
elect a Hegumen on the eve of the monastery's feast so that there
will be someone to preside. But he will resign the next day. As
Pro-hegumen (resigned Hegumen), he might, with an elected council, be asked to oversee the administration of the monastery. It can
readily be seen that such a system is open to serious abuses or at least
a certain amount of laxity. It is in the idiorrhythmic monasteries that
one finds some glaring economic inequalities and such indulgences as
smoking, eating meat, and reading newspapers. There were historical
reasons for the rise of idiorrhythmic monasticism in the fourteenth
century, and some idiorrhythmic monasteries are very fervent. But
today it is the cenobitic communities that are getting all the vocations and some of the idiorrhythmic houses have returned to cenobitism.

It has been with a certain amount of misgiving that I have decided
to share the pages of my journal by publication. They were not originally written with publication in view. Things had to be filled out
somewhat to be at all intelligible. Much of the lore was recorded for
its flavor more than for its content. It would take volumes to put ev-

erything fully into context. Entries which, standing by themselves
seem flat and uninspired, have immense meaning for the writer because they attempt to capture a moment of light, an insight pulsat-
ing with life, because it was a moment of communication with the
Beloved. The behavioral people tell us that in a conversation the
words are a very small part of the communication—the presence is
the thing that really communicates. We all know this from experience. And a journal only captures the words—the small part. And
these words—what there are of them—are words out of silence. It
was the silence that was more significant.

If one feels very vulnerable sharing a journal, that vulnerability is
heightened by this inadequacy of expression. But in the case of this
particular journal, there is one added fact that makes it even more a
limited and inadequate expression. It comes from a time of retreat
when the writer was purposely stepping back or out of his usual
world vision and concern and centering upon his own personal being
before his God. This leads to a certain tunnel vision, productive of
a helpful intensity during a time of retreat but crippling if it is carried
over into the pilgrimage of life. Furthermore, during this retreat, because of the place and situation chosen, what contacts were had were
almost exclusively with our Orthodox brethren. Other dimensions of
the writer's participation in humankind's struggle for divinization in
no wise surfaces.

Yet in spite of misgivings, I have decided to share these pages with
you and others. Even if it does leave me exposed and vulnerable—we
are all called by our Master to lay down our lives for one another—I
hope our good Lord will use this revelation of my weakness and
struggles and hopes and of his great goodness and mercy to bring a
little more hope and love into your life.

While it was not intended, my visit on the Holy Mountain seems
to have been a healing thing, a step, however small, in the coming
together in love of the separated sister Churches. By this frank and
humble sharing, perhaps the healing can be furthered. Mount Athos
is the heart of Orthodoxy. Many writers have previously tried to present it to the West. But I do not think that ever before has one from
the West been able so to experience it. As a monk who has long
lived the monastic life and was allowed to live within the Athonite
community for an unprecedented period of time, I have been able to
acquire a specially intimate acquaintance with life on the Holy

Mountain. Perhaps some of the details I share here will be of interest only to other monks. But my experience indicates a widespread interest in what goes on in monasteries and monastic life. Perhaps it is that bit of monk that resides in every person that is responding to something precious to it. I hope that what I am sharing will not in any way be misunderstood or cause any misunderstandings. I hope there is nothing that in any way will offend my Orthodox brothers and sisters, whom I sincerely love. I wanted to share very deeply their life; I am grateful that I was allowed to; I consider it a privilege. I want in no wise to be critical. But I do want to be honest and so I have let stand my own thoughts and feelings as they were expressed.

The journal has been edited very little. What has been added was added to make the material more intelligible or complete. The subtractions have been made to avoid too much repetition; there is still some of that, as I spontaneously re-expressed strong impressions over and over again in my daily jottings. There is one significant addition. I integrated into this journal, essentially in the section "Around the Mountain," updated pages from my 1973 journal in order to give a fuller picture of the Holy Mountain. At that time I did go all around the Mountain. This time—a retreat—I moved about as little as possible.

If in the course of reading the journal you feel at times a bit confused—or more than a bit—by the way dates and time change, by the inconsistency between theory and practice, by a sense of vagueness as to how it all fits together, please do not be surprised. That was certainly my own experience and in presenting the journal with a minimum of editing I hope to allow you to share in that experience. Mount Athos is in many ways truly another world, a world apart. It is good to sense that. At the same time, these entries, which speak frankly of the daily life of the monks even down to intimate and homely details, will explode some of the popular myths which surround the Holy Mountain, such as the oft repeated one purporting that the exclusion of females extends even to the animal kingdom. There are, in fact, lots of hens and mother cats who find their homes among the monks and render due service.

I have added at the end of this volume a glossary of places and terms which would be unfamiliar to the average reader. The first time each of these appears in the text it is marked with an asterisk (*). If all the Greek terms so commonly used had been deleted from the journal, it would have lost some of its flavor and lost some of its value for those who are reading it to increase their feel of their Orthodox brethren.

I want to express publicly my very deep and sincere gratitude to Archimandrite Aimilianos and his community. This man of God is one of the truly great persons I have had the privilege to know in my lifetime. His great love for me as a brother in Christ called forth the love and respect of his community and the acceptance of the brethren on the Holy Mountain. His kindness was fully human and reached down to details that only love can dictate. Not one of the least joys of heaven—if it does not come sooner—will be when we can fully enjoy our complete oneness in Christ. I thank all my Fathers and Brothers on the Holy Mountain.

I want also to express my gratitude to my own Father in Christ, Abbot Thomas of Spencer, another truly great Spiritual Father, and all my Brothers at Spencer, for allowing and supporting this time of retreat, and indeed my whole monastic life. And I must add a special word of thanks to my brother Father Robert, who produced the sketches for this volume.

And last but not least, a thank-you to Sister Mary Whalen of the Sisters of Providence of Holyoke for the many long hours of work and infinite patience it took to turn my raw material into a readable typescript. May the Lord reward her as only he can.

FATHER BASIL
Monk of Spencer

FIRST DAYS

Karyes

Monday, May 31, 1976

In ways it has been a busy day—in other ways a day filled with waiting and praying. Now I sit in Logan International Airport with an hour or so before the takeoff. I feel good, trusting, yet little spurts of nerves arise—so much ahead is question. What will the Lord ask in these days and months ahead? Very much, I hope.

Seven months is a big piece of life, but if, by his mercy, it is a time of real growth, new fuller commitment, the end of self-seeking, the beginning of truly seeking God—that's a lot. Ask and you shall receive. And so, Lord, I do ask. Create in me, Lord, a truly Christian heart, a monastic heart, a pure heart. After years of compromise in my monastic life, I hope, by your grace and life I can begin to live a total "yes." Help me, Lord. And make all my goings, like Mary's Visitation, a bringing of Christ with his joy and peace and grace to all I encounter. I renew my total consecration to you, Mary. And now I pray for the journey, for Germany, for Greece, for those I leave behind and those I will meet.

Tuesday, June 1 – A.M.

We are approaching Frankfurt. They have fed us too much on the plane and there was only time for two hours of sleep at the most. When we boarded they gave us, or rather offered us, newspapers. I took two. After spending a lot of time reading them, I turned to the Bible, which I much enjoyed. I am beginning the New American version. I wonder why I get so sucked into the "news." This morning my neighbor was reading *Time*. I found my eyes straying. Curiosity is very strong in me. This leads to distraction. Seek first the Kingdom—and all will be added. Your Father knows your needs. I shall work at constant prayer in full presence to the "now." Father, please help me.

Wednesday, June 2

꿈❧ We arrived in good time at Thessaloniki* but I had to wait a long time for the bus from the airport. Most took taxis. I was glad I waited—as a poor monk should—for when I arrived at the terminal, Dimitrios Maniotis was waiting for me. He looks very good, with a fine beard now. I was disappointed to learn that I had to wait till today to go to the Ministry of Foreign Affairs office. His father, a lawyer, investigated. We went to the Kaimakis house. Then I visited the Maniotises. Later Paul Kaimakis and I visited churches—some real gems of Byzantine architecture, though relatively little in good icons or frescoes. They eat very late here—around eleven. I got to bed near twelve after two long days.

This morning we celebrated the Ascension. All the children came to Liturgy* at Aghia Sophia. Father Kaimakis presided at the Liturgy. The sacristan spoke English and was very kind. It is difficult to know what to say or do. Feelings are very varied toward Catholics and toward Americans. Father Kaimakis expressed his surprise that I should be able to stay so long on the Holy Mountain. We shall see.

Mr. Maniotis took me to the Ministry office at eleven. There was much paper work. If one is a clergyman the Metropolitan has to get him permission from the Patriarch of Constantinople. Then the Ministry gives permission to stay on the Mountain, but for only four days. Then the police (on the other side of the city) give permission to go out to the Mountain. We returned to the Ministry office—two taxi rides across the city—to try to arrange for a longer stay, but got nothing more.

At one, everything closes down in the city for lunch and siesta. John Kanonides came at four and took me to his house. His father is a retired school teacher. He said I would always be welcome there. We talked for four hours. John is studying medicine and hopes to come to America after he finishes at the university. John represents that very small percentage of Greek students who are not all taken up with politics, but are dedicated to the Church and intent on leading a deep Christian life and working for the renewal of Orthodoxy.

We had ice cream and they invited me to dinner, but I had a date at eight with Dimitrios. He and I visited more churches and ruins, from the Roman period of Thessaloniki, and he spoke at length on art history. Also he voiced the Greek antipathy, especially strong among the students, toward Kissinger and America's intervention in the Cyprus affair on behalf of Turkey.

Thursday, June 3 / May 21

꧁ I arose around five and slipped out without disturbing my hosts. The bus left at six. It was warm and humid in the bus but the three-and-a-half-hour ride over the mountains was beautiful. Driving around many hairpin turns didn't seem to bother the driver. He kept up a lively conversation all the way. I am sure this long complicated journey is an important part of my retreat. A going out, a seeking, a feeling of loneliness, a certain dying to self, to known patterns, usual comforts, secure surroundings, into the unknown. I sense more the need of a certain stability, security, to be free to enter into deeper prayer. I am trying to pray constantly, but necessary attention to what is around me, which is prayer, drifts into curiosity and forgetfulness.

Ouranoupolis* has greatly grown since my visit three years ago. But the area down by the jetty and the old tower is unchanged. The little wicker chairs in front of the café are the same as the ones I sat on then waiting for the boat. And Mrs. Loch's door still stands open to offer monk and pilgrim a hearty cup of good English tea.

At eleven the boat left for Daphni.* Among the passengers was an American now living in Rome but originally from Newton, Massachusetts—Richard Kamm, a sculptor. Also, there was Father Athanasios, a monk from Simonos Petras,* who has gone with five others to help the depleted Monastery of Konstamonitou.* He is Secretary of the Holy Community* for this year. He welcomed me most warmly with the traditional offerings after we finally got to his office in Karyes.* But first we had a two-and-a-half-hour boat ride—a glorious and exciting experience: the fantastically blue sea and sky, the rugged mountain coast, the ancient monasteries, one after the other leaping suddenly into view or gradually arising on the horizon—a bite of pasta with the American sculptor, an hour bus ride up to

Karyes, and a visit to the police. And we lost thirteen days in the bargain—we are back to May 21.

Father Athanasios asked how long I wanted to stay, said he could give me only seven days' permission, then I would have to see the governor, who would readily give me up to a year. He also informed me that Father Vasileios, the Hegumen* of Stavronikita,* and Father Aimilianos, the Hegumen of Simonos Petras, were both away but would return in five or six days.

I took the bus at four-thirty, after a brief visit to the Protaton,* and then walked on down to Stavronikita. The situation is difficult here. Father Vasileios will be away ten days or more. Father Grigorios, the assistant superior, is very kind. And Father Symeon, from Athens, who speaks English, has been at pains to make me feel comfortable and welcome. But they have indicated in a tactful way that some of the community are opposed to my presence. This was evident at Vespers.* As I started to enter the nave with the other guests, a young monk went out of his way to ask each one if he were Orthodox, and when I said I was Catholic, he told me I could not enter but must stay in the liti.* Father Grigorios and Father Symeon were obviously embarrassed by this exclusion. The last time I was here I was allowed in the church with the others. I assured them I understood. Evidently there had been a discussion about my visit when I wrote to Father Vasileios. When I asked to stay until he came back, Father Grigorios told me it had been agreed that I could stay four or five days to visit with the Hegumen, and that was all. He suggested that I stay only a day now, go on to visit some other monasteries, and return for Pentecost when it would be possible to see Father.

There is a young French postulant, here seven months, Jean Pierre. He is very friendly and has helped give me a better idea of things. He had met Father Vasileios in Dijon but visited all around the Mountain before deciding to stay here.

The schedule at Stavronikita:

    2:30   Rise, prayer in the cell
    3:30   Services,* Liturgy, breakfast
  12:30   Lunch
    6:30   Vespers, supper, some chores and free time, Acathist Hymn,* Apodeipnon*

Monday, Wednesday, and Friday are fast days; on these days the monks take supper—as they do breakfast each day—informally, self-service, and the guests eat by themselves.

Friday, May 22

The American sculptor arrived for lunch.

I am having trouble deciding whether to go on to Simonos Petras and get settled there or to go on to Chilandari* to see Father Kallistos Ware or to the Skete* of Propheti Iliou* to see Father Seraphim. I think it might be good to visit Simonos Petras before seeing the governor.

The day is heavily overcast and there have been light showers, but it is cool. I have slept a lot, catching up on past fatigue. I realize how uncertainty and insecurity militate against freedom and peace to pray. One must be very detached, or questions constantly arise to the surface and one is searching for solutions and ways of handling the situation. I realize too what a creature of comfort I am. In a cell so sparsely furnished I do not readily settle down. The chairs are very small and awkward for me. The floor is linoleum. The bed has a spring that gives way too easily and a very thin mattress. Things are quite clean and well kept. Father Leo, the guestmaster and porter, does not seem very friendly but he does his work well. Under the regulations, which are posted on the wall—

RESPECT THE SILENCE.

DO NOT TALK AFTER EVENING PRAYER (but I heard a lot of talking last night).

WALK IN THE CORRIDOR ONLY WHEN YOU ARE PROPERLY DRESSED (I guess some were going to the washrooms with less on).—

there is written large:

STAY IN THE MONASTERY IS FOR ONE DAY ONLY.

At the point where the road for Stavronikita branches off there is a notice:

PLEASE DO NOT VISIT IN THE EVENING, ONLY THE MORNING, BECAUSE YOU MAY NOT FIND A BED AND IT WILL BE TOO LATE TO GO ELSEWHERE.

Father told me that last year some nights they had as many as forty bedded down on the terrace in sleeping bags and blankets. Tourism was so heavy last year that the Holy Community has succeeded in getting the civil authorities to agree to give permission to only ten foreigners a day and for a stay of only four days—it used to be for seven days. But Greeks are still free to come without permission. They try to keep guests at a minimum here and the atmosphere is very peaceful (on the surface—underneath I sense such tensions as I mentioned above; it is sad that prejudice or defensiveness or fear keeps these alive).

I still feel very uncertain about this whole retreat, where it will lead to. Hopefully I will find a climate of welcome and peace at Simonos Petras and get the permission from the governor and settle there quietly. Lord, I place my trust in you.

It is beginning to clear.

Find the door of your heart, and you will find the door of the Kingdom of Heaven. — SAINT JOHN CHRYSOSTOM

I am reminded of Saint Benedict's: there are never lacking guests in the monastery. There were five others at supper last night. By breakfast these had all left except for the one who made his Communion at the Liturgy. But four others had arrived. They left before dinner, but then three others came for dinner, including Richard Kamm. They left after dinner, but there were five more by supper.

After the monks took their supper, self-service, they set a table for us. While we were eating, a group of monks were in the corner preparing tomorrow's vegetables. While they sorted the beans, one of them prayed the Jesus Prayer aloud: "Lord Jesus Christ, Son of God, have mercy."

At Vespers the question of my retreat came clearer. I have to discern if I am to continue to let myself get involved in active works such as Canon Law, prayer workshops, etc., or seek a more contemplative life. There is the question, too, to what extent I should function as a Spiritual Father and otherwise be active in our own com-

munity and guesthouse. Much of this may be decided for me, for
certainly I must live in a very open docility to my own Spiritual Father. He respects my own discernment, but he must help in the discernment, too. Above all, my life must be a complete "yes" to the
Lord in everything.

※

It is getting dark. The sea, pounding on the rocks a hundred feet
below my window, is getting rougher. I will turn to Scripture and
prayer and then get some sleep before the 2:30 bell.

Saturday, May 23

❦ After the Midnight Service* and Orthros,* the monks went
to the chapel in the cemetery for Liturgy. There was a chill wind.
That may have been the reason Father Grigorios invited me in and
gave me a stall among the monks. Unfortunately I had to leave after
the Gospel for the hike up to Karyes. It was raining a little, so that
cooled things a bit, but I was very hot and tired when I reached the
capital. The bus was late in starting, but that did not matter since I
had over an hour's wait in Daphni for the boat. As I waited, I talked
with Tom, a young Orthodox from Australia, who was somewhat
mentally ill and was thinking of a monastic vocation. I wonder if
they give any thought to screening candidates here on the Mountain? He wavered for a time about coming with me to Simonos
Petras, but when the boat for Ouranoupolis was about to sail he decided to jump aboard it. For better or worse, the Mountain lost a vocation. May the Lord give Tom peace of mind and heart.

SIMONOS PETRAS

Simonos Petras

I got the boat to the Simonos Petras landing. A merchant in Daphni gave me a bag of fish to bring along and a letter. Fortunately, he said to leave the fish at the dock. The climb, over a thousand feet straight up in the noonday sun, with my bag on my shoulder, was a real workout—purgatory on the way to heaven.

The monastery itself is quite cool, catching the mountain breezes. It is very well kept. I received a cheerful welcome from the guestmaster, Father Theologos, and was given a room that looks out on the courtyard and the katholikon,* the main church of the monastery. I hope I will be able to stay here. Silence reigns here except for the birds, the wind, and the water.

Athos is a bit of paradise. The sea all around is deep green and blue. The hillsides are rich greens, with splashes of yellow as the gorse is in full bloom. Along the roadsides there are all sorts of wild flowers; around the well-laid-out vegetable terraces are carnations, roses, and geraniums. Unfortunately, tourists do litter—though actually very little. There are signs along the road asking for care—especially against fire.

Shortly after I got settled, Father Dionysios came along and we sat out on the balcony. What a view! I am sure I will never get used to it. It is just breath-taking: the sea a thousand feet below, Athos in all its grandeur soaring into the azure. Father Dionysios is a very kind, gentle, loving, and reverent man. He made me feel truly welcome. He is a young priest who assists the Hegumen in whatever way he is asked, is available to the novices and to all, and takes a special interest in foreign visitors since he can speak English well and has traveled in the West. He has his cell among the old monks on the floor below the hegumenate.* When the community came here from Meteora* about two and a half years ago, there were fifteen of these "granddaddies"—the oldest is now ninety-six. They were among the most zealot* community on the Mountain. But with great love they embraced their new Hegumen and his sons. And they have become more free and open. At their request Father Dionysios took up his abode in their midst, to be able to help them more readily. Some of them are so aged that they eat regularly in their cells and rarely or never come to the church for the Services. Father said that as I lived with them, I would get the feel of their community. I think I shall like that. He said that their Gerontas* liked me very much and that there would be no difficulty with my staying. He thought it would be the first time a Catholic hieromonk* stayed so long on the Mountain.

After Vespers and supper, Father Dionysios brought Father Maximos, and we had coffee on the balcony. Father Maximos is delightful and very friendly. He had known many of the monks of this community when he was at the university. He then entered Dionysiou.* After a year and a half as a novice there, he went to London to do graduate work in Byzantine philosophy. (It is more and more common for Athonite novices to complete their studies outside.) In England he was in contact with Father Sophrony's community at Tolleshunt Knights. When he returned to Athos he joined the community here.

Maximos told me a bit of Dionysiou. The Hegumen, Father Gabriel, is one of the oldest and most revered Elders on the Mount. He came in 1908 when it was still under the Turks. At ninety he still sings well, is first at the Midnight Service, works hard in the garden. The life there is the strictest on the Mountain, rivaling Megisti Lavra* in the length of its Services. The monks have long, hard hours of agricultural work both near the monastery and at the upper end of the peninsula. Perhaps because of the work demands, fewer join them than some of the other fervent monasteries.

※

At Simonos Petras they are about sixty, but some are novices and are away at school. It is a very young community for the most part.

※

Father Maximos, whose patron is Maximos of Kavsokalyvia* (whose life was published by the Bollandists), is librarian and looks after the foreign visitors. He assured me of my welcome and acceptance by the community, which is very united. I think I shall be very happy here.

Praise the Lord for his loving goodness!

Sunday, May 24

⟋ I arose at 3:45. I thought it was late and that I had not heard the bell and semantron* because Father Maximos had said that the Services would begin at 3:30. He had offered to wake me lest I not hear them. But hurrying to the katholikon I found only the ecclesiastikos* lighting the lamps. I had forgotten that time is taken somewhat loosely here. Also they are always translating from Byzantine time which seems to be about three and a half hours ahead of standard time at the present moment.

The ecclesiastikos has a big job. There are all the chores of any sacristan, plus. For every Service many lamps have to be primed, fed, and lit. Then, during the Service, he is constantly lighting and extinguishing lamps and candles. He also rings the bell and sounds the semantron three times before the Service and again rings various bells during the Service. In a way, he is the one who keeps the whole monastery going.

The Services began around four and went right through, with Liturgy ending around 7:30. However the "lunch" which followed was still really part of it. The acolytes led the way into the refectory with candles in hand. The censer was there, and before we finished, we all shared the blessed bread and were incensed and finally processed back to the church to complete our thanksgiving.

After Services I settled on the balcony with the Scriptures. These and William of Saint Thierry's *Golden Epistle** are the only books I brought, and I don't intend to get into the latter right away. I want to read the Bible through and especially get more and more of the mind and heart of Jesus. This is the most important thing for me.

I wasn't settled on the balcony very long before guests began arriving. But they respected my peace and left me alone. I was tempted to speak when I heard English being spoken, but I realized this could really lead to an infringement on my retreat if I started getting involved with guests. It could be very interesting meeting these fine young men from many countries and hearing their story. But that is not what I am here for. The guestmaster soon collected them for coffee, etc., and then lunch, and then they disappeared. For the most part, the monastery is very silent except for the moaning of the wind, which seems to be constant, the singing of the birds, and the cascade of water.

I took a little walk up the road to the cave where Saint Simon, the Founder of the monastery, first lived, praying the rosary as I went. The rosary keeps coming back to my hand. During the Services in church I use the komvoschinion* (the Orthodox prayer cord) and pray mostly the Jesus Prayer when I cannot follow the Greek chants. This morning Father Maximos gave me a small book for the Liturgy which helped, though I am quite familiar with it from our own practice at home. I pray the Little Hours* in my cell in the Cistercian fashion.

Today is the great feast of Pentecost in the West. I have a Pentecostal icon with me and lit a candle before it while I read the Mass of Pentecost in my cell, praying for a great outpouring of the Spirit on all, East and West, and especially on this retreat. Reading Acts and Jesus' Last Supper discourse, much spoke very powerfully to me of his mission and my election. There is great peace and courage to be found in the Scriptures.

After resting a while in my room I went out to the balcony to enjoy some quiet prayer over the sea. I had been regretting carrying along a coat and hat but today I was glad to have them. It was quite cool out on the balcony. Father Theologos soon came and offered me coffee, which came with the traditional sweet, ouzo, and water. I returned to the balcony and after a bit I was joined by the only novice at home at the moment, Charalambos. He is twenty-five and has been here ten months. He is not off to the university for exams like the rest, because he finished his studies as an electrical engineer before he entered.

Schedule:

3:30   Midnight Service, Orthros, the First Hour, Liturgy
       (Some go to work in the gardens early before the heat.
       On Sundays and feasts, lunch follows immediately)
10:30 The Third and Sixth Hours, lunch
6:00   The Ninth Hour, Vespers, supper
8:30   Acathist, Apodeipnon

Their free time is spent mostly in the cell, praying the Jesus
Prayer, the Psalms, or in whatever way they are led, and reading Sacred Scripture, the ascetics, the Fathers, theology, and philosophy,
and literature, including novels, for the Gerontas expects them to be
well rounded.

Father Maximos came with apologies for neglecting me all day. I
tried to assure him that no apologies were necessary; I was glad to
have time for prayer and reading. They will get used to a guest of
long standing and not feel so obligated, I hope. Father Serapion
joined us and invited us to his office. He is beginning to learn English. We talked together for quite some time, sharing many things:

They discern a monastic vocation by the signs indicated by Saint
John Climacus: desire to love and serve God without condition, fear
of hell, hope of heaven; more particularly, the ability of the young
man to familiarize himself with the monastery and its ways, becoming intimate with what he finds here, with the brothers, and above
all with the Gerontas. Father Serapion especially added: his ability
to grow in love. This community has a special character of family intimacy because the Gerontas knew most of the core group from early
youth and they all grew up together in the same neighborhood. Following one of the traditions, the Gerontas has already nominated his
successor as Hegumen and is training him. He hopes in a few years
to retire as superior and live in greater solitude while still serving this
community and others as Spiritual Father. There is real warmth and
openness among the brothers.

The novices are developed according to their abilities and gifts in
the way the Lord is leading them, even if this means going outside to
study. And the duration of the novitiate varies from man to man. In
fact, most of them will be finishing at the university during their novitiate. They may have a particular canon of prayer, but primarily
they are being led to adopt a monastic outlook. In this and in other

ways Simonos Petras is to some extent unique on the Mountain. When the community first came here, the monks visited around, not seeking a better monastery or community, but sharing with their new brothers and then returning home. This made a strong impression on the other communities on the Mountain.

I like all that I find here. There is certainly much that is similar to home and some things I would like to see more fully at home.

✳

They have an abundance of good water here. The excess from the spring on the mountain cascades down to the sea, adding its music to the symphony of the wind. The monastery is perched on a huge granite outcrop that springs out from the mountainside. The donkeys roam the hillside with bells on their necks to make them easier to find. They amble home to eat and drink. They make me think of man, naturally turning to God for all, ringing his constant little bell of prayer to let God know where he is.

✳

It is hard to believe that it is less than a week since I left Spencer. So much seems to have happened. I am seven hours difference and seven thousand miles from home, picking up relations of three years past, and living in another world. As I sit on the balcony over the sea, it seems like a dream come true. I realize now what an audacious thing I have done in abruptly dropping a very busy life and putting myself in a position of complete inactivity, quiet, solitude, isolation —in a sense—and rest for a prolonged period, with little escape. I have to be careful not to seek or find escapes, even such as writing this journal or sharing with the monks. It is probably more of my heavenly Father's great careful love that is keeping these first days so full so I can taper a bit. I will have some activity next week, going to Karyes and then on to Father Vasileios and maybe Father Kallistos. But once I get back here it should be very peaceful.

✳

Father Serapion has charge of the administration while the Hegumen is away. But things are so developed that the monastery proceeds much on its own.

✳

Shortly before Vespers, Father Dionysios found us with a tray of coffee and sweet pudding for me. After Vespers and supper I went to my cell to read the Gospels. There were four other guests at supper. In spite of the monastery's remoteness, guests do come. There were six or eight for lunch. Those staying overnight are older Greek pilgrims. In the refectory the Hegumen has his own little round table at the head, before the year-round icon (depicting all the feasts of the year) and the seven-branch candlestick. The priests have a table in the middle before him. The monks are on each side. Also along the side, after the monks but at separate tables, are, on one side, the novices and, on the other, the guests. I am given the first place at the guests' table.

❊

I frequently catch myself racing ahead in thought, planning next week's trip or going home, etc., escaping from the glory of the "now," seeking the security of plans and mastering my own destiny. Help me, Lord, to live free, with you, in the "now," safe in the confident knowledge that all is in your hands and it will unfold far better than I can plan. I think of how providential it was that a member of this community was invited to the Oxford symposium and I was able to do a service for him and get to Meteora, thus preparing a place for me here these three years later. I have every reason to trust God; in all ways, he has led me. How good he is! For those who love God, all things work together unto good.

Monday, May 25

We arose around four this morning. As the Services progressed, Father Maximos came and told me they would be long since we were celebrating the third finding of the head of Saint John the Baptist. (The first two findings are celebrated earlier in the year —February 24, I think.) Saint John is very popular in Greece, with many feasts. I think this is especially true for the monks. I know I look to him as a special patron and I am happy to be able to celebrate a day in his honor at the beginning of this retreat. (My Abbot was chosen on the feast of his beheading.) During Orthros there was veneration of his relics. We finally finished a little after eight.

Father Maximos prepared a breakfast for me: a large cup of coffee (he had apologized earlier about their little cups and promised to get a large one for me—I guess this is just another "bigness" that is associated with Americans or the West), some bread, a sweet made of sesame seed with peanuts in it, and water—more than enough to hold me till lunch at eleven. Food begins to take a disproportionate place in a life that is emptied of all activity but prayer and *lectio*.* Even as I sit on the balcony, odors from the kitchen below come up. And two hundred feet below I can see Father Myron picking beans in the handsome kitchen gardens. Though the monks eat only twice a day here (and once on Mondays, Wednesdays, and Fridays), they are constantly offering me a "coffee," which always comes accompanied by sweets, etc. It is one of the concrete ways they express a love and kindness that is just overflowing. I have found here at Simonos Petras the kind of community I have always idealized—a community that really runs on love. There are no strict rules or expectations. The men come to Services because they want to, they do their work because they want to, they keep silence and prayer because they want to. It is very much a family. And as Father Maximos put it, "Naughty children are not thrown out of a family." But I have not seen any "naughty children" yet—though there is freedom to speak in church and refectory in a way which we would not feel comfortable with in our Western monasteries. Last night as we were getting ready for Apodeipnon, Father Dionysios, who was to preside and who was standing out in the middle of the church, did not hesitate to turn to me and inquire how I was doing—if there was anything I needed, etc. It did not seem the least out of context here. It is family, love in God's family, that prevails.

※

I have been a bit baffled by the question of how many monks are in the community, because each gives a different number and explains the various reasons why so few are home. Actually, there were only ten at lunch today—only three or four at the Third and Sixth Hours. But then I reflected on my answer when they asked how many are at Spencer and find it also baffling. If we count all on the books we would be over eighty (I don't know precise numbers, either, although I know and love each one), but that would give a false impression. Of the fifteen or so away, some are only off to school for the moment, others are to be away for longer periods. Among these latter there are differences: those assigned to serve our nuns at Wrentham or in another monastery, etc., and those abroad. Then should we count the brothers at our annex in North Carolina, etc. So here they have the same situation. Some might count the Father with the nuns or the six at Konstamonitou, others might not. Father Serapion said they have ten novices, but some of these are still at the university or in military service; only one is here at the moment. Once one receives the habit, he is a monk and is expected to stay in the monastic state for life, but he may move from monastery to monastery or to a skete or hermitage or to ministry in the city, etc. (Simonos Petras has a house and church in Thessaloniki, with a priest, and another in Athens.) Thus, in one sense, even our postulants at Spencer would be considered monks since they received a habit and are usually "tonsured" and stay in the monastery; but in another way only our solemnly professed are monks, committed to the monastic state for life, and that is the way we usually look at it canonically. We might parallel simple profession in the West to the taking of the rason* or to the receiving of the Little Schema* by Orthodox monks, and making solemn vows to receiving the Great, or Angelic, Schema.* In sum, there is no simple way to draw exact equivalents juridically, but in the reality there is very much—all the essentials—that is the same. We come out of one common living tradition.

I think that in our monastery at Spencer one has every opportunity one has here for living a full, intense, monastic life. The difference lies in this, that at Spencer one also has ample opportunity to get caught up in the world through newspapers, magazines, trips outside, neighbors, and friends. Such opportunities are not so available here, with the result that all the monks are more obviously one in seeking the goals of the monastic life. This leads to a lot of support in being faithful to the essentials and experiencing oneness and security, even with maximum freedom in observance.

As I was eating the breakfast Father Maximos offered me, I looked into the guest book. From the numbers on the diamonitirions,* the permits to visit the Holy Mountain, it seems about 2,500 have visited the Holy Mountain in the first five months of this year, about 650 have come to Simonos Petras, and relatively few of these have stayed the night here. It is a difficult house to reach and has no art or library treasures because of fires. Most of the present structures, apart from the thick outer walls, are less than a hundred years old.

❋

Some hours after lunch, Father Dionysios joined me on the balcony with coffee. I had seen for the first time a group of monks playing together—laughing and joking and chasing after each other. On Athos it is rare to see young monks smiling; they are a rather serious lot. But Simonos Petras is something of an exception. It turned out it was Dionysios, Maximos, Serapion, and a couple of others. As we talked about it, there came to mind the texts "Unless you become as little children . . ." and "Simple as doves and wise as serpents." As Father Serapion remarked, "Monks are little children. They play, and never dream their Father may have problems." There is a strong family spirit here. Yet the world and, here in Greece I am told, not even the bishops understand such a life free for God. This is one of the reasons why Father Aimilianos allows his sons to continue at the university. It helps their families to accept the idea of their being monks from an early age. He accepts novices at fifteen and even younger and thinks this is good for having a true family. Yet he also appreciates study and learning and sees the value of education. However, there is no general rule requiring it of all. It is encouraged according to one's ability and attraction.

❋

There are three sketes near the monastery. Two were inhabited before the community came and their occupants are zealots. The third is used by a part-time hermit of the community.

❋

Father Dionysios spoke of the saints who have lived here. Saint Gregory Palamas occupied a cave just over the hill. Saint Nectarios is especially close to Father Dionysios for he knows personally a spiritual son of the Saint who is still Gerontas at Paresus, an island off the coast of Greece. The saints are very much alive here.

❊

The monk has three treasures: the Services, Communion, and the Jesus Prayer. They sing the Services with enthusiasm and joy here. All are encouraged to come to Orthros, Liturgy, and Vespers. For the other hours they are free to pray in their cells. Father Dionysios' cell is really a chapel, with many icons, a lectern, lamps and candles, and a choir stall.

❊

Father Dionysios is so beautifully open, generous, and encouraging. He said he thought that God would so greatly reveal himself to me during this retreat that I would have to hide my face and that he would surely make known his will for me. I do trust he is right.

❊

After Vespers Father Maximos and Father Serapion asked me to go for a walk. We went to a high outlook from which we could see the next monastery. The view was another of those breath-takers: Grigoriou* clinging to the rocky coast, Athos soaring up behind, a very rich and handsome mountain, laced with all sorts of colorful marbles and graced with a halo of white clouds.

Father Serapion first asked many questions about my own monastery. I had to describe its location. We went on to discuss why Cistercians usually located in valleys. Then he asked about the structure of the Order. Then about its characteristics. I summed them up as seeking to live the Rule of Saint Benedict fully, union of the abbeys to help preserve fidelity, poverty, and noninvolvement in churches, etc., and the mystic emphasis of the Cistercian Fathers, especially inspired by the Song of Songs. Father Serapion became very interested. He asked if we still had men living the mystic life and if we had always, in our Order, monks with the special gifts found in the early Fathers. I was happy to be able to say "yes" and tell them of Bernard of Clairvaux and other early Fathers, and then of some of the monks of our own abbey like Father Bernard and Brother Patrick and some of our brothers with the gift of healing. He wanted to know if we were familiar with Gregory of Nyssa's commentary on the Song of Songs and how our Fathers commented on it. I told him of how they regarded the literal sense as the rind and emphasized the spiritual senses, the allegorical and the moral, also touching on the anagogic, or that sense of things to come.

Father Serapion went on to explain how novices among them are first trained in ascetic practice and communal prayer and only later formed in the precise way of the Jesus Prayer. At first the novice is left to use it and the Psalter as well as he can in his cell prayer. The two Fathers asked of our use of the Psalter. This led to my telling them of our way of using the Scriptures in dialogical prayer. This was something new to them and I had to explain at length. Father Serapion asked how in such prayer one was preserved from the noetic and one's own psychological deceptions. I said we judged by the fruit, and I also introduced them to Centering Prayer.* As I started to discuss this, we entered upon a discussion of the Divine Indwelling. We understand this to come about with grace. But for the Orthodox the Uncreated Divine Energies of grace are just a beginning and the Indwelling is the highest state, coming only with perfect love. They see the Orthodox Fathers insisting on complete purity for contact with God. I said I thought the West emphasized more God's coming to sinful man in the Incarnation, the outreach of the Prodigal Father.

The bell for Apodeipnon cut off our sharing. We had to head back to the monastery or we would find the gate closed and be locked out for the night. We all felt it had been a very good sharing and wanted to continue. Father Serapion has a very keen mind. It is a pleasure to discuss things with him.

As it is a fast day, the monks have had no regular meal this evening. But when we returned, they brought a big tray to my cell. The workers were eating in the guest dining room and a couple of them were arguing very loudly, not uncommon for Greeks. Fortunately, the workers very rarely come to the monastery itself but stay up in the forest. There are two young Americans staying overnight. I have to resist the temptation to get involved with them. The involvement with the monks is already enough. I trust it will lessen, too, as the time passes and the retreat will deepen. I am longing for more depth of prayer and experience of God, but all seems to be just a quiet openness to his pervasive presence. I do not spend special time "centering" as I do at home. The whole seems centered already, except for occasional distractions. At the Services I am able to just be in God's presence, uplifted by the whole atmosphere of prayer and carried by many Kyries* and Doxas.* It is filled with praise.

❧

As I sit on the balcony I watch the many birds—swallows, pigeons, gulls, etc.—flying about beneath me. Today I saw an unusual russet bird gliding effortlessly for all the time I could see it. I thought of it as myself in this time, gliding effortlessly on the mercy and love of God, free from all care and effort, just moving along with his grace. It all seems almost too good to be true. The trouble with us is that we don't accept and believe that wonderful bargain that that good Jew, our Saviour, struck for us—a hundredfold in this life and life eternal, too. I am certainly getting the hundredfold. I trust I'll get the life eternal, too. I would like to see all my brothers get a chance for such a pilgrimage and retreat. Dionysios told me he and his Hegumen went to the Holy Land last year and now they are going to send two each year. I would like for us to allow two of the brethren to go each year on pilgrimage to Jerusalem, Athos, Rome, and some of our European monasteries. How it would enrich their lives and the whole community. Such pilgrimages certainly are in the early monastic tradition, even if Saint Bernard did not favor them. Above all, we need to become as little children and not depend on our own plans and efforts, but freely receive of the abundance the Father wants to give us. That is why I think the idea of a Spiritual Father is so important—so men can learn how much a father and the Father loves, accepts, and wants to give.

It is very late (monastically speaking), so I had better finish and get to bed.

Praise Jesus Lord!

Tuesday, May 26

After finishing writing last night I went out along the balcony to the washroom and was overwhelmed by the beauty of the moon on the sea amid the quiet murmuring of a creation entering into night. This is truly a paradise.

The rising bell rang at four but the bell for Mesonyktikon* not till nearly five as it is a ferial day with shorter Services, finishing before eight. I find that Athonite time changes from day to day. It seems one can only go by the bells, although the brothers do wear watches. There must be some master clock they set them by. I will have to ask more about this—and many other things.

After breakfast (it was served in my cell, as it was richer than the other guests received and included cheese and an egg—why do they feed a monk better, one who should fast more?), I sat on the balcony reading Genesis and watching the three pilgrims of the night leave. As they wended their way down the steep winding path and got lost among the olive trees I thought: how like life. We are all wending our way along. Each tends to experience himself as the center of it all. But seen in perspective, we are but pilgrims, each, on the path. And a loving Father looks down with love and concern and blesses us. Abraham's election, the election of his people, is very much here. What a blessing from the Lord it is to be on the paths of Athos or those paths of life that go in peace and lead to the Temple of the Lord. The three lads went along, very carefree, especially the young one from New York, totally enjoying the experience of each moment and ready to move on to the next. This is the way our Father wants us. Totally in the present, fully receiving and enjoying his love. We are so often missing much of the present because we are busy planning ahead or regretting the past.

I wonder if this journal is getting in the way of the present? I begrudge it the time, even though I have all the time in the world. Time is passing too quickly. I am eager for God to act. I want more time for prayer, for reading, for being. Fill each moment with yourself, O Lord. You are with me as I write and maybe will help me put everything into perspective as time moves on. Now it is mostly just recording the surface experiences. They have to be handled before the way to the depths is free and uncluttered.

The food is ample and good, well prepared but with the necessary monotony of a vegetarian diet: vegetables, salad, bread, cheese, and wine (on nonfast days). Olives replace the cheese on fast days, but olive oil is forbidden—a real fast for Greeks since most things are prepared with lots of oil. In the evening, pasta, beans, or lentils. I thought I would lose weight here, but as things are going, I shall gain because I get little exercise.

It is quite cool, probably because it has been overcast much of the time and there are strong breezes. This monastery is well placed to get the full benefit of them. I was regretting carrying a coat—now I am very glad I have it, and a hat, too.

❊

Although I had been aware of the Greek theology of the Uncreated Divine Energies—though I must confess I do not fully understand it; it probably is not supposed to be fully understandable—I was not aware of how closely this is related with the spiritual doctrine that stresses the Divine Transcendence, the awesomeness of God that fills the Services with *Kyrie eleison** and *Doxa Patri.* . . . This is what places the Divine Indwelling as an ultimate grace, given only when the creature is wholly pure and there will be no admixture of evil and divine in man. It also leads to that reverence of the Eucharist that keeps the faithful away. I am happy to see here at Simonos Petras that they receive more frequently, three or four times a week.

❊

This afternoon Father Dionysios came to tell me that the Hegumen had called and will arrive tomorrow. Yes, they have a phone! Most of the monasteries have them now. They even have a road from here to the port at Daphni and a Land Rover. Although I had the pleasure this afternoon of seeing two monks ride in on mules. They were going at a sprightly pace, bells jingling, and a third mule behind with the baggage. The Hegumen proposed that I make a tour of the Mountain before settling in here. I think they have difficulty grasping the idea of a retreat. A pilgrimage to the icons and shrines is the usual thing for the devout Orthodox—not settling down in one spot for quiet and prayer. You can do that at home. They are constantly apologizing for leaving me alone all day and I am rejoicing in it.

❊

Father Maximos came for a few minutes before Vespers. We

talked about the Great, or Angelic, Schema. The tradition on the Mountain is that it is the only one and received right after novitiate, which is usually one to three years in duration. A later tradition, more current elsewhere and brought by this community from Meteora, has three steps: novitiate in secular clothes, the Little Schema, and then the Great Schema. And some monasteries have introduced a stage between the novitiate and the profession of the Little Schema, when one receives only the rason and the skouphos* without making any promises or being tonsured. They have this at Grigoriou. The Great Schema is considered to be a sacrament restoring baptismal innocence, a solemn commitment to the monastic way of life. The Little Schema is called an "engagement" for the Great Schema. It seems, in fact, very like our arrangement of simple profession as an engagement toward the consecration of solemn vows when the cowl, or cuculla,* is received.

❊

After supper tonight Athos was clothed in clouds and a rainbow reached to the end of the peninsula, as a setting sun bathed all in warm light and a full moon shone above the clouds. There is a small chapel of the Transfiguration atop the Mountain. Father Dionysios tells me it must be rebuilt every year for the feast because lightning destroys it. That is easy to believe. It is fascinating here to see a sky full of stars and yet flashes of lightning as the clouds from the west bump the high peaks. "Holy Transfiguration" is the right titular for such a chapel and for the heart of monasticism. We, unlike Peter, have been allowed to build a tent and are invited to dwell as fully as we can in the Divine Cloud. Praise the overwhelming beneficence of our God.

STAVRONIKITA

Stavronikita

Thursday, May 28

﹏ At Apodeipnon Tuesday night Father Dionysios told me I must go to see the governor at Karyes in the morning. At the end of Orthros on Wednesday Father Maximos had breakfast for me. I left some of my things in my cell and started out with a lighter pack, down the hill for the eight o'clock boat to Daphni. It was very cool. Again I was glad to have my coat.

While waiting in Daphni for the bus to Karyes I spoke with a young Jewish student from Great Neck, New York, who had graduated from Stony Brook and had received a United States government scholarship to study Arabic in Alexandria. After finishing his studies there, he came to the Holy Mountain. Now he was going to Nepal to learn what he could from the holy men there. He had hoped to spend a year in a kibbutz in Israel, but he has been accepted as a graduate student in anthropology at the University of Pennsylvania. Tuesday night at Grigoriou he spoke with a retired Greek who had been living at the monastery for two years. The gentleman had told him, "God became man so that man could become God." The student asked me to explain this for him. While I did, he listened with great attention. Please God, seeds of faith are being sown.

On the bus I met a tall, lanky Dane with silver rings in his ears and purple trousers, eating tomatoes and half a loaf of bread which he had bought at the port. I told him there was a Dane at the Skete of Propheti Iliou.

❊

On the way to Karyes our bus passed two helicopters parked near the academy at Aghiou Andreou.* An official Bulgarian contingent had flown in to visit the Holy Mountain. The governor later assured me the visit was purely political and cultural, not religious, though one of the party told him quietly that he was a believer and wished that he could venerate the icons.

When I arrived at the capital I went directly to Father Athanasios' office. He was working on the account books with a pocket calculator. A beautiful old monk from Chilandari was with him. They greeted me fraternally and served the usual refreshments. At that point, the day's early group of visitors arrived, about twenty-five, mostly German. Father Athanasios had to issue the diamonitirions for them. We then went to the governor's office. His secretary greeted us warmly and used his little English to very good effect to make me feel very welcome.

After a short time Governor Tsamis arrived. He is most gracious and kind. He asked how long I wished to stay and instructed his secretary to prepare the permit. Then we went into his private office, while good Father Athanasios waited most patiently. The governor had studied theology at Yale for two years in the 1960s. He has been a lay preacher and continues to teach Sunday school even though he is now a professor at the University of Thessaloniki, as well as governor of the Holy Community.

The governor and I talked about many things. First of all, the recent developments on the Mountain. Since 1973, when Father Ephraim arrived at Philotheou* with twenty young monks, he and his group have been trying to live there the full hesychast* tradition of Saint Gregory Palamas. The tradition is also having a strong influence on the renewed life at Stavronikita. There are many other signs of hope. Relations are opening up with Russia. Fifteen monks are expected to arrive next week from Russia and there are plans to send a delegation from the Holy Mountain to visit the Moscow Patriarchate.

The governor said he recognized the Catholic and Protestant communions as true Churches. While he realizes that Orthodoxy is closer to the Catholic Church, he feels emotionally more comfortable with the Protestants because he studied with them. He found it hard to understand how the Catholic Church has gotten so involved and disturbed by questions of birth control and contraception. The Orthodox Church leaves these matters to the conscience of the individual. If one has questions he can talk with his Spiritual Father. For the Orthodox, marriage has not been tied up with procreation but is a thing of love—a sacrament of the love in the Trinity. I told him we were rapidly moving in that direction. In spite of recent Roman documents, most of the faithful and most priests hold that the couple themselves must make the decisions in these areas. He brought forward other minor areas that caused concern among the Greeks, saying at the same time they did not fully understand the context within which the Catholic Church had to work in America. They were disturbed by "guitar Masses" and also bishops, like Archbishop Robert Sanchez of Santa Fe, New Mexico, getting too much down among the people. The basic attitude of great reverence seems to constantly be at the heart of the different approaches. Undoubtedly, we in the United States have gone too far in familiarity in some cases, but there is a need to bridge the gap between the Church and the common man. The governor agreed but would make the bridge longer than we. He felt that a priest or bishop getting close to the people might at first attract but in the long run would not sanctify. They have had this experience in Greece. I wonder how true that might also be in America.

We would have happily gone on longer, but the governor's luncheon guests were arriving.

The governor then had his driver take me to the Kellion* of Saint Nicholas. The Elder there is Father Charalambos, a spiritual brother of Father Panteleimon, the Elder in Boston, and Father Ephraim, all sons of Father Joseph the Hesychast at New Skete.* There is an English monk there, Father Nicholas, who was with Father Sophrony in Tolleshunt Knights for a couple of years before coming to the Mountain two years ago. He had been a Jesuit, steeped himself in the early Fathers, and finally decided to change to the tradition he felt more consonant with what he found in them. I was welcomed by the Elder with the usual refreshments.

As he could not directly find Father Nicholas, he sent Father Anthony to speak with me. Father Anthony is a Greek who lived in New York for some years. He was very friendly and told me about the kellion. A kellion is a small community with its own Elder—this one is one of the largest, with eighteen monks—dependent juridically on a monastery but actually quite independent. As they have no land holdings, they have to earn their living by crafts and their garden. This kellion is very well kept and has beautiful gardens. With such a Spiritual Father as Father Charalambos, life here is lived in the hesychast tradition with great intensity.

Father Nicholas finally arrived. We were soon engaged in serious conversation. He felt the logical conclusion, under the Holy Spirit, for one who has entered into the mind of the Eastern Fathers and draws sustenance from the Byzantine Liturgy and icons is to take the leap and become Orthodox, in spite of the ecclesiastical confusion involved in the different jurisdictions, etc. He argued this on the basis that spiritual practice flows from doctrine and that the doctrinal differences are significant in this respect. When I asked for an example, he pointed to the heavy emphasis on law and order in the Roman Catholic Church as flowing from the concept of the *Filioque*,* that the Holy Spirit proceeds from both the Father and the Son. He didn't really satisfy me as to why this is so. It seems to me that, first of all, the law-and-order emphasis is not from doctrine but rather from Roman culture; secondly, it is fast passing out of the Western Church; thirdly, at least in the areas of discipline and rite, the Orthodox monks are more tied up with rules and regulations than we are at the present time. In fact, I have to smile at times when I hear someone speaking of our being "law and order" and then go on about their many rules and regulations for fast days, and the like. But it is true, as Governor Tsamis pointed out, the Roman Church certainly has, through Aristotelian influence, gone too far in its moral regulations or, to be more precise, has gotten too detailed.

It came time for Vespers. I started to follow Father Nicholas to the chapel, but was informed that non-Orthodox are not admitted. I asked if we could continue our discussion after Vespers. The Father said we could not. I asked to stay for the night and was told there was no room for me. I was disappointed, as I would have liked to have gone further into our sharing and also have had a word with the Elder. So I headed up the hill towards Propheti Iliou.

As I arrived in the courtyard of the skete, Father Seraphim and Father Adrian came out of the building. Father Seraphim had been a monk of Saint Tikon's Monastery in Pennsylvania. He changed to the Synod* (the Russian Orthodox Church-Outside-of-Russia), went for a time to Saint Sabbas near Jerusalem, and then came here six years ago to keep this skete alive. Father Adrian is here for only a short time. He is from Father Panteleimon's community in Boston. There are also a novice, Father John, and an elderly visiting monk who will leave shortly. After a refreshing drink of orange juice (one of the many American influences in this skete), we went to Vespers. This is a Russian skete historically, though dependent on the Greek Monastery of Pantokratoros,* so the Service was in Slavonic. I cannot understand this language, but the polyphony even with this small group was beautiful, a real invitation to worship.

It being Wednesday, after Vespers we had fast-day fare—lentil soup. Father Seraphim inquired about the American political scene. He spoke of how America hurt the Greeks in Cyprus, blockading the area while the Turks parachuted in. He went on to lament the many ills in the world today. Petitionary prayer is a very important part of Father Seraphim's life. During the whole of the Midnight Service, Orthros, and the First, Third, and Sixth Hours, Father is making preparation for Liturgy, placing all the petitions on the diskos* (the paten).

As it got dark, Father Adrian opened a can of apricots and got out some Greek sugar cookies and we settled in the main reception room of the guesthouse. Father Adrian had been a novice at Chevtogne* in Belgium in 1965. At that time, a number of novices left to become Orthodox. For seven years he functioned as deacon in the Synod in New York and then joined Father Panteleimon in Boston.

As we ate, we talked about the Spiritual Father. To have one is a rather awesome gift, yet one that every monk truly needs. This man is to be entrusted with one's whole self in the Lord. He should be a man who is always in the presence of God, never in the way, allowing God's gifts to flow through, seeing all the need of his disciple and applying the Word of God to it. The Spiritual Father must be a man with a very pure heart. There are few, because few are willing to pay the price for this. It is a fearful thing when one asks you to be his Spiritual Father. How do you know if this is God's will? That you are ready for such a service? I want to ask the Fathers here on the Mountain more about this.

❊

The saintliness of a life is transmitted from him who has achieved it to those who come within his circle; for there is truth in the Prophet's saying, that one who lives with a man who is holy and clean and elect will become such himself.

— SAINT GREGORY OF NYSSA

❊

We retired about ten and the bell for the Midnight Service sounded about two this morning, Thursday. After the Liturgy we rested again for a few hours and at nine rose for breakfast. Father Adrian fixed an American breakfast for us: cheese omelette and Nes-

café, with some canned fish from Russia as a side dish. During breakfast we talked about how the Spiritual Father in the hesychast tradition of Saint Nilos helped the beginner. This skete was started by
that great Spiritual Father, Paisios Velichkousky, in 1756. He was in
a way even too much for the Holy Mountain and moved back to
Moldavia. The group he left behind him at the skete grew, and in
time Josephite ritual monasticism* replaced the hesychast tradition
here. Although the monks are now so few in number, they still try to
carry out in full the later Josephite rule. But Father Panteleimon is
in the hesychast tradition. In this tradition more time is spent in the
cell, less in liturgical Services. At first the novice is given the lives of
the Saints to read and the ascetical teaching of the Fathers. The *Orthodox Word* offers good material for this in English. Then the novice is gradually led into the Old Testament.

I realize how we tend to neglect these sources and go right to the
Gospels. But our Cistercian Fathers used the Old Testament a great
deal and were, we might say, specialists in the Song of Songs. Saint
Bernard in his commentary pointed out that Ecclesiastes is for the
beginner, Proverbs for the one moving along, and the Song of Songs
for the one striving after perfection. During these days I have been
reading the Old Testament from the beginning, experiencing again
the gratuity of God's great love in my creation and vocation as one
with that of my people—we are all Semites spiritually, as Pius XI
said. I think I am going to bring in the Old Testament more when
giving guidance.

The novice is also gradually introduced to the Jesus Prayer with
the rope* and the metanias* (prostrations). As Father Adrian and I
spoke of this, Father Seraphim came in with the biggest prayer rope
I have ever seen. It had three hundred large knots. The novice was to
be on penance that day and was to do three hundred metanias during dinner—quite a penance for an older man with a rather ample
girth.

❊

I had hoped to stay at the skete until Saturday but the rule allows
only one-day visits in sketes, apart from special permission from the
Hegumen of the monastery on which the skete depends. So about
noon I went down to Pantokratoros. The guestmaster, Father
Sabbas, received me most warmly, didn't ask the usual question—

"Orthodox?"—fixed me a good lunch, and then took me to a fine large room that has three windows overlooking the sea. There were clean linens on a bed turned down for my siesta and a sink with running water—luxuries not previously met in my travels on the Mountain.

There seems to be no one in this monastery who speaks English and no other visitors so I am getting some real peace, sitting on a balcony over the sea. These past days seem to have been more sharing than retreat. But that should pass when I get settled at Simonos Petras. The fact that discussions keep getting back to doctrinal questions indicates that, at least in the Orthodox mind and perhaps more than we are usually conscious of, spirituality is an expression of doctrine. Thus there is a legitimate question as to what extent we Catholics can use the spiritual writings and practices of other traditions in an integral way. This is a very far-reaching question, with considerable significance, which I want to explore further.

Pantokratoros is a very well-kept monastery by Athonite standards. The courtyard is brightly painted in white and blue (the Greek national colors) where it is not brickwork. There are citrus trees—orange, lemon, and lime—set in wells and a magnificent magnolia. The outside of the monastery is being refinished now with cement and painted the usual dusty red. There is a pleasant sun house out in front of the main gate, overlooking the sea. I discovered another quiet lookout a little further down the cliff, but when I went there after Vespers I found an old monk catching a smoke. He seemed startled to see me so I passed on and went back up to the sun house to continue my reading of Acts in preparation for the Feast of Pentecost on Sunday.

It is very hard to believe I have been on the Holy Mountain only one week.

※

Silence and solitude are the supreme luxuries of life.

— Thomas Merton

Friday, May 29

The bell sounded after four and the semantron about half

an hour later. Services ended a little after seven with the Epistle and
Gospel of the day, but no Liturgy. Breakfast was coffee, bread, honey,
and olives.

Honey is being developed more on the Mountain. There are many
hives between Daphni and Karyes. I saw new ones being unloaded
from a small freighter at the port. The Mountain is so full of wild
flowers that the bees have lots with which to work.

I enjoyed a quiet morning out on a little terrace over the sea, reading Acts. How much the Church of today and the Church of the
Council of Jerusalem have in common: the traditionalists, the move
to greater freedom, the compromise documents. Although it has its
very real drawbacks, compromise is precious; it allows each to both
give and receive.

Father Sabbas fixed me a good dinner: fried potatoes, lentil soup,
pasta, fresh bread. Although it is less than an hour's walk along the
coast to Stavronikita, the day was hot and the trail rugged, so I decided to take the easy way. We took the boat together at three—actually it arrived very late so I sat on a rock, talking with Father
Sabbas and praying over Stavronikita which we could see in the distance, praying that my visit would be blessed, the Spirit would be
poured out, that love and joy would prevail. And the prayer is being
answered.

I gave Father Sabbas a small offering. He was very pleased and
paid my boat fare. He is from Crete. He asked me to bring his greetings to Father Panteleimon, the guestmaster at Zographou,* who is
his friend and made the prayer cord he is using, a very nice one.
That seems to me a very meaningful way to bind friends together.

❄

It is good to be back at Stavronikita. Father Vasileios is still away.
He is part of the three-man delegation that annually goes to the
Greek Prime Minister in Athens to settle affairs between Greece and
Mount Athos. The Prime Minister keeps them waiting sometimes.
Father Vasileios hoped to be back tomorrow for the feast, but it
could be yet another week, according to Father Grigorios.

Father Symeon welcomed me with the usual refreshments. As we
sat in the lodge Father Hieronymos came in. He is a theologian. We
talked about the theological differences between the Christian East
and West and their effects on our spirituality. Father Symeon thinks

that the doctrine of the *Filioque* tends to divide God; that we West-erners ignore the Father, put all our attention on the Son, and put humanity at the center. He pointed to our art—meaning the Italian masters—exemplifying this, in contrast to the icons. Also, our rejec-tion of the Palamite* theory of the Uncreated Divine Energies at the Transfiguration, with the distinction between the unknowable Es-sence of God and contact with God through these Energies, has its effect on our attitude toward God and worship. It seems to me that the East does have a greater sense of God's transcendence and more of an attitude of reverence—although at the same time there is a re-markable informality and humanness in the way the monks relate to each other in the midst of the Services, with their moving about, comments, and conversations. The West tends to put on a little more formality in church—at least in some countries and churches—yet the basic stance of its outlook and prayer is a closeness to God in Christ. I think we could use some of the Greek insight into God's transcendence, and here I think using their spiritual writings could help. What is found in their spirituality does not contradict our posi-tion, it merely complements an emphasis. Father Symeon com-mented that we did not accept Gregory Palamas as a saint in the West. I realized then that neither side has officially accepted the saints of the other since the division, although we readily acknowl-edge the great holiness of Orthodox spirituals right up to our own time, such as Father Silouan. We finally agreed that it was not for monks to get taken up in theological dialogue or controversy—our concern should be in spiritual sharing. We went on to talk about achieving constant prayer through the Jesus Prayer, the types of read-ing we do, and some of our experience with the Eastern religions.

I was given a small room with an interior balcony. There are four other guests at the moment. Everything is very clean here. I like their little katholikon very much. It is the smallest on the Holy Mountain. The frescoes are excellent and the katholikon is bright enough to really be able to enjoy them. There is a beautiful odor about the katholikon—maybe from the constant use of incense, or perhaps they have perfume-giving relics. It has a whole atmosphere of prayer. They do the Services very well—more slowly than most and very reverently.

After supper I spoke for a while with Jean Pierre. Then Father Grigorios, the acting superior, came. We had just begun to get into a conversation about the Divine Indwelling when it was time for the guests' supper and then Apodeipnon. We promised to continue.

The sun is always there. The layers of clouds are gradually blown away and the light becomes stronger. We can concentrate on the removal of the clouds or on the growing light.

Silence is the very Presence of God—always there. But activity hides it. We need to leave activity long enough to discover the Presence—then we can return to activity with it.

Stillness is present throughout the run at every point. But if one only runs, he never knows stillness.

God is present in all beings, but we will never be aware of him if we never stop and leave behind all beings to be to him.

Still I am too busy, too active—not enough of the silence and solitude that opens the depths, exposes the sin and need and the Presence. After Apodeipnon I went out on the balcony over the katholikon. The Lord came in power. My whole being longed to be dissolved and be in complete union. I could not read as I usually do before retiring. I finally went to bed and continued in Presence. How I wish my every moment could be in this painful, sweet state. *Mane nobiscum, Domine*. Remain with us, Lord.

Only he who perseveres in watching [vigils] can comprehend [grasp] the glory and the power that is hidden in the monastic life. — ISAAC THE SYRIAN, *Logos 29*

Saturday, May 30

 The bell rang at 2:50; the Midnight Service began an hour later, giving the monks time to pray in their cells. Each has a rule from the Gerontas to do so many komvoschinions and metanias in his cell morning and evening. After Orthros we went to the cemetery chapel for Liturgy. In the midst of it, a pilgrimage led by a young Bishop with about twenty priests arrived and crowded in with us.

At the end of the Liturgy the koliva* was blessed. This is a special kind of sweet cake made of whole grain, sugar, and spices. At lunch we shared it as a sort of dessert. It celebrates the victory of our dead. The dead hold a special place in the lives of the monks here and in the other monasteries on the Mountain and throughout Orthodoxy. The graveyard is a special place of meditation. There are benches there to sit and meditate. There is also an open grave with a ladder. One can go down into the grave and sit on a little stool or lie on the bier. The simple grave cross is there, too, and a small icon shrine with lamp and prayer books. The cemeteries are small. After a time, when the wind and the rain has worn away the monk's komvoschin-ion which has hung on the cross marking his grave, the bones are dug up, sorted out, and placed in neat piles in the charnel house under or near the cemetery chapel. Sometimes the monk's name and date are written on the skull. The Orthodox monk's attitude toward death is like the rest of his spirituality, filled with fearful reverence and awe—the meeting with Christ the Judge. Here, too, I see a difference East and West, for in the West we tend, at least among monks, to see death as a fulfilling passage, a step further in the completion of the Paschal Mystery, a falling away of the veils, finally seeing the Face of Christ. Lord, let me see your Face. I see all of life, in a way, as a waiting for that blessed moment of revelation. The passing moments of light and vision in prayer are but the whetting of the appetite for more, the increasing of the desire. Lord, I do long to see your Face.

I have to struggle at times with the luxury of my present position. I think of how many harried Americans pay thousands of dollars just to have a few free days or weeks in the midst of some of the peaceful beauty I find here. And here I am steeped in it with nothing to do but let it fill my being with the message of his beauty and love. It is a real "honeymoon." I think of my niece who was married earlier this month and got a few days in Bermuda and then back to school, work, and busyness. And here I am, the poorest of the poor, allowed to enjoy all this with my Beloved day after day. He certainly is true to his word: a hundredfold in this life—on every level. Yet I have to struggle a bit at times with the Martha in me that says, "Couldn't you be loving him just as much while doing something to help others?" Yes, I am sure, by his grace, I could. But he has in his wonderful love allowed me to choose this better part for this time. I love the beauty of your place and the goodness of your love.

❋

About an hour before Vespers Father Grigorios came with Father Paisios, and Father Symeon joined us. Father Paisios is considered the greatest Father on the Mountain today. He lives as a hermit about a half an hour from the monastery. He comes in on Saturday evening for the Agripnia,* the All-Night Vigil, and Liturgy.

We talked about the Spiritual Father. If the disciple gives himself fully to the Father, the Father must give himself fully. He must seek within to see if this relation is wanted by God. His own heart must be very pure—no human motivations or seeking of personal gain or fame. The Father must stand before God for his son pouring out prayers for him, making good for all his son's sins, bringing him forth through pain and suffering. He best teaches him the way of prayer by his own love of prayer, evoking in him a desire to pray without ceasing. By obedience to the Spiritual Father, the son learns to be in submission to God and to humble himself. He must obey in all that is not immoral or heretical. If the Father is wrong, God will win out. If later in life a son loses his Father, it is good to choose another. If he does not, he still must seek advice of others and be in submission. Father Paisios' final word: "Let us pray for the Light of God."

❋

Vespers were short and there was no Apodeipnon because of the Agripnia. There are ten laymen here tonight and two visiting monks, one a cantor who came to help with the Vigil and the other a deacon. There are twenty in the community, counting two visiting monks and two novices. Two or three more are expected to join soon.

Pentecost, May 31

❧ Father Vasileios returned late last night.
The bell sounded at 11:20 and the semantron fifteen minutes
later. The Agripnia was magnificent. Many rich chants, much incense, the lights of the corona,* the swinging of the chandeliers,* the
procession with the icon, the blessing of bread, wine and oil. There
were three concelebrants and two deacons. Different monks took turns
leading the different parts. At the beginning of Orthros, Father Paisios led the singing of the Alleluias. He has a very pleasant voice.
The cantor and Father Grigorios have very rich, full voices. It was altogether a wonderful night. When the Liturgy ended about 6:30
A.M., the bells rang out and we processed to the refectory with incense, candles, and the Hegumen with cope and crosier, for a festal
meal, again with much singing and ritual. Father Symeon read part
of Saint John Chrysostom's first homily for Pentecost from Migne's
Patrologia.

❊

It was a busy day for the guestmaster. A dozen pilgrims came at
two and had to have lunch. Then three boatloads came for a shorter
visit. Father Kallistos Ware and Professor Philip Sherrard, who have
been working at Chilandari on the English translation of the *Philokalia*,* came for the night. After supper we talked on the terrace.
We discussed again the question of Catholics using Orthodox spiritual writings. It was agreed that spirituality and practice do and
should flow from doctrine. And therefore it is understandable that
some Orthodox feel that Catholics should not use the Jesus Prayer or
any of the writings and practices of the Orthodox Church. But Father Kallistos and Professor Sherrard felt that the massive bulk of
our doctrine is one. The areas where we differ are comparatively
small. A person truly seeking and guided by his Spiritual Father will
surely draw out the good that God wants him to find in these writings and practices. These should be available to Catholics and other
true seekers. In this regard Father Kallistos recounted an incident at
Chilandari. A young English pilgrim was about to leave to visit
Philotheou and Father Kallistos was warning him that he would not

be admitted to the katholikon there during the Services. The Elder, who was standing by, expressed his disagreement with such policies: "Good things should not be hidden." The Elder went on to recount how the Russians were converted when Saint Vladimir was allowed to assist at the Liturgy in Aghia Sophia in Constantinople.

Father Kallistos feels the contribution of the *Philokalia* is not so much the techniques for prayer which people tend to emphasize, but the presentation of the role of the Spiritual Father. He feels that the renewal of this role is the great need of Christianity today. Here on the Mountain wherever there is a good Spiritual Father, there is a lively community. This role of the Spiritual Father seems to constantly emerge in our conversations here.

❋

The monk from Aghiou Pavlou* who came for the Feast of Pentecost was driven off in the tractor cart. The deacon, Father Joachim, has come from Saint Sergius in Paris. He will be staying.

❋

Hesychasm*—quiet, inner peace, silence attained by starchestvo*— manifestation of thoughts and constant prayer—the Prayer of Jesus.

At first starchestvo is more demanding—going each evening to the Gerontas and exposing to him all one's folly, grime, filth, stupidity, vanity, frivolity. At first there are many thoughts, but gradually they quiet down. At first he asks only those that seem most alien, most embarrassing—the ones we least want to reveal. Sometimes he has a word of advice, sometimes he encourages, sometimes scolds. Sometimes he says nothing but dismisses us with a blessing. Quite gradually comes emptiness—room for prayer—purity of mind and heart.

At first the Jesus Prayer is less demanding. In the morning and in the evening we are to say five komvoschinions, with prostrations. Each prayer is to be said slowly, meaningfully, before the icon with the little metania. At the end of each komvoschinion, ten prostrations: knees and knuckles and forehead to the floor. If there is time, other periods in the cell before the icon in the same manner. But as we go about during the day, at work, and even at the Services, we keep the little cord discreetly in hand, if possible, and the Prayer welling up from the heart to the lips. In time the Prayer will simplify

—sometimes "Jesus, mercy" or just "Jesus" or just "Mercy." More and more constant. And then the silence. The heartbeat says it all. The breath carries it from the depth and back into depth. The great quiet, the great peace, silence—hesychasm.

❊

When the heart begins to recite, the tongue should stop.

❊

Thoughts are enemies who are bodiless and invisible, malicious and clever at harming us, skillful, nimble, and practiced in warfare. . . . A person whose mind is caught in thought is distant from Jesus; a person with a silent mind is with him.

— HESYCHIUS OF JERUSALEM

❊

I am so full of thoughts, projects, ideas, things to be done. I am hardly ever fully present. Distracted at Services, at prayer, at *lectio*— never there—dissipated, shallow. Lord, have mercy.

Monday, June 1

❧ The Services were quite long—over three hours—and then a very fine lunch at 8:30 A.M.

I spoke for a time with Père Basile, a Swiss who is ecclesiastikos. He also paints icons and does some scholarly work. I promised to send him David Goldfrank's study on the Rule of Joseph of Volokolamsk.

❊

When I woke up this morning I was moved to kiss the Cross I wear and I realized that if one really loves Christ, he wants to share in his sufferings. After I washed I sat down to read the Scriptures. I was at Chapter 5 of Romans: "More than that, we rejoice in our sufferings. . . ." I am afraid I am far from that. I realize that when I have to plan something, instead of keeping the end fully in view and planning as to what is best for attaining that end, I look too much to my own comfort and try to plan the way it will be easier for me. I

don't think I consciously shirk my duty because of cost, but I am not
as completely a "yes" to Christ as I could be because of selfish con-
siderations. And I do think I fall down in prayer and reading because
of this, too. The long Services are very demanding. To stay at attention in one's stall through several hours and continue fervent prayer
in spite of fatigue and physical pain calls for a bit. I am afraid I do
not do too well. At home where the Services are shorter and I am
fully involved, it is difficult enough. Here where I am not allowed to
actively participate but must stay with it the best I can, I tend to fall
by the wayside at times. I try to move with the sentiments of the
chants as much as I can and fill in with the Jesus Prayer or other
prayers I know by heart or just to be before God in the prayer of the
community.

❋

Although I feel quiet and peace, I perceive that I bring with me
some of the restless urgency of our Western world. In my contact
with the Spiritual Fathers, I am eager to get as much as I can. But in
their practice, they are content to give the disciple but a word and
let him chew on it for a time and then return for another. The disciple in his reverence considers it a privilege to be able to approach the
Gerontas and receive a word. The Fathers realize that growth and insight come from God and they are willing to abide his time. I see
that in working with my sons I have been too eager to see them
move on, too eager to impart knowledge. For the future I will try to
move more at God's pace, be content to give a word, and let it be
used by him as he sees fit. Also, I note that the Fathers are slow to
give their time to the disciple, not out of any unwillingness to give or
lack of openness to the disciple. But they have engendered in
them this reverence and contentment with a word. And they realize
they can better serve their sons by prayer and sacred reading—growing themselves—than by a lot of talking. I should have reverence for
my own time and guard it with due care and not let it be taken heed-
lessly. Yet the Fathers do not hesitate to spend moments in leisure
with the brethren, enjoying pleasantries, etc. There is a full humanness about them.

❋

There was a lot of commotion late this morning, with all the bells ringing, as the Minister of Northern Greece arrived for a brief visit. He greeted me in English. I then retired to my room for some rest. Suddenly the door opened and there was the Minister, full of apologies for barging in. He wanted to see how the monastery looked from my balcony.

For the most part the day has been very quiet and peaceful. I finished Acts and am now into Romans. I had intended to read the Old Testament first, but I left my Bible at Simonos Petras to cut down baggage weight, so I have only my pocket New Testament. It is providential as it is good to read Paul and be centered with him in Christ these days of Pentecost. I hope I will be able to read through the Old Testament and come again to the New before I complete this retreat. I want to enter into the fullness of salvation history and let it come alive in me.

Tuesday, June 2

꘍ Half a month already gone! Lord, have mercy.

This morning before the Midnight Service there was a solemn blessing of water with a sort of litany of saints and then a sprinkling and anointing with the water. It reminded me of what we used to do on the Vigil of Pentecost. It is a good time to renew Baptism, because we have been baptized in water and the Holy Spirit.

Father Grigorios took me to see Father Paisios, about a half hour over a mountain trail. Father Paisios is the Spiritual Father of Father Vasileios and Father Grigorios and many others. Father Paisios had once been a hermit on Mount Sinai. There he contracted tuberculosis and had to return to Greece to have a lung removed. When he had recovered sufficiently, he came to the Holy Mountain and lived in a skete as Elder, with Vasileios and Grigorios and another. When disciples came in greater numbers and the diminishing community at Stavronikita had faded out of existence, the Holy Community asked him to come here. He sent Father Vasileios with the others and returned to the eremitical life. That was in 1968.

Father Paisios received us warmly. He is a small, lean, graying man, looking much older than his fifty-two years. While we prayed in the rugged little chapel with its screen of modernized icons, he prepared the usual coffee and glasses of sweet, cool water from the well. We sat outside the cell on stones which he had covered with cardboard for us.

I questioned Father Paisios on his life: I don't remember; I am an idiot. Then on continual prayer: First you must find tranquillity and simplicity—to be free for prayer and know yourself; second, you must know the mercy of God; third, you must know that prayer is not a burden but a rest. If you want to pray continually, you must be free from responsibility. If you cannot be free, you must further the possibility for others and you will share in the merit of their prayers. The worst thing is a superior who does not appreciate prayer. If you feel the call to constant prayer, you should be insistent with your superior to be free, but in the end you must obey—he has the responsibility before God.

The young can have illusions and seek mystical experience for the wrong reasons. A dirty child trying to snuggle up to a king will be repulsed, but if he peeks from a distance, he will be called, cleaned, and welcomed close. As Father said this, he acted it out, first crouching down behind the large sleeve of his rason and peeking out from behind it, then throwing out his arms in great glee as if responding to the call, and then rocking an imaginary child in his arms close to his heart. The totalness of simplicity! One does not quickly forget lessons taught with such charm.

There were many other things we spoke of. With emphasis he said we should disorganize our life in the monastery, leave all the military regimentation behind in order to find spiritual freedom. But even the monk enjoying constant prayer should have his canon* of prayers for the Church, benefactors, etc., and after that he is free. He spoke especially of metanias and prayer on the rope. I noted that his thumbs were very callused and almost doubled in thickness. I suspect this is from making many metanias.

Reading, he said, is important, but practice is more so—"Be a 'philosopher' not only in your mind but also in your life."

During the summer Father Paisios receives many pilgrims, but otherwise he is free. A novice, about to depart for exams at the university and military service, arrived with a basket of fruit and vegetables from the monastery, which cares for Father Paisios' needs. As we left, he went part way with us and gave me a small plaque which he made. There is an impression of Mount Athos on it, with Mary hovering in the sky over the Mountain. We returned to the monastery hot and tired but spiritually refreshed.

I think of the four-day retreat I led for some Benedictines just before I left the United States—they seemed like very fruitful days. I would like all days to be fruitful in that way. But those days could be what they were because of what went before. There must be seed time for harvest, and fallow time, too. I haven't gotten to the section on the jubilee yet in the Old Testament, but it applies. Yet in fallow time, the good earth is longing for the fruitfulness. Paul tells us all creation is yearning for the fullness of the Redemption (Romans 8:22). It is now a fallow time for me. Yet I find in me this yearning, even a little restlessness, longing for the fullness, for getting on with the filling out of the Redemption in myself and others. May this time lead to very great fruitfulness.

Petitionary prayer—I think we have to make more of it. It is true that it is not in the words but in the heart. God does not look to what we say but how we hold people and needs in our heart. He sees this as we stand before him, and we need say nothing or, at most, Mary's "They have no wine" or the sisters' "Lazarus, whom you love, is sick." Yet I think it is helpful for us in developing that heartfelt care and concern to formulate our prayer of petition. We should make more of the Prayer of the Faithful. I should take time to formulate more explicitly my intentions for Liturgy as the Orthodox priest does at Prothesis,* the preparation for Liturgy. The Anglican monks of the Holy Cross have a period of fifteen minutes before or after Tierce when they simply hold up to God the petitions they have received. I find in these days I am praying more frequently, more explicitly for my Spiritual Father and my spiritual sons, for my community and family, for those who have committed themselves to my prayers and those to whom I have been called upon to minister, to so many needs and peoples and all mankind. Lord, have mercy.

A practice here on Mount Athos is that during the Prothesis, when the priest is putting the small pieces of bread on the diskos, at one point he rings a bell and all bow in silence, remembering the liv-

ing and dead they wish remembered at Liturgy while the priest puts
portions on the diskos for them.

❊

Father Grigorios told me the blessing of water is done about once
a month to have a supply of holy water. The monks who do not receive Holy Communion, besides receiving the Antidoron* from the
priest at the end of the Liturgy, also drink a bit of this water. It is
kept in a special shrine where there is a fresco of the Baptism of
Jesus. But Father Grigorios said they do not think of the rite as a recall of Baptism, as we Western monks do with our weekly blessing
and sprinkling with water.

Wednesday, June 3

☙ The bell rang an hour earlier than usual (1:50 A.M.) and
the Services began at 2:50, ending at 6:15. The reason—a gasoline
motor used in the bakery broke down and had to be loaded on the
boat going to Ierissos,* to be fixed. The boat was due around 6:30
and many hands would be needed to load it, as it is very heavy. The
tractor pulled it down to the port in a cart, then the monks put ropes
around it and put a long pole through the ropes so many could lift it
aboard. I like the flexibility here where the Superior can adjust the
schedule easily to needs and the monks take it quite simply in
stride.

❊

An old monk, Father Enoch, was the only visitor last night. He is
considered a very holy man. He lives alone near Karyes. It is quite evident that he is most welcome here. He came simply for supper and
Apodeipnon, slept, and left right after Liturgy. With a sizable bag
over his shoulder, the climb to Karyes would be quite a penance for
the old man of eighty. But this is the sort of thing monks do on the
Mountain.

❊

When I went down for dinner there was a young pilgrim from
Texas there, Charles Crowley, a beautiful, open lad who had just

finished at the Quaker college in Indiana and was going to enter Andover Newton in the fall. He hoped eventually to teach but felt a call first to minister and experience the vitality of his theology. After lunch we shared for a time the differences we experienced between the Orthodox and Western Christian approach to God. I was also able to share with him our ways of dialogical reading of the Gospels and Centering Prayer. He hopes to visit Spencer after I return.

❊

I talked for over an hour with Father Vasileios. He is insistent that the way to unity is for monks to live truly spiritual lives and become true theologians like Father Paisios. The deeper one enters in the Spirit, the more he seeks the truth.

Father emphasized the importance of the whole man entering into prayer. He is opposed to Christians using Yoga and Zen, techniques which are associated with other cultures and cults which he sees as having something of the devil in them. I am afraid I cannot fully agree with him here, but I certainly agree with his follow-up question: Why not use our own Christian tradition of metania? For the beginners he prescribes fifty full prostrations and five komvoschinions, making the little metania with each careful recitation of the Jesus Prayer.

He affirmed the need for great freedom in the monastery. On work days they have lunch at 10:30 to allow about four hours work after Liturgy. They have Liturgy every day and all are expected to attend. In practice, all receive Holy Communion on Saturday, other days only one or two receive, with the permission of the Gerontas.

For reading Father Vasileios urges especially Isaac the Syrian—the prime influence on Father Paisios and himself it would seem—warning, however, of the eremitical orientation. He feels Isaac is fully developed, very current, and alive, completely psychologically balanced. Also he encourages the reading of Saint John Climacus, Saint Gregory Palamas, and Saint Symeon the New Theologian. Evagrius is out among Orthodox because of his condemnation for Origenism, but his teaching on prayer is introduced under other names, such as Saint Nilos, by different Fathers.

Father Vasileios insisted that though the lives of monks, East and West, are similar, the spirit with which we live is different. The Western concept of the Church tends to destroy the mystery. We must remain where we are in our respective traditions, yet change to become truly united. We were talking in the library which is well stocked with Patristic writings, including Migne, *Sources chrétiennes*, and others published in the West. In regard to *Sources chrétiennes*, Father Vasileios noted that the notes are very extrinsic. Scientific work does need to be done—but the Fathers are fire and we must let ourselves be inflamed. Each young monk should be guided by the Gerontas in the Father best for him. Some of the more simple cannot follow Saint John Chrysostom, but the more dedicated need this kind of spiritual food.

❊

As I sit in my room I hear the same kind of evening sounds I hear at home: the birds singing, someone hammering in the distance, and a power saw off in the nearby woods. With all the differences, there is still so much here that is very much as at home, even down to the details.

The food here is excellent, especially this week, which is a festal week with no fasting. Yesterday we had some very good fish with a fine tasty sauce. And there is a good red wine. They have their own flock of chickens to provide them with an abundance of fresh eggs. The food is well prepared. Like all monks, though, they eat very quickly. They also do what we used to do: serve very large portions to each and leave an empty dish into which each one can spoon what he does not want.

❊

A young Greek who has been here all week is fasting today and made his confession this afternoon in preparation for Communion tomorrow. The Sacrament is still so unapproachable for the Orthodox. We Catholics certainly could use some of their reverence, but I think the Lord in the Gospels shows a constant desire to be close even to us sinners.

❊

In order to walk, one must take the first step; in order to swim, one must throw oneself into the water. It is the same with the Incarnation of the Name. Begin to pronounce it with adoration and love. Cling to it. Repeat it. Do not think that you are invoking the

Name; think only of Jesus himself. Say his Name slowly, softly
and quietly.

※

There is a polish for everything that takes away its rust; and the
polish of the heart is the Invocation of Jesus.

※

When the heart begins to recite, the tongue should stop.

※

When occupied with self, you are separated from God. The way
to God is but one step, the step out of yourself.

Thursday, June 4

꧁ Tomorrow will be the twenty-fifth anniversary of my entering the monastery—a cause for much thought and prayer. I am offering today to the Lord, especially in reparation for all the sins, faults,
and failures of these years. How poor has been my response to such
great love. I hope tomorrow will indeed be by God's grace a new beginning.

※

After lunch I sat for a time in the cemetery. The sun is very hot,
but there is a gentle breeze fluttering about and there is no humidity,
so it is quite comfortable in the shade. A bit of the heavenly life is
my present state, just being before God, receiving all, and enjoying
him. But there are great differences, to say the least. I have no spiritual body—how well I know that—but a very physical one that is a
weight on the spirit in more ways than one. There is a basic contentment, to let things be as God would have them—Thy will be done.
Yet deep within me there is also the desire to be finished with the
pilgrimage and be with God. I realize more the meaning of Saint
Benedict's final words: "Through *patience* we share in the Passion of
Christ." Here we monks have our quiet role in bringing the creation
to its fullness. By love, prayer, and presence we make Christ's saving
Passion present to our times, to the pilgrim Body.

❄

The monastery is so quiet most of the time it could be taken to be abandoned. Little is seen of the monks. Three laymen do most of the gardening. The monks seem to be kept busy within: cooking, cleaning, baking, secretarial work, icon painting, study, and mostly praying in their cells. Before and after meals there are little gatherings on the terrace. (The view from the terrace in front of the gardens is considered to be one of the most beautiful on the whole Mountain—across the blue waters of the northern sea to Iviron,* then up the green slopes to Philotheou and beyond that to the soaring magnificence of Mount Athos itself, crowned with clouds in the azure skies. A real invitation to "lift up your hearts.") And, of course, there is always a monk in the porter's lodge to welcome the visitors.

❄

The daily cross:

The vertical—following Christ to heaven.
The horizontal—my own tendencies and desires.

I can escape the cross by not following Christ, forgetting his call, dropping the vertical out of my life. But the horizontal has no destination—ultimate frustration—that is hell.

To carry the cross daily:

consciously choose to be a Christian.
follow Christ—not by the feet but by ideals and principles.
read the Scriptures to see what Christ wants.

It is the way to love.

❄

Till your untilled ground,
Sow not among thorns. — JEREMIAH 4:3
    — purity of heart to receive the Word.

❄

The mind is filled with thoughts that create a gulf between man and God. Empty the mind; in the stillness you will find union with God.

AGHIOS
PANTELEIMONOS

Aghios Panteleimonos

Friday, June 5

One of the things I think the Lord is trying to say to me very strongly in this retreat is to hang loose and move with him. When I got up I expected another quiet day at the Stavronikita and possibly another chance to talk with Father Vasileios. During Mass he sent for me to say he would be leaving in a few minutes for Athens and would be back in five or six days. I could return to see him later. If I had had more warning, I could have driven to Karyes and down to Daphni with him, but it was too late to get my few things together and be off with him. So after Liturgy and breakfast, I started the climb to Karyes. As I walked along the road I said the Jesus Prayer, as has become my habit. I find it very easy to pray constantly here. The whole atmosphere is so charged with prayer. It seems to be so in harmony with prayer—as it were, impregnated by it. The climb was difficult. Although the sun was not yet hot, it was very humid. I stopped at the Kellion of Saint Nicholas to speak again with Father Nicholas, the English monk who had lived with Father Sophrony in England for two years before coming to the Mountain. He had planned to stay with his Elder until he reposed and then come, but Father Sophrony told him not to wait any longer. This separation from his Spiritual Father is one of the sorrows in his life. Father Sophrony is one of the few who really understands East and West.

We again found ourselves speaking of the Spiritual Father. The strength of the Spiritual Father is the strength of his prayer. When one loses his Spiritual Father he realizes a great loss. The Father has learned the way through his own struggles, sufferings, and prayer. Thus each Father has to some extent his own way. One who has grown in the cenobium* will know and teach that way. Another will perhaps emphasize the Jesus Prayer more. Even in idiorrhythmic* monasteries there are some very good Spiritual Fathers, like Father Maximos at Iviron. But their disciples usually defer to them only with regard to their spiritual life and canon of prayer. The good of obedience, which is so central in Orthodox monastic practice, is to some extent missing in the idiorrhythmic monasteries, though there may be hidden saints there. (Father Nicholas told me how Father Paisios after three years at Esphigmenou,* asked to be allowed to seek an Elder in the desert. He went to a saintly old monk who was becoming very feeble and sick. The two of them went to live in Philotheou, which was at that time still a lax, idiorrhythmic monastery, and they lived in a hidden way a very ascetic life.) But in the cenobium or kellion, one lives in complete obedience in every regard.

We spoke again, too, of Western Christians using Orthodox practices and spiritual writings. I think we agreed the full living out of the Jesus Prayer was impossible outside of a hermitage or a monastery geared to it. Or a society open to such as was Russia. Father Nicholas felt there are still places in Serbia where lay people can do this. For the rest, the use of the Jesus Prayer becomes usually little more than a sort of ejaculatory prayer, sometimes combined with metanias or put in rhythm with breathing or perhaps used as a sort of mantric prayer, but not used in the fullness of the spirit of the tradition. The full spirit of the writings, also, escapes one who is not living the fullness of the tradition, with the Church and its Sacraments. (Of course Father Nicholas and I have different positions on what that means.) But Father Nicholas felt it is good and profitable for Westerners to use these writings. Truly seeking, they will find much. It seems to me the writings do complement the strong emphasis on loving intimacy found in our tradition with a certain reverence. I do personally feel they have a lot to offer us. We agreed there was nothing contradictory here.

Father Nicholas asked about my monastery—what young people are seeking when they visit or seek to enter. I said I thought in part it is the stability present there in the midst of a very unstable world; but more, the evident love and peace and joy that is present there. They are received with love and given care. Those who are serious about entering are brought more into contact with the community and can see in the seniors, like Father Bernard, the beautiful fruit of this kind of life.

I shared with him a very real question in my own heart. How, while remaining fully true to what we should be as monks—for otherwise we are of no use to anyone—can we be more to those who are seeking and searching? The gurus and swamis use mass media, organization, techniques to attract these young people to their response.

We have a fuller response and one that the Westerner can so much more fully and easily integrate into his native culture. Yet I fear many of those seeking have written Christianity off as having failed. We have so few real Spiritual Fathers to respond to so many. I don't think it is because God is not willing to give us many more—all we need—but few of us are willing to pay the price necessary for such paternity. Father Nicholas felt such a question would not even occur to an Orthodox monk. He simply lives his life as a monk. Another caution Father Nicholas offered in regard to reading the Orthodox Fathers was that Westerners without guidance often took up very advanced writings which, without guidance and due preparation, could lead one into illusion. I asked where one usually begins in his tradition. He mentioned the writings of Dorotheus of Gaza for his novice (coincidentally today is the feast of Dorotheus), of John Climacus, of Theodore the Studite, and of course the Gospels. He thought the idea that the Gospels should be put off, which I heard from one Father, was not good.

With the hope that we might meet again I took my leave and walked through a desert area, where there are a number of hermits, to Aghiou Andreou near Karyes. The formerly gigantic Russian skete with the largest church on the Mountain fell into emptiness when Russians could no longer come. Recently it was opened in part as a minor seminary for Northern Greece. The hope was that it would offer the monks opportunity for study and also perhaps produce some monastic vocations. But so far, neither has happened. It was a poor time for a visit, as the students were getting ready to go home for vacation. There was a busload of them with me en route to Daphni. In fact, the bus left over an hour late, waiting for them to get themselves and their baggage together.

An American monk asked me to get him a prayer rope and have it blessed at the grave of Father Silouan, so I decided to go to Aghios Panteleimonos* to visit his grave before returning to Simonos Petras. The fifteen monks who are to arrive from Russia will make little impact in this massive monastery that could house a couple thousand. I am sure the guest house could easily bed down a thousand people. But only small sections are being kept up.

Saturday, June 6

I think the Lord must be laughing at me. As I walked around Aghios Panteleimonos yesterday afternoon I became quite depressed. In 1965 over half the main monastery burned down. Two years later a wing of the guest house also burned down. Little has been done even to tidy the ruins. All the surrounding buildings are empty and falling down. The frescoed interiors of the used part are cracking and peeling—it is a very desolate scene. The cemetery is at the highest point of the property. I could find no way to get there through the ruins. I was anxious just to get away from the place. I wondered if the Lord brought me here to show me what my twenty-five years really looked like in his sight. I remember reading Paul the other day—how we all build on the foundation that is Christ, but with different kinds of material: precious gems, gold, silver, stone, wood, stubble. In the end we will be saved, but only through fire—and each one will have to sustain his loss according as he has built. How have I built? Is so much of it stubble, needing to be burned away? I am afraid so.

I went to the katholikon for Vespers. It was not open. A monk directed me to the top of the monastery where I found another immense church—actually a double church; rich in gilt work and nineteenth-century naturalistic icons. Four monks were singing Vespers and two pious Russian émigrés were attending. After Vespers I met the émigrés. They had been living in Brussels for forty-five years and come here each year. They served as my intermediaries with the monks who spoke only Russian. The welcome was warm. We went down to the other church where a larger group was now celebrating Vespers. They asked the priest who was incensing the icons if we could venerate the relics. He took us behind the screen and we venerated the skull of Saint Panteleimon and many other relics—of Saint John the Baptist, Saint Basil, and so on.

As we left we met the Hegumen, Archimandrite Avel, a relatively young Russian who has been here about six years. He was most friendly. And in our conversation we discovered we had entered the monastery at the same age. He invited me to the refectory and sat me at his own table. After supper we visited the bell tower. They have an immense collection of bells, the largest on Mount Athos. The biggest weighs eighteen tons. The Hegumen had a cell prepared for me in the monastery and insisted that I stay till Sunday. It proved to be the cell farthest from the destroyed part, with the windows overlooking the sea, new clean sheets, and for the first time on Athos a large comfortable chair. As I settled down for the night I had to chuckle. Maybe in all this the Lord is showing me his world, so full of the havoc of sin, and how specially he cares for me, providing a quiet, beautiful corner for me in it. In any case, his love is beyond all telling. And even as the needs of men press upon us, we can rest confidently in his love. "What can separate us from the love of Christ?"

The Services began at five this morning with a few more monks attending, ending with the Liturgy around 8:30. The singing on the whole is a bit rough, but a young tenor sang the Cherubim Hymn with great beauty.

Of the twenty monks here, there are only two that could in any way be considered young. Most are very old. It has been a quiet day of prayer. Although I have nothing to do but pray and read, I seem to get little reading done. The long Services in church and the quiet prayer in the cell fill the hours. Today I said the Rosary. I have been using the prayer cord nearly constantly since I came to the Mountain. It felt good to take up the beads for a change. It took a couple of hours to move through the fifteen mysteries. I think though I shall use the beads more.

I am happy to see efforts being made here and elsewhere to prevent fires and fight them, since the monasteries have suffered so much from fire. Here they have put in an extensive system of large pipes throughout the building, with frequent openings. At Pantokratoros, in the outer porch of the church, there is a portable fire pump made stationary with a lead hose right into a well. The future will perhaps be spared from a repetition of the past.

I feel a touch of homesickness at times as I see the boats go by heading for Ouranoupolis and look forward to the day I will be heading home. It is good to know I have a home. I appreciate more the asceticism of those monks called to be pilgrims for Christ, ever on the move, dependent on their hosts, never sure how long they will be in one place and when and where they will move on. In a sense, that is the way I have been living these past few weeks. It calls for great detachment, taking each moment as it comes. Letting the Father, who provides for the birds, provide for one's everyday needs. He certainly has been providing well for me. It is a new experience for me. In the past my trips have all been carefully planned out and, in a sense, from the very first day, I was already on the homeward journey. Oftentimes my eagerness to get home would get the better of me and I would omit some of the last things and head straight for home. This time there is going to be a lot of emptying before the homeward lap. One of the temptations I have to resist is beginning to plan the homeward journey. One of the things I think the Lord wants to teach me is to live freely and wholly in the *now*, with him, and not miss the present because I am in the future. Sufficient for the day is the evil thereof—and the grace, joy, and peace of it, too.

There is no problem getting exercise here. My room is over a hundred steps up from the katholikon. But it is important to get exercise. The diet is rich. Fish and eggs at every meal, along with pasta, salad, cheese, abundant wine, and excellent bread. It is not surprising that I have seen here some of the stoutest monks I have seen in my life. The deacon, I am sure, is as much around as he is tall.

I found one of the stout Russian monks working placidly with a tiny trowel and a pan of cement, patching some cracks in the stairway, seemingly oblivious of the mountain of ruins around him. His humble labor seemed something like a pebble in the face of a flood. Yet there was something serenely beautiful in his quiet labor. "It is better to light one candle than curse the darkness." I do not know if his work was being done in obedience. I am not sure if there is much obedience or discipline here or if there is a true Staretz,* or Spiritual Father.

After Liturgy this morning we venerated the skull of Staretz Silouan. Already in his time the place might have been in decline. There were over two thousand here at the turn of the century. Then World War I called away more than seven hundred, practically none to return and no new ones allowed to come from Russia. It was all downhill after that. Yet in the midst of it all, Father Silouan achieved eminent holiness, and I am sure others did, too. And today there is Father Seraphim who has been here fifty-five years and radiates holiness. Environment can help or hinder, but not prevent the growth in holiness.

Before supper there was a brief service—only thirty-five minutes.

After supper Father Seraphim invited me to his cell for Nescafé—something very special on the Mountain. I see how they keep the old monks limber; his cell at the other end of the surviving building—at the point where the fire was stopped—is fifteen steps higher than mine. Quite a climb for an old man to make several times a day.

Find the door of your heart and you will find the door of the Kingdom of Heaven. — SAINT JOHN CHRYSOSTOM

The essential part is to dwell in God, and this walking before God means that you live with the conviction ever before your consciousness that God is in you, as he is in everything: you live in the firm assurance that he sees all that is within you, knowing you better than you know yourself. This awareness of the eye of God looking in your inner being must not be accompanied by any visual concept, but must be confined to a simple conviction or feeling. — THEOPHANE THE RECLUSE

The Staretz Parphenil of Kiev likened the flowing movement of the Jesus Prayer to a gently murmuring stream. The invocation of the Name is a prayer for all seasons. It can be used by everyone in every place and at every time. It is suitable for the beginner as well as for the more experienced; it can be offered in company with others or alone; it is equally appropriate in the desert or in the city, in surroundings of recollected tranquillity or in the midst of the utmost noise or agitation. It is never out of place.

The principal thing is to stand before God with the mind and heart and to go on standing before him unceasingly night and day.
— THEOPHANE THE RECLUSE

It is a great illusion to imagine that prayer time should be different from any other, for we are equally bound to be united to God by work in work time and by prayer in prayer time.

Sunday, June 7

༄ When a pond is greatly agitated by the breezes and the wind, one can throw in a pebble or even many pebbles and there is no noticeable effect. When a pond is perfectly at peace and one casts a pebble into it, the gentle waves spread in every direction till they reach even the farthest shore.

I have noticed in the greater quiet that thoughts for better or for worse are much more perceptible, carrying so many resonances. When we are in the midst of a busy everyday life, so many thoughts go in and out of our minds and our hearts that we do not perceive the effect they are having upon us. But when we come to achieve a deeper inner quiet, then we are much more discerning. The way is open to following even the most gentle leadings of the Spirit and to avoid even the most subtle deviations that are suggested either by the self or by the evil one. By deep prayer, with the help of the Holy Spirit, we can hope to so establish this deep inner quiet that even in the midst of everyday activities, this lively sensitivity will remain and all activities will be guided by the call of grace and the leading of the Holy Spirit. This is really the fruit of hesychasm.

❈

The great bell rang last night at 8:30 for the beginning of Agripnia, the All-Night Vigil, but actually they broke off at about two this morning. At nine the Hegumen led a pontifical celebration in the upper church, while the Archpriest led one in the katholikon in Greek. One has to admire the heroic efforts of the holy remnant here. With only twelve or thirteen able monks and most of these very old, they continue to celebrate the full Services in Slavonic in the upper church and in Slavonic and Greek in the lower church of Saint Panteleimon. Only the full Greek Service in the church of the Dormition has been dropped. There seems to be only one monk left who sings in Greek and he is kept busy in Saint Panteleimon's. The way these old men continue during the long hours in choir praising God and praying for all says much of the meaning of monasticism.

In the monasteries where there is Apodeipnon, the Acathist Hymn is prayed before it. In the others it is said before Vespers.

Today it was celebrated pontifically in the upper church of the Protection of the Virgin. In the lower church there was a special veneration of the relics of Saint Panteleimon. It is the Feast of All Saints, and I was glad to be able at this monastery to honor Father Silouan on his feast.

In the course of the afternoon I took a walk around the cemetery and the extensive buildings, discovering some new wild flowers, especially one bush of yellow flowers with long streaming red pistils—truly beautiful. How the Lord lets the abundance of his magnificent beauty even adorn ruins! It is certainly what he does in his mercy in our poor sin-scarred lives.

Aghios Panteleimonos is certainly a place not to be forgotten. There is good fellowship among the monks here. The Hegumen always carries his crosier as he walks about, but it is a formality that does not impede fraternity. There was a solemn meal after Liturgy today, with cope, candle, bells, and all. There is something tragic in seeing a stooped old monk function as an acolyte. The younger ones were ringing the bells.

After dinner a large group of military arrived by boat. All the bells were rung. The monks seem to try to be good to government personnel. The young soldier stationed here is very well treated by the Hegumen.

Four or five of the monks came from Russia only three months ago. They know no Greek.

I will be glad tomorrow to return to Simonos Petras. It seems a bit like home for me now. I hope I will be able to settle quietly there for the rest of my time on the Mountain.

When you pray, you yourself must be silent . . . You yourself must be silent, let the prayer speak. — COLLIANDER

Prayer is God who works all things in all men.

— SAINT GREGORY OF SINAI

❊

To stop the continual jostling of your thoughts, you must bind the mind with one thought or the thought of One only.

— THEOPHANE THE RECLUSE

BACK AT
SIMONOS PETRAS

Grigoriou

Monday, June 8

I was surprised when the boat arrived at Simonos Petras and many got off. Last time I was the only one. This time a couple of monks, a group of students from Aghiou Andreou, and some tourists and pilgrims alighted. If the hundred plus steps at Aghios Panteleimonos keep one trim, the climb from the port to the monastery of Simonos Petras is killing—over a thousand feet straight up an old donkey path.

Before I left Aghios Panteleimonos, Father Seraphim gave me some picture postcards of the monastery and the other Russian monasteries. The Hegumen gave me an icon of Saint Panteleimon. When I finally reached Simonos Petras, Father Theologos, the guestmaster, welcomed me very warmly and soon I was back in my cell, had a good wash and rest, and enjoyed a big bowl of lentils.

In the course of the afternoon, some twenty officers arrived from the military school at Thessaloniki. They were invited into the choir. At the close of Vespers they venerated the icons after the priests, before the rest of the community. I like the way in general that visitors here are brought into the Services and even asked to read, etc. This is common on the Mountain, at least in regard to Orthodox guests.

After lunch Father Dionysios brought along Professor Apostolos Karpozilos from the faculty of Byzantine studies at the University of Thessaloniki. He has been here for a week to explore the archives and see if any of the material is worth publishing. He found some later material of interest which he will indicate to colleagues, but nothing of note from his own earlier period of expertise. The fires have destroyed most.

We had a long talk. He had studied at Yale and was eager to talk to an American. He will leave shortly to take a post at Ioannina in the Western mountains of Greece—at one of the three small, relatively new universities founded in the hope of developing other areas of the country. Until recently there were only two universities (Athens and Thessaloniki) and students tended to come to the cities and stay. Professors still tend to commute from the two great universities to the new smaller ones. Apostolos thought it would be good to locate in Ioannina to help develop a new center of cultural life there.

We talked about many things.

The professor indicated how Saint Gregory Palamas did not in fact break with tradition but rather systematized and refined a tradition long alive among the monastics, alongside the more commonly accepted ecclesial tradition. In doing this, he faced, besides the opposition of the Westerner Varlam, also that of the other Orthodox tradition and the Greek Thomists. But monasticism since the tenth century (and not just because of spirituality but also because of economy—the monks had immense landholdings and systems not unlike those in the West), was coming into its own. Earlier, in a situation where Christianity and paganism were often mixed, the Bishop chosen was a local man who could defend the territory and, later, was chosen as a reward for imperial service. But in the tenth century the practice of choosing monks as Bishops began to prevail. As a result, Palamas' teaching was quickly accepted as the doctrine of the Church by an almost wholly monastic episcopate.

We touched a bit on charismatic leadership, not only in the Spiritual Father but also in the secular sphere, among professors and presidents. Europeans generally find it hard to understand the American situation where election is a popularity contest. In Europe they seek a man who has quality and charisma. Just as the Spiritual Father is chosen by the seeker as one who has the sincerity and the abilities he needs to find in a guide, so the professor's status is judged by his learning and ability. The president of Greece is a man of extensive education and culture. American leaders seem shallow in comparison.

The awakening climate in the universities is very important in Greece, quite different than that in the United States. The students are not apt to take much of a turn toward the Church, which compromised itself with the 1967–73 dictatorship in Greece. Nor monasticism, which had compromised itself with the Turks through the centuries and then played it cool with Greek liberation in the early years of this century in order to safeguard extensive landholdings. Before World War II only a very few from pious families, and some others who were unfit for life in the world, came to the monasteries. After the war, for ten years or more it was impossible. Now, with some good Spiritual Fathers, some are coming this way. But most students will turn to politics and social reform. A big difference from the American scene is that the young people here are not rebelling against their parents and their parents' generation. The family is still very solid and elders are respected and loved. Also, the students belong to well-defined, already established political parties with clear Marxist and democratic principles. They have been effective, proving to be the only group who was free enough and strong enough to oust the dictatorship. They have no desire to turn to the communist socialist world, but wish to create something that puts Greek interests first. They want to stay aligned with the West if America will adopt a policy that will let Greeks have the last say in what concerns the Greeks.

I think Apostolos summed up Simonos Petras well in saying, "They want to live the fullness of the tradition in a human way. While there is much that can be criticized about Mount Athos, what better has anyone to offer the world today? They may retain the tradition in a somewhat static way, but where else can we find it? All come here to find it. They have this role to play in the ecclesiastical and cosmic scheme of things. And the monks receive a grace from the Lord to live out this life and achieve great sanctity in doing it. Mount Athos has to be seen in the light of the whole."

After the Liturgy today I looked up at the Cross and spontaneously there came from my heart the words: "You did this in memory of me." Jesus was mindful of me as he hung on the Cross. Great is his love.

A man who has committed himself to the way of interior attention to himself, must above all entertain the fear of God which is the beginning of wisdom. — SERAPHIM OF SAROV

Tuesday, June 9

Apostolos was working on an English introduction to a new critical edition of the letters of Joannis Mauropous (died c. 1075) and asked me to go over it for him. That kept me up till midnight.

We went over it this morning and after lunch until he took off on a mule to get the two o'clock boat at Daphni. Father Myron walked down behind the mule and rode it back—Greek hospitality is really something! Daphni is ten kilometers away!

Here I sit on the balcony over the sea, sipping coffee, feeling the warm sun, and the cool breeze—enjoying this bit of paradise. Deep down in some little corner of my soul there is a voice urging me to feel a bit guilty. It is perhaps that streak of Jansenism in all of us, a bit of fear. To be holy it has to be hard, painful. We tend to find it difficult to simply receive good things, especially when they are so completely undeserved. We have to learn to accept good things from the Lord, our loving Father, as well as bad. Yesterday it was a killing climb in the hot sun. Today it is a bit of Tabor at the top. They should be received with equal love and gratitude. It is precious to share in the saving plan of the Lord, whether by suffering or by joy. Perhaps we feel safer with suffering because we know our ability to be selfish. But we are, in fact, although more subtly, equally capable of being selfish in our sufferings. It keeps getting back to becoming the child for the Kingdom of Heaven, accepting with love all our Father disposes. This is what pleases, merits, saves. "I do always the things that please the Father." Our Model said that. "Learn of Me. . . ."

I am happy to see Father Myron coming over the rise of the hill, now on top of the jogging donkey instead of running along behind. The students have been helping Father Kyrikos with the guesthouse sheets—endless numbers of them. Guests are certainly never lacking. At lunch there were two besides Apostolos and myself. One, a sociologist from Montpellier, in France, affirmed he had no faith—just came to see an interesting corner of the world. The student from Brussels said almost the same. Most of these tourists never come to Services. The monks make no effort to invite them or to let them know when they are—and some monasteries forbid them to attend. The Services are long, and the tourists would be distracted distractions. I admire the great patience of the guestmasters, especially Father Kyrikos, who greets all with warmth and smiles, hastens to get coffee and sweets and then a meal for each one who comes. Of the many things one can learn from these monks, hospitality is certainly one of them.

I also can learn from the brothers here something about fraternal love. There is a warmth among them that is extraordinary, yet with a certain reverence for each other, a care and a kindly concern. And a time for playfulness, too.

After supper, Father Dionysios and I spoke for a while. He told me Archimandrite Aimilianos' father is in America now, visiting his daughter who lives in Detroit.

They are going to give me a new cell in the other building where it will be quieter and I will have a private balcony, so will be less apt to be disturbed by the many guests. It will be next to the cell that Saint Nectarios used when he was here. One is close to the saints here. Father Aimilianos' father was born in Cappadocia, the land of Saint Basil and Saint Gregory, and slept by the latter's tomb as a boy. Father Theologos, who grew up with Father Aimilianos and became an Archimandrite before coming here to join the community as a monk, has a brother who is an Archimandrite and cares for the tomb of Saint Nectarios.

Father Dionysios then introduced me to two young Finnish students. They had come because they are close to the community at Uusi Valamo in Finland. Before World War I there were a thousand monks in the community. By World War II there were only three hundred; today there are six. One of the monks there is an American, Father Anthony. He converted from Catholicism fifteen years ago and came to Uusi Valamo two years ago. Father Anthony read my article in *Sobornst* about Meteora and wrote the monks here about coming for a visit. He is the one who directed the two students here. One of them is studying for the priesthood, the other, photography. They are both active in trying to promote Orthodoxy among the youth in a country where most of the population belong to the state church that does not have much spiritual vitality. They feel the key to spiritual renewal is the Tradition and the Fathers. Unfortunately, there is little in Finnish of the writings of the Fathers; they depend much on English and Russian. The *Way of the Pilgrim* will be published in Finnish for Christmas.

The monks at Uusi Valamo are very poor. They are swamped by visitors—over thirty thousand last year. They have a guesthouse for sixty. Most of the monks are very old. The Hegumen is eighty-four and the oldest monk is one hundred and three. Their Archbishop is very supportive of them and plans a new church for them soon. Not far away from them is a convent of almost twenty nuns, equally poor. The community had been very wealthy before the wars, with twelve sketes, extensive lands in Russia, a small fleet of ships, etc.

❊

Through the remembrance of Jesus Christ, gather together your disintegrated mind that is scattered abroad.

— PHILOTHEOS OF SINAI

❊

The remembrance of the Name of God utterly destroys all that is evil. — BARSANUPHIOS

❊

The Jesus Prayer holds in itself the whole Gospel truth. It is a summary of the Gospels.

❊

The Name of Jesus present in the human heart confers upon it the power of deification.

Wednesday, June 10

Do not trouble about the number of times you say the prayer. Let this be your sole concern that it should spring up in your heart with quickening power like a fountain of living water. Expel entirely from your mind all thoughts of quantity.

— THEOPHANE THE RECLUSE

❊

Do not contradict the thoughts suggested by your enemies, for that is exactly what they want and they will not cease from troubling you. But turn to the Lord for help against them, laying before him your own powerlessness; for he is able to expel them and to reduce them to nothing. — BARSANUPHIOS

❊

I am back to the Old Testament again. What is striking me very strongly in Genesis and Exodus is the reality of vocation and divine election. God makes his choices and everything depends on that.

Even when he gets angry with Moses for not wanting to accept his mission, he yet does not repent of his election, and Moses yet becomes one of the greatest figures in the history of man. If we are wise, we learn to go along with God without a struggle. He made us. He has a role for each of us in the working out of his plan. Paul speaks of eternal election, too. Most of us tend to squirm a bit at our lot and think things would be better if the Lord got somebody else for our job and let us try another role. One of the graces I hope to get out of this retreat is the grace to see things God's way and move with it without reservation, whatever role he may ask me to play, whatever painful or humbling limitations this reveals in me. Praise him! *Doxa si, Kyrie.*

✻

After lunch I had a long talk with the Hegumen, Archimandrite Aimilianos—the "old man" (Gerontas), as they call the Spiritual Father here—although he is younger than I. His welcome was very warm indeed, and very loving. He assured me that that is the feeling of his whole community.

He went on to explain something of the general climate I would find on the Mountain, which represents a true living Orthodoxy. The monks do not have an order depending on the law. Rather, their order and unity come from the realization, under the light of the eschaton,* that they are one body with all the Orthodox of all times. The present unfolding events are but the doorway of eternity. Many of the monks on the Mountain sense, in a very deep way, the hurts of the past *as present.* Today, Roman Catholics sense a great closeness with the Orthodox, but the reverse is not so for the Orthodox, who have an outlook much more conditioned by the past. If the tourists increase, if the roads are put in (very bad things), or if any evil befalls, the monks here are ready to blame it on the Pope. And there is no possibility to open these monks through arguments or logic.

It is an unheard of thing, never done before (if one discounts the medieval Benedictine foundations), that a Roman Catholic monk should stay so long on the Holy Mountain, as I have proposed to do. When this was proposed, many raised difficulties. Father Aimilianos said his own monks sense it as painful that I have to stand apart in church and refectory; but we all have to be sensitive to the historical situation. In any case I can plan on staying here quietly until after the Feast of Saint Mary Magdalen, July 22 (that will be August 4 in the civil calendar). Then, depending on how things develop outside more than in this monastery, he will say if I can stay longer. He thought it would be good to have some experience of other monasteries, especially Philotheou, where the Hegumen is truly a spiritual and grace-filled man. He felt that Stavronikita has a bit of Western flavor. Each monastery is much colored by the person and teaching of the Hegumen. Westerners sometimes find it difficult to understand this great variety in such unity. The whole Mountain is as one family.

I expressed my desire to talk more about Father Aimilianos' teaching and ways of prayer. He said it is a very weighty theme and difficult, because ways of prayer are so intimately bound up with the doctrine and the psychology of the outlook. He thought, for an individual in the West with good will, it could be fruitful to draw from Orthodox sources. But for a brotherhood to try to live in Eastern ways could be dangerous and forced and truncate growth. I stressed that my desire to enter more into their ways and traditions was not so much to practice or imitate but, in the light of a different way, to see my own way more clearly and fully and also to appreciate more and glorify God for what he is doing in their midst.

The Father showed great concern for my comfort, stressed again and again I should ask for anything I need. He wanted to know if I wanted a supply of food or of Nescafé for my cell, etc. Continually, in every way, he expressed love and concern and care. That is the climate here.

While we were talking, Father David came in. He had just returned from exams at Thessaloniki. He is English, a convert from Anglicanism in his teens. He became an Orthodox priest in Holland, where he taught statistics at The Hague. He joined the community here a year or so ago, and the Hegumen sent him to the university for theology. We interrupted our conversation for some time to welcome him. He was given the usual refreshments. He brought a stack of letters from Father Aimilianos' spiritual children. I expressed sympathy to the Elder with all that mail to answer. He replied that he is not expected to answer it. He places their confessions and concerns in his heart in prayer, and soon they will write to thank him. Only rarely does he write a response. That seems like a good way for a Spiritual Father to function!

The community has a sort of city monastery, or metokion,* in Thessaloniki—Aghios Charalambos. The priest there, Father Hilarion, is from Canada. Brothers who are in the city stay there. The people come for Liturgy and confession, but it is not a parish as such.

Father Aimilianos said I could determine my own attendance at Services, only to be discreet in my presence, as that would be most acceptable. What I understood the Father as saying when he said that order came from being one body—and not from law—is that he had to be sensitive to the feelings of the other monks on the Mountain. He explicitly said they would not be able to keep me with them as long as *they* would like.

His parting wish was that Christ might evermore be between us— not that he was not already, but that we might enjoy an ever greater union in him. The Hegumen is a very wise Spiritual Father. He knew it would be helpful to my peace and prayer to know exactly where I stood and what to expect. Superiors sometimes keep their subjects in suspense, thus trying to exercise more power over them. But a good Spiritual Father has no desire for power—although in fact he may have considerable—the power of love; his only concern is for the good and peace and growth of his sons.

❄

There were a dozen guests at supper tonight. I guess the days when I had the guesthouse to myself are over, with the increasing influx of summer tourists. They come from distant and diverse places: Australia, Finland, the United States, Great Britain, France, Italy, Poland, and, in great numbers, Germany.

❄

If I feel pain at times at being put in a corner or excluded as a "heretic," I can readily accept it in a spirit of reparation for all the past sins against unity of my own Church. Even so few years ago as when I was studying theology, our theologians and even papal documents did not hesitate to exclude these holy monks and all their brothers in Orthodoxy from membership in the Body of Christ. How the Lord puts up with us! We can be consoled and take courage in seeing his patience with the first Bishops, the holy Apostles, who had their share of false zeal.

※

After supper I moved to my new cell. It is in the newer building. The top floor is the Hegumen's apartments. The next, for the old monks; then our floor, for the long-term guests (usually monks, clerical students, candidates); below, the cells of the monks. There are only a couple of others on my floor so it is very quiet. I was delighted to find a shower in the otherwise quite primitive washroom.

※

Trees which are repeatedly transplanted do not grow roots.
— SAINT GREGORY OF SINAI

※

Shining through the heart, the light of the Name of Jesus illuminates all the universe.

Thursday, June 11

It is the feast of Saints Bartholomew and Barnabas, so we started earlier—4:15—and finished about 8:30, with the Hegumen concelebrating with Father Dionysios, Father Theologos, and two deacons. After lunch I had coffee on the balcony with Father David. We talked about a good many things.

Father Georgios, who had been a professor at the University of Athens, became a priest and monk. He continued to attract young people and finally started a monastery on the island of Evia. In 1974, when there was an extensive change of hierarchy, he came to the Mountain to Simonos Petras. Grigoriou was asking for some young monks, so Father Georgios was sent there with his disciples. He was soon elected the Hegumen of that monastery. Unlike most of the other Hegumens on the Mountain and perhaps because of his background, he frequently speaks to his community, which follows very traditional lines. There are fifteen older monks remaining from the original community at Grigoriou who still to some degree look to a Spiritual Father from New Skete, although many of them have turned to the new Hegumen. In addition, there are about twenty-two new monks. Among them there is a young Peruvian convert there, Father Symeon, who speaks English very well. Father David likes Grigoriou very much and has urged me to visit there.

Simonos Petras has also sent a group of monks to Konstamonitou because there was a very fervent group of old monks there who were not attracting any new men. The monastery is somewhat off the beaten track, up in the desert area. They quickly chose one of the newcomers as Hegumen. They had appealed for monks from Simonos Petras, because, they said, they wanted to become another Simonos Petras. I think in time Simonos Petras will have a very extensive effect on the whole brotherhood on Mount Athos.

Father David explained to me how every monk is supposed to be signed into some monastery. This gives the Hegumen thereof jurisdiction over him. There are many cases, especially on the Greek mainland, where men are signed into a monastery only because they are celibate. "It is not good for man to be alone," so a priest must either be married or belong in some way to a monastic community. Father David himself is still canonically a member of the small community in The Hague. As it is a very poor community, he continued to lecture on statistics at the university there for ten years after he became a monk.

In the more traditional style of Services at Grigoriou, a choirmaster goes back and forth between the two sides of the choir, singing everything in a quiet monotone, and usually only a small group gathers around the kilrosi* (lectern) on each side to sing. Here at Simonos Petras they use a choirmaster only at Agripnia, and all the young monks gather around to sing with great energy, more the way we do in the West. The monk who does not sing moves along with the general movement of the Services in his prayer, but does not necessarily follow all the words or ideas. There is a lot of repetition which allows one to enter more deeply into the meaning of the texts. While there are advantages to spacing the liturgical hours out through the day as we do, when they are put together as here, one gets a Service long enough to be able to go quite deep.

After I took leave of Father David I returned to my cell. Shortly thereafter there was a knock and there was Father David with his wonderful warm smile and a tray of French fries, wine, and olives. He explained that at this season, Tuesday and Thursday were only minor fasts and I had missed out on my wine and oil because the community was fasting in preparation for Communion on Saturday. (Lunch had been potato soup, bread and water, with the koliva blessed at the end of the Liturgy in honor of the Apostles.) They are really too good to me here—and my waistline is in danger of showing it!

In the Services today the Apostles actually got second place to the Commemoration of Mary—"Worthy Art Thou . . ." This commemorates an event dear to the hearts of the monks on the Holy Mountain. In one of the small cells near Karyes, a young monk was praying Vespers alone in the absence of his Elder. A stranger appeared and, before the hymn to Mary, instructed him to say the "Worthy Art Thou . . ." After three efforts at repeating it—the lad wasn't too apt a student—the visitor, Archangel Gabriel, wrote it on a stone. The icon before which the youth was praying was later taken to the Protaton, the church in the center of Karyes, and is in the sanctuary there. On Mount Athos, commemoration of this occasion is given priority over the Apostles. For Athos is Mary's garden.

❊

When we have reached love, we have reached God and our way is ended. We have passed over to the island that lies beyond the world where is the Father with the Son and the Holy Spirit.

— ISAAC THE SYRIAN

Friday, June 12

Shortly after Liturgy, word came that Metropolitan Ezechiel was arriving. The monks were scurrying about just like at home. Soon they were out with crosier and cope for the Metropolitan, singing their welcome—all the bells ringing. He was met at the church door by a priest fully vested, with the Gospel Book and acolytes. The chandelier was set swinging, and all the relics were brought out. After the singing and the blessing, the Metropolitan and the Hegumen exchanged greetings. They went to the guesthouse for refreshments and an hour or so later all the bells rang again as the Metropolitan started off down the hill with a group of monks on his way to the next monastery. Coming up the hill was an old monk with a group of young students in tow. Another group of youngsters had arrived from the other direction with the Metropolitan's group. A parish priest came with still another group. There were thirty or forty youngsters for lunch.

❋

Psalm 61 speaks to me in a special way these days:

Hear, O God, my cry;
    listen to my prayer!
From the earth's end I call to you   (In some respects the Holy Mountain seems to be at the earth's end.)
    as my heart grows faint.
You will set me high upon a rock;   (Simonos Petras is built on a giant granite outcropping.)
    you will give me rest,   (That, indeed, he is doing.)
    for you are my refuge,
    a tower of strength against the enemy.
Oh, that I might lodge in your tent forever,
    take refuge in the shelter of your wings!   (That certainly is my prayer.)
You indeed, O God, have accepted my vows;   (I have been thinking a lot about that since this week I marked twenty-five in the monastery.)
    you granted me the heritage of
        those who fear your Name.
Add to the days of the king's life;   (Basil [Vasileios] = king)
    let his years be many generations;
Let him sit enthroned before God forever;   (Amen, amen, amen.)
    bid kindness and faithfulness preserve him.
So will I sing the praises of your name forever,
    fulfilling my vows day by day.

Psalm 62 goes on to say: "Only in God is my soul at rest; from him comes my salvation. He only is my rock and my salvation, my stronghold; I shall not be disturbed at all." That is the reality. When I leave this rock, I will still have a rock to stand on: Christ, the Lord, who will always be with me.

❋

It is not enough to possess prayer. We must become prayer—

prayer incarnate. It is not enough to have moments of praise; our whole life, every act, every gesture, even a smile, must become a hymn of adoration, an offering, a prayer. We must offer, not what we have but what we are. — EVDOKIMOV

❊

This afternoon two more groups of students arrived—around fifty or sixty. I am impressed how the monks quietly provide for them. The church gets crowded. One group went on to the next monastery for the night.

After supper I took a walk up to the ridge, as I do most evenings. I met one of the very old monks, who shuffles about the monastery, on his way to the cave of Saint Simon, the founder of Simonos Petras. I wondered how he ever managed the rough road up the hill. He went on even higher to visit the monks who live above the cave. These old monks are really amazing.

When I returned I was invited to have coffee with a young Dutch professor of biochemistry from Leiden, Leon Oten, who was drawn to the Mountain by its natural beauty, so striking for a Dutchman from his own flat country. He did decide to stay the extra day so he could be present at the Agripnia for All the Saints of the Holy Mountain.

❊

Thoughts are enemies who are bodyless and invisible, malicious and clever at harming us, skillful, nimble, and practiced in warfare. . . . A person whose mind is caught in thought is distant from Jesus; a person with a silent mind is with him.

— HESYCHIUS OF JERUSALEM

Saturday, June 13

Other visitors are constantly surprised when they hear I am staying so long on the Mountain. I didn't realize it would be such a unique thing. I hope that besides being a good retreat for myself, it will be a meaningful ecumenical presence.

The Hegumen presided at the Liturgy this morning. He does it with such dignity and grace that it is a special joy to be present.

A group of students stayed for lunch. The youngsters yesterday ate the monks out of bread, so the baker made hot rolls for lunch.

After lunch I spoke briefly with Professor Daniel Sahas from Waterloo University near Toronto. He has been there for seven years, although he is a Greek native. He is just completing a sabbatical in Greece with his wife and two children. His wife, like him, is specializing in Islamic studies. He told me that Father Georgios, the Hegumen at Grigoriou, had been at the theological seminary in Richmond, Virginia, for a year.

❊

With the influx of students and visitors at Simonos Petras, my place in the refectory has been changed to the other side with their own candidates and novices. Visiting monks usually are right with the monks, but because I am "heterodox" they have to keep me apart. Yet they are concerned that I am well cared for and not unduly disturbed by the other guests. It is very quiet and peaceful in the house where I have my cell.

❊

A short while after lunch Father Dionysios came knocking at my door with a tray. There are a couple of mulberry trees near the monastery. One has white berries, the other black. He had picked a dish of these for me. And there was a side plate of nuts, a sort of almond. He has a most beautiful smile. His eyes are so clear—they tell of pure joy. The brothers here seem truly to find their joy in making others happy. Sometimes we—and I am afraid I have to say "we" in this case—do things for others more for our own sake than for theirs, to sort of prove to ourselves and to assert to others our value, that we are worthwhile, that we are needed. There is none of that here. It is just pure gift. I am in what is a good position for me to be in for a while, where I can give nothing but my prayers and love—and I am not fooled by their worth—and have to receive everything humbly, gratefully. It is good, because at home I tend to be all-giving, always trying to do for others. I need to be less independent and realize that one way of giving is to receive, because it gives another the joy and opportunity of being a giver. Every giver needs a receiver. If I may so express it, this is why God needs us—to receive his great bounty. "Unless you become as little children. . . ."—I think that is what he is trying to say. We have to be done with all pretense at being in any way independent of God our Father.

Before Vespers Father Dionysios was at the door with coffee and stewed peaches. There was only a short Vespers and a good meal in preparation for the Vigil. It is the Feast of All the Saints of Mount Athos. It is joy to be in their midst for this feast, to be in their house. After supper I walked up to the cave where Saint Simon lived until he saw a star on the mountain and received directions to found this monastery in honor of the Birth of Christ. I lit the lamp there before his icon. Although this monastery is dedicated to the Mystery of the Nativity and there is a special veneration of the founder, the secondary patron is that Woman-Equal-to-the-Apostles, Saint Mary Magdalen. I did not know this when I chose to come here, but I am very happy about it. It was on her feast I received the habit, which in the East is considered the making of the monk. She is an excellent patron for this time of retreat, when, more than ordinarily—although it has always been my ideal—I choose her "better part." May she obtain for me the grace I need to stay quiet at the feet of the Lord, wholly open, letting him do what he wants within, for his will's accomplishment, for the glory of the Father.

Sunday, June 14

The bell and the semantron sounded for the Agripnia at 9:20 last night. The katholikon was crowded. The monks certainly know how to celebrate and create a climate of celebration and prayer. The bells, the semantron, and tinkling bells on cope and censer, clouds of incense with its uplifting odor, the candles, lamps, and swinging chandeliers reflecting in the gold and silver icons and in the silks and gems of the rich vesture; the many varied chants, the processions, the symbolic use of bread, oil, wine, and grain, each emerging out of the dark shadows of a medieval church and for a moment holding their own in the unfolding drama of praise and worship. It is truly Byzantine and even heavenly splendor, as the saints look serenely on from the icons. After about an hour the Hegumen made the rounds, exchanging words of greeting with the guests and encouraging the singers—who needed little encouragement. As Father David said to me: "We enjoy doing a Vigil." And it is quite evident. I think that is why I enjoyed it so much. The great Vespers lasted two and one half hours. Then we settled down for a quiet hour of Psalms. Virtually all the lights were extinguished. Things came alive again with the lighting and swinging of the great chandelier and the singing of the *Polyelos** (Psalms 134 and 135) with the Alleluias. At this point, with the careening chandelier and corona casting wild shafts of light into the shadows, and old monks hanging on to the kilrosi, joyfully bellowing out the Alleluias, my profane mind rose to say that the party had reached that point! But the night was still young and the oldsters gave way to the youngsters to continue the Alleluias in a somewhat more sedate voice. The Hegumen made the rounds again, encouraging, exchanging a word, waking up a couple of young guests who had settled in their stalls during the Psalms and had not risen since.

After forty-five minutes of Alleluias we moved into Orthros, with Father Myron coming forth with the censer. Father Myron is one of those vital sorts of young men (once he was cook, baker, gardener, infirmarian, pharmacist, and econome* of the monastery—all at the same time!). By the time he had finished incensing the icons and people, everyone was fully alive. To see him is better than a cup of Nescafé. He exudes vitality and energy. Things finally wound down at 3:30 A.M. and we went to our cells for rest until near seven, when bells and semantron recalled us to the katholikon for the First Hour and the Liturgy, concelebrated by five priests and two deacons. From church we went to the refectory for a solemn meal and its accompanying ritual, and then back to church for the closing litanies— another three hours. Yes, the monks know how to celebrate! They did this for the saints. It is hard to imagine what they do at the Pasch!

Leon Oten and Daniel Sahas left after Liturgy. I got some rest until Father Maximos arrived at my door with coffee at two. I am going to be spoiled by so much kindness and service!

Monday, June 15

෴ Up till now, apart from some bits in the Fathers, about the only thing I have been reading is Sacred Scripture. But working my way through Leviticus, I must confess I haven't been getting too much out of it. So I am beginning to read a bit of William of Saint Thierry's *Golden Epistle*. Today, though, is the Feast of the Prophet Elisha, so I skipped ahead and read about him in the Second Book of Kings. I was struck how in the cure of Naaman, the general almost missed out. He had his own preconceived idea of how God and his servant should go about things. But God often accomplishes what we want through the ordinary things, the ordinary means, and we can miss out because we are looking for something special or out of the ordinary. It is interesting too, how Naaman, for civil reasons, asks leave—and apparently it is granted—to continue to bow down in the temple of Rimmon. God and his prophets are so much more open and understanding than his ministers sometimes have been.

❄

I am finding good things in William, too. His advice about praise is useful now: "Disregard praise, and love in those who praise you the good which they love in you" (*Golden Epistle*, 14).

The monks here may never have heard about the psychological school of affirmation or the House of Affirmation. But they know about it in practice. They learn it from the Gerontas whose whole person affirms. And the goodness they affirm really radiates from themselves. They are men of love and joy, truly seeking God with most generous hearts.

❄

It is for others to serve God,
    it is for you to cling to him;
    it is for others to believe in God, know him,
        love him, and revere him;
    it is for you to taste him, understand him,
        be intimate with him, enjoy him.

—Golden Epistle, 16

That certainly corresponds to my aspirations. The contrast might be applied to Orthodox and Western monks, but I would be slow to apply it. The monks here do seem to emphasize serving and reverencing, as does the whole of their monastic tradition, but they surely are seeking, too, that intimacy that we desire. The emphasis might be different, but I do not know if there is any substantial difference. I think we more readily apply Moses' words: "The Lord himself will fight for you; you have only to keep still" (Exodus 14:14). Rather than struggling to overcome all the sin and evil in us, all our bad tendencies, we seek to enter into the Divine Presence and be to God: "Be still and know that I am God." Instead of struggling with self to kill the old man ("mortification"—to make dead), we simply ignore him with all his beautiful or not so beautiful thoughts and feelings and desires and turn our whole attention to God. In a struggle for self-mortification there can still be an awful lot of self—we can even be quite proud of our accomplishments in this—at least, our attention is still on self. We perhaps know from experience how much more annihilating (in the literal sense of the word) it is to be completely ignored. If somebody attacks us or fights with us or even damns us, he is at least paying some attention to us and acknowledges that we exist. When we are completely ignored, we simply cease to exist. It is a step beyond death. So by ignoring self and turning our attention fully to God in silent, attentive prayer, we truly die to self and live to God. We come to taste him, understand him, be familiar with him, enjoy him.

※

As I was sitting on the balcony I could see Father Myron far below on the terrace, irrigating the vegetable garden. He was completely oblivious of my presence. My heart was filled with love for this wonderful young monk, and I prayed for him and thanked God for him and blessed him. And I thought this must often be the way it is with us and God. As we go about our daily doings, often not explicitly mindful of him, he is looking down on us with love, blessing us, very pleased with us as we do ordinary everyday things for him. We are far more loved and cared for than we can ever realize or appreciate.

※

I have gotten into pretty much of a settled routine now—it doesn't take long—blending with the rhythm of the community life here:

4:15 Rise, prayer in the cell

4:45 Midnight Office, Orthros
      First Hour (on Monday, Wednesday, Friday, the Third and
          Sixth Hours are added here)
      Liturgy
      Coffee   Tierce (I like to say some of the Offices* from
          our own tradition)
      Scripture, prayer

10:45 Third and Sixth Hours (on Monday, Wednesday, Friday re-
          placed by the Paraklisis*)
      Lunch
      Write in journal   Sext
      Rest
      None, Scripture, William of Saint Thierry, prayer

6:30 Ninth Hour, Vespers
      Supper
      Walk
      Scripture, prayer

8:45 Acathist Hymn, Apodeipnon
      Read, sleep

One of the reasons I have chosen to read William's *Golden Epistle* is because William, coming from the fullness of the Benedictine-Cistercian tradition, is in this *Epistle,* writing for Carthusians who live in cells. I am very much in a cell here. And, in general now, with the change from the dormitory to cells, so are most Cistercians. We need to develop a Cistercian theology or spiritual practice for the proper use of the cell. William speaks a lot about the cell in this letter, so I am hoping to get some good insights from him, for now during this retreat and for later on when I go back to my cell in Spencer.

❉

I witnessed a little drama today that probably tells the story of some of the desolation seen in the depleted monasteries. The lock of the door of the cell of the old monk down the hall jammed. He set about trying to fix it with his knife. Soon he was banging at it, and two panes of glass fell out of the door and broke on the floor. By the time he gave up, he still had a door that would not latch and a couple of missing windows. If the situation here was as it had been a couple of years ago, with only a few old monks in the community, he would have had no one to turn to. He probably would have abandoned the cell, leaving it to the ravages of time, and moved into one of the many empty cells. But fortunately, a wonderful young community has come to care for these precious old men—and to receive from them a rich heritage.

※

After Vespers I gave Father Eliseos a postcard reproduction of an icon of his patron Saint, Elisha, clinging to the cloak of the great Prophet Elijah, who was ascending in a fiery chariot. It is an eighteenth-century Russian icon. I don't think Father Eliseos had seen it before. At the same time the Hegumen sent me a gift of candy, probably from the feast-day celebration for Father Eliseos.

※

I took a walk up to the cemetery. There is an open grave from which the monks recently dug up the bones of the Archimandrite Charalambos, the former Hegumen, who died on May 23, 1973, at the age of eighty-three. The grave is not deep and one can still see the remnants of his habit, vestments, shoes, and belt. I don't know what the origin of this practice of digging up the bones is. Perhaps it was just a practical necessity because of the limited space in the small cemeteries on the Mountain. They certainly do not leave the bones to rest long. The heavy calcium content of the soil, they say, causes a body to decompose very quickly. With all this, the monk is kept very close to: "Remember, man, that you are dust and to dust you shall return."

Tuesday, June 16

☙ Today is a very special day at home in Spencer. Brother Basil is being ordained to the holy priesthood and Brother Paschal to the diaconate. In spirit I am very much with them there, realizing that oneness we have in Christ. It will be a great joy to concelebrate with Basil when I return home.

※

I am in admiration of the flexibility and hospitality of this community. We started services a half hour earlier this morning so that a visiting priest, Father Nephon, could celebrate the Liturgy and make his boat to Ouranoupolis. He is a priest from Athens who started social ministry for homeless girls there twenty years ago. It has been very successful. It is one of the few social outreaches of the Greek Church. Father Nephon is not highly educated, but is a man of true apostolic zeal. The community showed great interest in his work, asking many questions. He and this community are truly signs of hope for the Greek Church of tomorrow.

❋

I finished Leviticus and moved into Numbers. It is good to be on the move again toward the Promised Land. Like Peter and Paul, I hope to learn something from these poor sinners, who are God's chosen, for my own journey. The thing that stands out in my mind from Leviticus is God's tremendous, detailed, loving care, exerting every effort to help these people realize their great dignity as his chosen people. If we could only get a good grasp of what really happened to us at Baptism, when we became by an eternal providential love not only adopted children and heirs but, in some deep way we will never truly fathom, one with every Son of God who already possesses and is all that God has and is! "O Christian, know thyself, know thy dignity!"

❋

Father Dionysios came along with some coffee in midafternoon and we talked for a while. He told me a bit more about Father Nephon. He came from a wealthy family. At twenty he decided to become a monk and a priest. He went to study theology at the University of Athens, but he became interested in the plight of young girls who were left, for one reason or another, to the streets. He started a home for them. Realizing that if he went on to get his degree in theology, he might be made a bishop, he left off his studies to devote himself totally to being a father to these girls. He found women who were ready to dedicate themselves to this work for God and set up households each with a dedicated woman who would be a mother to a group of seven girls of varying age. He tried in every way to make it possible for the girls to live a very normal, completely non-institutional life. The girls are encouraged to study at the university or abroad. Some have become nuns and Father Nephon now has a convent. But this was not his aim. He just wanted these unfortunate girls to have an opportunity to become happy, creative women in whatever vocation God gave them. Today he has over one hundred girls in households.

※

Father Dionysios told me a little more about Father Melitos, a simple old monk who was with us at the feast and asked me why I didn't become a Christian. He is actually a member of the community, one of the original ancients. For years he prayed God to send them some young monks. In 1948 a hermit came and told them God would. When? They had to be patient and prayerful. The monks were yet to be born, grow up, go to the university, and finally become monks and then come to the Mountain. He wondered if he could hang on that long.

When the monks came from Meteora, he saw it as an answer to his prayer and the fulfillment of the prophecy. Early this year he asked to retire, to live apart. He asked a young monk to teach him to sing so he could sing the Morning and Evening Services in his hermitage. He may not have a particularly good ear or voice, but he certainly enjoys singing—and everything.

※

The monks received a letter from America addressed "To Any Monk, Holy Mountain, Greece." The writer had read the *Way of the Pilgrim* and was asking some rather searching questions. The monks replied, telling him that God is with him, and as he seeks, God will reveal himself and all truth to him. They suggested he read the Gospels, Saint John Climacus, and Saint John Damascene, and the story of Barlaam and Josaphat because it contains a basic Christian catechesis. They then related a story from the early life of Saint Nectarios. When he was around twenty and in Athens, he fell on hard times. He had been supporting himself selling cigarettes, putting in the little packages Scripture verses. These became very popular, but his success aroused jealousy and he was beaten down. Finally, in midwinter, he found himself without food, clothes, or fuel and quite unwell. So he wrote a letter to God, telling him of his needs, and addressed it to "God in Heaven." On the way to post it, along with others his teacher had given him, he fell. The letters were scattered and he hurt his leg. He limped home, only to be beaten by his teacher for failing to post the letters properly. Meanwhile a good man found the letters and took them to the post office. He noticed the one addressed to God—and knowing the post office could not deliver it, he opened it and read it. Then he gathered up food, clothes, medicine, etc., and left them at Nectarios' door. The Saint was sure they came from God, as indeed they had.

I enjoy talking with Father Dionysios. With great simplicity and clarity, he lives in and shares the tradition, yet he is fully alive to the present. He has over one hundred cassettes of talks by the Gerontas on all the traditional themes of monastic life, bringing them to the present and enriching their practice with current theological and psychological insight. The nuns at Ormilia* are transcribing them. It would be wonderful if we could get them translated and available in English.

※

There is an unusual young man living with the monks now. George had become possessed by the devil. As a last resource he came to the Holy Mountain and was directed to Father Paisios. Father received him with great affection and gave him all he could and then sent him to a monastery telling him to return in a few days. In the meantime the devil came in many forms to torment Father Paisios for trying to help the boy. When the boy returned to Father Paisios, he was very depressed and wanted to die. Father Paisios sent him here. As he walked along the mountain paths, the devil constantly tried to get him to cast himself down off the high places. The community here has embraced him with love. There have been frequent exorcisms but the struggle still goes on. In time, hopefully, with the love and prayers of the brothers he will be wholly freed from the evil one and able to give himself fully to God. Stories like these make one realize how close the life here on the Mountain is to that of the Fathers. It is really the same.

※

The aim of every monk and the perfection of his heart tends to continual and unbroken perseverance in prayer—and immovable tranquillity of mind—lasting and continual calmness in prayer: for this are all our exercises of the monastic life undertaken.

—SAINT JOHN CASSIAN

Wednesday, June 17

〰️ It is hard to believe that a month has already gone. I feel as though I have hardly gotten into the retreat. The days pass very quickly, with the long church Services, prayer in the cell and on the balcony, reading Scripture. There is a temptation to want to see the results, see something happening, something coming out of this retreat. But rather, it is just a quiet resting in the Lord. At the Paraklisis today we read again the Gospel account of Mary at the feet of the Lord. May this word come alive in my life and in my heart.

There are two novices at my table in the refectory. The one visited Meteora a few times while studying English philology at the University of Athens. Then he was called to military service. When he was released, he came straight to the monastery here. His parents had been calling the Gerontas, asking when he would come home. Finally he called to tell them he was going to stay. They were not too happy about that. He will go home after a bit, to visit with them.

The other novice has a very beautiful voice. He was singing at the Paraklisis today and I was enjoying it. Then he was called out and Father Simon took over. Father Simon is living tradition. He is one of the old monk-priests who was here before the community came from Meteora. In fact, until last year, when Father Myron took him to the hospital in Thessaloniki, he had not left the Mountain in the thirty-five years he has been here. He knows the whole typicon* by heart and has taught it to the young monks down to the last *Kyrie*. He is the one who can always find the needed book or the special troparium,* the one who generally keeps things going in the choir even though his legs are so weak he can no longer celebrate the Liturgy. He has a very strong voice, but it, too, has suffered with time. To the human ear the novice's voice is by far the more pleasing, but to the ear of God . . . ? I suspect the one he has been hearing regu-

larly for thirty-five years, day and night, comes to his ear with that
something special of an intimate friend.

❋

I shared that beautiful passage from William of Saint Thierry
with Father Dionysios. He agreed with me. It speaks as much to his
heart and the ideal of the Orthodox monk as it does to us. There is
something paradoxical here. The monk stands before God in an attitude of profound reverence, with Doxa and Kyrie constantly on his
lips. And yet during the Services the monks circulate freely in the
church, come and go, talk with each other and the guests—very
much at home in their Father's house. It is the same with the Hegumen. He walks about with crosier in hand, very much the prelate.
The monks bow profoundly before him and kiss his hand. Yet there
is a warm, spontaneous relation and affection between them and
him, and they can be very free in his presence. I think there is something very good here, a successful hanging-on to a balancing of poles,
both with their essential values. Either one alone would cause imbal-
ance. It is a kind of healthy and happy integration we all need.

❋

There is a monk in the community who has not been off the
Mountain in fifty years and has never seen an automobile.

❋

Saint Nilos of Kavsokalyvia in the seventeenth century foretold
that the Mountain would go into decline and there would only be
old monks left, and then young monks from outside would come to
save it. Many of the monks on the Mountain see this community as
the fulfillment of that prophecy.

Thursday, June 18

Mario Goerig and I had supper together last night and then
we walked up to the cave of Saint Simon. Mario is interested in
becoming a Cistercian monk at Mariawald.* He has just finished his
third year of theology at Jerusalem and has two more years at Frei-
burg. He is taking the opportunity to see other monasteries and mo-

nastic traditions, which is very wise. He has visited Bellefontaine*
and Latroun* and the Orthodox monasteries in the Holy Land. He
will go on to Italy to visit the Camaldolese hermits.

This morning we had breakfast together on the balcony. Later a
troop of German Boy Scouts arrived in uniform. It is certainly a
wonderful thing for these boys to have the opportunity to experience
not only another country and culture but, I might say, another
world. This small monastic realm, where the Gospel is the law, is certainly something apart from the rest of our poor world. If men could
but believe and accept in practice the law of Christ, all mankind
could enjoy the peace and beauty that prevails on the Holy Mountain.

※

Yesterday used to be the Commemoration of Saint Paul in Western liturgy. As I was meditating on his great love of Christ, I decided
I would devote the afternoon Scripture prayer each day to the Gospels. It was a good decision. They are so powerful. God is truly present in his word. He does not so much reveal thoughts and ideas to
us—if we would truly listen—but rather himself. And then we can
but "be silent and know that he is God."

I had hoped to read the whole Bible during my retreat but there
seems little hope for that. God is so present here that much time has
to be spent just being present to him. The whole scene from my balcony—the truly Holy Mountain, the deep blue calm of the sea, the
rich greens of the hillside—all call to be present to him, and time
slips away.

※

It was just a year ago today that I was praying by Father Paul as
he breathed forth his soul to the Lord. May he intercede for us all.

Friday, June 19

☙ This is a kind of special day, a day of grace for me. It used
to be for us the Feast of the Visitation (July 2). May Mary bring
Christ more and more into our lives. It was on this day, twenty-three
years ago, that Abbot Edmund decided I could make my vows as a

Cistercian—a very special gift from the Lord—the confirmation of a beautiful vocation for which I can never thank our good God enough.

❄

After the Liturgy the Hegumen sent for me and we spent the morning together—a very real grace.

The Hegumen asked me what I found alike and what different in our monastery at Spencer and this one. I find a great similarity and yet differences. The spirit of love, joy, and prayer that prevails here is the same as at home. There are superficial differences such as the Services being grouped together here, giving long stretches in church, the mixing of guests in the house (church and refectory especially), the talking in the cell area. More profoundly, I indicated three differences which he commented on at length.

1. The paradox of profound reverence toward God, which is in so many ways expressed in their Services and their lives, and the great freedom and ease in church as they wander about, come and go, and talk. Father began to speak about the differences of mystical approach in Orthodoxy and the West, Protestant and Catholic. (At first I did not realize he was addressing my comment, but as he drew it all together, I was amazed at the integration of his thought.) In some places in Greece the pietist movement, largely influenced by the Protestant West, has sought to bring quiet and order into the churches. But this is not what you find in the villages and monasteries.

Father went on: as one opens to God, God seizes the soul and takes it beyond concepts and ideas to the sweet inner experience of himself. When this experience passes, the man is desolate. All creation has lost its taste for him. He would have the bonds loosed and pass to the heavenly kingdom. He would go to a cave where he can weep and sigh for God. But he takes on an eschatological outlook. He sees all in the fullness of the risen Christ—the flowers, the flying birds, the swinging chandeliers, men, the angels, Christ, the adorable Trinity—all one in a communication of love. They are all very much in Christ in God, and so when one goes to church to adore, he experiences the oneness of all this. This is not something that is achieved by conceptual theology—it is communion. One nearby may be asleep. Let him sleep. What is more natural than to sleep in one's Father's house? The activity in church may be due to the weakness of the human spirit or the Divine Spirit or simple needs. The church is not something outside the ordinary life of the monk. His whole life is in the church. And ordinary needs continue: to arrange the Services, to find the right texts, to remember something and tell a brother, to go to take care of something, etc.

The simple man may not be able to express this so well, but it is common among the Orthodox, though experienced in various degrees of intensity. The "saying" of prayers and the "carrying out" of Services is a foreign attitude coming from the West. For the Orthodox it is a question of attitude, one of adoration, worship, presence to God. Without this, Orthodoxy would end, the inner life would be lost, the Church would turn to social activity.

2. The second point I made had some of the same paradox in it: how the monks so reverence the Spiritual Father and yet are so familiar with him. More basically though, I was concerned with the role of the Spiritual Father in monastic life.

Father Aimilianos began to respond by saying that what the Councils are for the Church, the Spiritual Father is for the individual. The Church—the Councils of Bishops—has never legislated in regard to the Spiritual Father. Nor does it interfere with his role. The faithful go to church for the Services, Baptism, Eucharist, Penance, but for their spiritual life they go to an Elder. The recognized Elders drew people from all sides, men like Father Simon of the Monastery of Pendeli.* The Orthodox Church has suffered many influences from the West: during the Byzantine period in the tenth century; during the Crusades in the twelfth; in the thirteenth and fourteenth centuries among the Slavs, and especially with the Uniats* of Poland; and after Greek liberation from the Turks in 1830, when the new German rulers brought Protestant ministers. Today most Orthodox theologians study in the West, and most of the theology taught in Greek universities is influenced by Protestantism. But the common people have kept free from this, for they look to the Spiritual Fathers.

The Father noted that in Orthodoxy one never goes to join a monastery. Rather, he seeks or finds a Spiritual Father and then stays with him whether in a monastery or a city.

I asked how one could discern that it was God's will that one serve as a Spiritual Father.

The Father replied that this is a question an Orthodox would never think of asking. Christians have received the freedom of the Spirit. If one wants to be a monk, he becomes a monk. The invitation is given to all. But one does not become a Spiritual Father because he seeks it or wants it or desires it. It is quite the contrary to natural fatherhood. There, the son becomes son through no will of his own. It is the father who decides to be father and brings the son into being. In spiritual paternity, it is the son who seeks, and the Father comes into the role of paternity only with anguish and fear. It can come about in two ways. The son comes seeking, the Father takes him to his own Father who, rather than accept the new son, blesses his becoming the son of his son. Or, more often, the Father will come to recognize that in fact God the Father through his Son, Christ, has spirated life into this seeker through him and he is in fact a father. He can only accept the reality, knowing that the life comes from God the Father, and all else will also, because the Father will be with him every step of the way.

I asked if when one loses his Spiritual Father—if he dies or goes into the desert—he chooses another?

This is a cause of immense sorrow to the son. He can have only one father, as Saint Paul says. But he will not be without someone over him, walking in the way of obedience. The community will choose a new Hegumen. With his will, if he is able, the monk will turn to him as Father. In any case he will obey him. Maybe, in time, he will find another and discover that he is his true Father, rather than the first.

3. The third difference I remarked was the great freedom here, where no one is required to go to Services, meals, work, etc. Among us, all are expected at choir, to be there on time, to sing, to be at the refectory, etc. We are afraid if we allow such freedom, everything will go to pieces.

The Father thought it would be good if we could find more freedom in our monasteries, but if we went as far as the Orthodox, we would be out of spirit with the Roman Church and people would take it as laxity. I said I thought such freedom worked well here because there is a deep unity since the Hegumen is also the Spiritual Father of all. The Hegumen replied that where this is not so and there are various Spiritual Fathers, there is still no problem unless the monks are not fervent. The Hegumen has the last say in obedience and the monks accept it. He pointed to the actual situation here. The old monks here are fervent. He does not know who is their Spiritual Guide. They come to him for all permissions. When they hear he is planning to do something, they talk among themselves about it and often against it. But once he decides for something, they accept it from their heart.

The old monks have a great devotion to the typicon. When the new group came they were still fairly active, and whenever someone made a mistake, three or four would rush out to correct him and the Service would stop while there was a discussion on the point. There was one old monk, who died last year, who used to stay out in the liti by the stove with some others who were warming themselves and chatting. But he would hear everything in the Service. Whenever he heard a mistake, he would come rushing in. The Hegumen did make some changes to meet the needs of the young community. The old monk would come rushing in as soon as he heard the change, but when he was told the Hegumen decided it, he immediately accepted it. True freedom enables one to obey.

If the Hegumen asks a monk to go into prison for six months, he will go. If he refuses, the Hegumen will say "all right." There is no force or compulsion. But the monk will go because he is asked.

We could have gone on but the lunch bell rang. The Hegumen speaks with much energy and enthusiasm, his face, his hands—very expressive. He sits behind a small table as prelates are wont to do here. And there is always some coffee or juice. But all the formalities are in fact transcended by really loving, caring communication. There are interruptions by phone or at the door but the Father always picks up right where he left off. He speaks with great clarity and order. His beard is beginning to gray a bit and the creases at the corners of his eyes have become more pronounced. I am told he suffers from ulcers, but his vigor seems to belie it. The diet here is about the worst possible for ulcers—a couple of heavy meals a day, widely spaced, with lots of beans and wine. He actually does not come to meals in the refectory very often, so I hope they are giving him a more suitable diet in the hegumenate.

The community here is certainly blessed, and many others are too, with a very wise and holy Spiritual Father. As he shared with me this morning on the mystical life, there was no doubt that he was speaking from experience. He stressed, again and again, joy and freedom and entering into the heavenly dance. One could set laws and regulations, but the mystic cannot be bound by them. He must follow the movement of the Spirit. He is like David before the Ark; he must take off his clothes and dance before the Lord. Those looking down from the windows cannot understand and despise him. He has entered into the water until the water has wholly engulfed him and he is aware of nothing else.

In regard to the role of the Spiritual Father, Father Aimilianos recommended my reading Saint Symeon the New Theologian and the chapter to pastors at the end of Saint John Climacus' *Ladder*.

If one comes on retreat to Athos expecting to find someone to guide him like a retreat master or director in the West, he will be disappointed. The monks gladly share on the level of spiritual reality. But if one places a personal question or concern, they humbly refer him to the Spiritual Father. The Spiritual Father is to be approached with humility and reverence. He listens lovingly, takes all in his heart, and brings it to the Lord. But he is usually content to give but a "word" in response, leaving it to the Lord to unfold its meaning and to answer all one's needs.

Father Aimilianos is indeed like the scribe who is learned in the Kingdom of God of whom Jesus speaks—he is "the head of the household who can bring forth from his storeroom both the new and the old (Matthew 13:52)."

❋

Father David told me of another aspect, as it were, of this spiritual paternity which shows how much it is a part of the Greek Orthodox culture. At Baptism the godfather stands for the child—not his own parents—and from henceforth has a special relation to the child which takes precedence over even that of the natural parents. His wife becomes the godmother. At the wedding, after the priest, it is the godparents who, before all others, exchange the crowns on the heads of the couple. If the couple have difficulties, it is to the godfather they go for mediation and advice.

Saturday, June 20

 Father Maximos joined me at supper last night. He explained some of their practices for me.

Koliva—a sweet mixture with whole grain in it—is blessed at Vespers on Friday and given out as we leave. It is blessed again at the Liturgy—usually in the cemetery chapel—on Saturday. The grain represents the soul. It is eaten in celebration of the victory of the just in heaven (it is also blessed on feasts of the Saints) and in petition for the souls in purgatory. By legend, its origins go to the time that Justinian the Apostate tried to kill off the Christians in Constantinople by poisoning the food and grain in the markets, but the Patriarch was warned in a dream about it. In fact, its actual origin is unresearched. It seems to me it may flow out of pagan funeral rites that have been baptized. There are two special All Souls' Days—one in great Lent, a week before All Saints', and another on the eve of Pentecost. But every Saturday outside of Paschal time is celebrated for the dead, unless a great feast intervenes. Legend among the people has it that during the fifty days of Easter all souls are freed from their pains but their sufferings return at Pentecost.

The origins of the monastic habit are also not researched. The skouphos may come from the Turks, but the rason most certainly does, being the court robe of Islamic judges which was adopted by Christian priests in the cities. Only after the liberation of Greece was it generally required of priests to wear it. The sostikon* is simply the traditional robe of the monk.

On Monday and Wednesday before lunch we have a Service, the Paraklisis, in honor of Mary, the Mother of God, as Mount Athos is hers. On feasts, the Gospel account of Mary's choosing the better part, which is used at the Paraklisis on Monday and Wednesday, is added to the Gospel of the day. On Friday, the Paraklisis is celebrated in honor of the Founder of the monastery. On these days the Liturgy is usually celebrated in a chapel, and the Third and Sixth

Hours are said there before Liturgy while Orthros and the First Hour are being completed in the katholikon.

❋

There's some concern about the future of the Mountain. The present government in Athens, which is very strong and vigorous, wants to settle with a certain finality the question of relations between the Holy Mountain and Greece. Popular belief is that the monks are fabulously rich. The government would like to get an accounting of the monasteries and begin taxing them. The monks are, of course, eager to maintain their independence, which already has been greatly lessened. Before, the monks owned most of northern Greece. When three million Greeks were expelled from Asia Minor in the 1920s, the government took the monks' land to settle them and now pays an annual sum to the monasteries in compensation for their lost revenues. The monks still do possess some valuable land in Greece, especially the northern coast of the neighboring peninsula. Loss of regular revenues and the imposition of taxes would certainly limit the monks' ability to continue to govern the Mountain as they wish.

Since the liberation of Greece from the Turks the government has required all members of the monasteries to be Greek citizens. Around the turn of the century Russia sought to get an opening into the Mediterranean through the Mountain by sending literally thousands of monks. Many were expelled between 1914 and 1917 and laws were passed against more Russians coming. But other Orthodox can come. Some think that if many of the Orthodox in the West who want to come, do in fact come, it will strengthen the independence of the peninsula. But it would mean having monasteries where the Services are celebrated in English and in French.

Also of concern to the Athens government are the Mountain's underground resources. The wealthiest gold mine in ancient Greece was at the border of the monastic domain. It is felt certain that there are rich veins of gold on the peninsula and also uranium and possibly oil deposits. There has been talk of the government taking over all Church property including the Mountain, which would enhance the government's wealth tenfold. It seems to me, though, that if the monks are faithful, they can count on Mary to protect their domain for them.

❋

Father Aimilianos is going to Moscow later this month with a delegation from the Holy Mountain. A novice, Heracles, had to take his papers to Karyes for passports—a jaunt of seventeen and a half kilometers. Here, as elsewhere, novices never know what they will be asked to do next.

❊

As I sit on the balcony a large flock of birds, maybe fifty or sixty swallows, swirls around in large circles swishing past my observation post, sometimes in silence, more often with a terrible shrieking. They are like the many thoughts that go swirling around in my head, sometimes making an awful racket. The best thing with both is just to ignore them and rest in the deeper silence of presence where God so truly is. So, too, with all the other things going on around me: the chattering of the old monks upstairs, the monk practicing singing downstairs, the activity in the vegetable patches, the visitors coming up the mountain path, the coming and going of the boats—whatever —they are all just swirls with little meaning in themselves; but when perceived—if they are to be perceived—from the core of inner presence, they do have meaning as part of the saving dance of creation that prepares for the heavenly dance of the elect.

I sometimes tend to feel sorry for the humble laymen who work at lowly tasks here on the Mountain. Most monasteries have a few, working in the gardens or woods or in kitchens, etc. And there are the boatmen and the bus drivers who go constantly back and forth. That is what they have chosen to do, just as we have chosen to be monks. I may feel infinitely more blessed in my vocation, and certainly it is a most beautiful gift from the Lord. But who is to say which is more significant in the working out of the divine saving dance of creation? Each has its place. Only the love of the dancer counts in the end. One's steps may be awkward and seemingly graceless, but what is in the heart? God knows—that is what matters!

❊

"Do not wonder what others are like but to the best of your ability what they may become through your influence."

— William of Saint Thierry, *Golden Epistle*, 21

❊

". . . men who are satisfied with essentials and seek a voluntary poverty." — *Golden Epistle*, 23

❋

I expected to find much more austerity in this retreat than I am finding. Oh, there are certain asceticisms for me: the general strangeness of things, longer choir Services, constant use of a foreign language, somewhat more primitive facilities than we are used to at home, different hours for meals, the different kinds of food prepared differently—though well prepared and plentiful—and the absence of loved ones. But I am certainly surrounded by love and concern and a constant effort to make me feel at home and comfortable. Lots of silence and leisure. No phones, mail, and few visitors to concern me. A quite adequate cell—whose unclutteredness makes me feel embarrassed about the abundant clutter in my cell at home—with a balcony view that competes with anything any travel agency could ever offer. A bit of the hundredfold, indeed. The Lord makes a very good offer, too good—so we are very slow to buy it: "Whoever gives up . . . for my sake will receive a hundredfold in this life *and* life eternal." Yet I catch myself constantly hanging on to things. Even here, how quickly I get things set up in my cell; a routine sets in; things have their place and I expect them to be there. And I catch myself making plans for the trip home and after. All little hangings on to self, instead of a complete letting go and living fully in the enjoyment of his outpouring hundredfold. One area in my life that certainly needs reform is the area of "seeking voluntary poverty."

Father Maximos invited me to go with him to Dionysiou next week for their patronal feast, the Birth of John the Baptist. (Maximos was a monk there one and one half years before going to England to study.) The monasteries celebrate their feasts in a big way. They bring in special singers from the sketes and kellions who can sing special chants that are used on such occasions. The singing is done more slowly and fully than in ordinary Services. The Agripnia might last ten to twelve hours. Monks and laymen come from all around for them. I told Father Maximos to ask the Gerontas if I should accompany him. I am very content to stay quietly here, but they show constant concern lest I feel left out or unattended. Father Athanasios, the former secretary of the Holy Community, arrived this afternoon with Father Justin, Simonos Petras' representative at Karyes, to plan the mission to Russia and to celebrate the Feast of All the Saints of Meteora. We will have a solemn Vigil tonight.

Sunday, June 21

༄ The United States is celebrating its two-hundredth anniversary today (July 4). Not so long by Greek standards. Yet something to be grateful for. I do not think of myself as particularly patriotic, but being in the midst of other nationals, I realize how much of an American I am. Americans have a different way of looking at the rest of the world and even at the moon now. I feel a certain compassion for the Greeks and citizens of other nations that are small and relatively weak. They want very much, and properly, to experience their own independence and to make their own decisions. But they are caught up in the world politic where others actually make the decisions. And there is little they can do about it. Cyprus is a case in point. Both sides, Greek and Turkish, looked to the United States and the choice not to intervene made by the United States was fairly decisive in the affair. I fear the decision was more guided by money and oil concerns than by right and justice, but maybe it was the best one. These affairs are complex. If the United States had intervened or actively helped Greece, the problem could have escalated out of control. As it is, it is now fairly well contained and this might be the best for general world peace. But it would be good to see us Americans really stand up loud and strong for right and justice for all concerned.

Today, here, we celebrate the Feast of All the Saints of Meteora—a special feast for this community. The solemnity was heightened by Father Theophilitis' receiving the Great Schema. This must have been decided just last night because Father Dionysios told me on the way to the Vigil and Father Maximos told me at the Vigil. We started about nine last night and broke off at three this morning, to resume at seven and go on till eleven. The profession took place at the Liturgy after the small entrance before the readings. Father Theophilitis, dressed only in a simple robe and barefoot, was led in by two brothers. After many prostrations, venerating the icons, and reverencing the Hegumen, he stood before him at the holy doors. (I was happy to see the deacon spread a little mat over the cold marble under his bare feet.) The Hegumen gave a carefully prepared talk which he read from notes. Then the profession took place, through a series of interrogations. Father's robe was taken off and the Hegumen tonsured him. This was especially interesting. Archimandrite Aimilianos first stressed that by tonsure, Father Theophilitis placed himself under Christ and his Gospels in total obedience. To emphasize this, he rapped the Gospel book with the scissors repeatedly. Then he dropped the scissors on the book and they fell to the floor. Father Theophilitis picked them up and gave them back to the Hegumen, signifying his complete willingness to be tonsured and come completely under Christ and the Gospels in the person of the Hegumen. This was repeated two more times before the Hegumen cut Father Theophilitis' hair. Then he was clothed in a new robe and sandals, the analavos* (a black scapular with special red embroidery and strings attached), a belt, rason, skouphos and veil, and mandyas* (a pleated black cloak), all of which had remained on the altar through the night. He kept the veil on even during Communion. At the end of the Liturgy he was given a cross and lighted candle with a prayer cord attached to it. During the thanksgiving prayers the monks came and kissed his cross and embraced and kissed him. We then went to the refectory in procession for a festive meal. The Hegumen gave another longer talk on the profession with the new professed sitting at his table. There were more rites, then back to the katholikon for more swinging of the chandeliers, litanies, and prayers over the professed.

As we celebrate this feast, still savoring last week's, I begin to appreciate more what a rich heritage we are called into when we are called to become monks. We enter a great assembly of Saints and we can blend our poor offerings and prayers into their great choir of worship and praise and share in the fullness of their prayers and merits. It is a tremendously beautiful gift from the Lord to be called into this company. In the West we are not generally sufficiently aware of the heritage that is ours. We should celebrate the feasts of our Saints and Founders more fully and get more in touch with them. This realization is one grace I will take away from this retreat.

I was glad to learn they have a couple of "coffee shops" around the house where the monks can get a cup of coffee when they feel the need. In the midst of an All Night Service it can be a real help. I was amused last night watching the cantor cope with a monk who is not blessed with a particularly good voice or ear but likes to really sing out. So like home!

※

During lunch Father Dionysios had a small cassette recorder on the table taping the Hegumen's talk. I am glad they are getting his talks on tape. I hope some day we can manage to publish some of them in English.

※

The new professed received a new name—Basil! I gave him a small icon I had with me of the three Hierarchs.

※

After supper Father Maximos served coffee in the courtyard to Father David, Mario Goerig, Archimandrite Germogen (a Polish monk from Rome who is writing on a history of the Orthodox Church in Poland), a German friend, and myself. When I related how I was particularly impressed by the tonsure service, Father David told of his in the monastery at The Hague. As a further expression of the new professed's determination, the Hegumen, after simply dropping the scissors the first time, tossed it some distance the second time, and the third time gave it a real heave. Father David could not find them. Fortunately, it was the Feast of the Transfiguration and there was a pair of scissors on hand to cut the blessed grapes for distribution. Father David brought these scissors back to the Hegumen, only to be charged with a lack of docility right in the midst of his professing it.

We discussed the relation of religion to culture and the need of Orthodoxy to be able to separate itself from Byzantine culture, to take root in other cultures, or allow new cultures to develop.

Monday, June 22

As a result of fatigue and feasting I had a bout of sickness this morning. I also have some sort of allergy which is causing me to break out all over. Father Myron gave me some pills for it. I hope they work.

I had breakfast with the same group that was at last night's coffee. We talked about the differences in our practices relative to the Eucharist: concelebration, reception of the Sacrament, fasting and preparation for it, reservation of the Sacrament.

Orthodox Church law only requires complete fast from the previous evening. In practice, since Communion became rare, the faithful began fasting three or six days in preparation. Here where frequent Communion is developing, this is more left aside, though one can get fasting food—free from oil—from the kitchen if he requests it. There has always been something of a double standard, as this extra fast was not expected of the priests on the Mountain who usually celebrate quite frequently, even daily.

The Eucharist is reserved under both species. On Holy Thursday the Sacred Bread is dipped into the Consecrated Wine and then carefully dried and kept for a whole year. The Orthodox insisted that this reservation is only in order to have the Sacrament for the sick, not for veneration. The veneration is to the altar, or to the Gospel book on it, which represents Christ. In fact, though, the Sacrament is reserved usually in a very finely wrought tabernacle kept under a glass dome and with a lamp burning. So there is certainly respect and reverence for the sacramental Presence.

I spent the rest of the morning talking with Mario about the differences and similarities between the two Churches and their expressions of monasticism. Also we talked about the Christian use of Zen and similar Eastern practices. He will be doing a two-week Zen program with Father Gregory Wett of Beuron* when he returns to West Germany.

✵

The hesychast is one who says "My heart is strengthened" (Psalm 57). The hesychast is one who says "I sleep but my heart watches

(Song of Songs 5:2). Close your cell door to your body, the door of your lips to words, the interior door to spirits. Hesychia is worship and uninterrupted service of God.

— SAINT JOHN CLIMACUS, *The Ladder of Divine Ascent*, Step 27

❊

The hand at work, the mind and heart with God.

— THEOPHANE THE RECLUSE

Tuesday, June 23

Among the visitors today there is probably the oldest monk on the Holy Mountain, Father Ananias, who lives near Karyes in the kellion in which Saint Nikodimos dwelt. He is one hundred and ten years old and has been on the Mountain since 1886. Despite his great age, he rode over from Karyes on horseback 17½ kilometers. There are also some Anglican theological students from Yorkshire interested in ecumenical dialogue. And a Greek priest with a group of students. Groups like this have been frequent. It is a good sign to see young priests and students taking a serious interest in the Holy Mountain and monastic life. The monks reach out to them, too. Last night after supper you could see monks with one, two, or several students, sharing with them.

During Apodeipnon almost every night the monks have to get out the relics of the monastery for the visitors to venerate. Relics mean a great deal on the Holy Mountain. Here at Simonos Petras they have a couple especially significant ones: the second largest relic of the True Cross on the Mountain. When the monastery burned down a hundred years ago the Hegumen took this and another relic to Russia to raise money. On one occasion the crowd was very great and the relic miraculously rose up into the air so all could see it. The miracle caused much excitement and the Hegumen got enough money to rebuild the monastery and put up a new wing. The other very significant relic is the right hand of Saint Mary Magdalen. It still has the flesh on it, keeps normal bodily temperature, and gives off a beautiful odor. It is considered one of the most significant relics on the Mountain and is the reason why Saint Mary Magdalen is the secondary patron of this monastery.

❋

Today a number of monks have gone to Dionysiou. Many are flocking there and extra boats are running from Daphni. Tomorrow is the Feast of Saint John the Baptist (June 24). They have in that monastery a hand of Saint John the Baptist and this day is celebrated as their patronal feast.

❋

The various methods described by the Fathers (sitting down, making prostrations, and other techniques used when performing the Jesus Prayer) are not suitable for every one. Indeed, without a personal director they are actually dangerous. It is better not to try them. There is just one method which is obligatory for all: to stand with the attention in the heart. All other things are beside the point and do not lead to the heart of the matter.

— THEOPHANE THE RECLUSE

Wednesday, June 24

🍃 We started Services a little earlier this morning, but they were not that long so we finished the festive meal by eight. It makes for a rather odd day when lunch is over by 8:00 A.M. and you have a ten hour afternoon. I guess the best solution is the one adopted by many of the monks—take a good long siesta.

❋

My life these days could probably be best described as just lying around with the Lord. This "better part" or "best part" of Mary's is not always the easiest. Mary Magdalen had lain around with other men for years to get money to buy what she wanted and to prove to herself her worth in the experience of power over men and her allurement. Then she found love. And her whole being was centered in her Beloved. No longer did she need anything for herself. It was all in him. Our temptation is constantly to prostitute ourselves to activity to have something in hand to assure ourselves of our worth. Instead of forgetting self—dying to self—and finding everything in him. He may well then direct us to activity; but it will be all the same—an attentive eye of the servant on the Hand of the Master as we go about it, instead of on ourselves.

❊

The fifth joyful mystery of the rosary is the carrying out of the fourth, the Presentation of Jesus in the Temple. Mary offered to the Lord God what was most precious of all he had given her—his very own Son. And she gave him back to him. We can only give God of what he has given us: thine own from what is thine own we offer to thee . . .

Life then moved along quietly for a dozen years. Then suddenly the Father took what had been offered. "Did you not know I must be about my Father's business?" No, Mary did not understand. We offer ourselves to the Lord, and life goes quietly on, and we think he is accepting the offering—and he is—but suddenly, one day, he moves in and makes his claim in a way we least expect it, and we—not he—are lost. I am in my fourth decade; what does the fifth decade hold for me? For many of my friends—Tom Merton, Odo Brooke, Basil Morrison—it included a real finding as they entered into Life.

❊

The fifth, tenth, and fifteenth decades of the rosary are all findings. The fifth, the obscure, confused, not too well understood finding of this groping, searching life of faith. The tenth, the essential way to finding the source of all our finding, when Christ himself found all: "Father into thy hands. . . ." And the fifteenth, Mary's full finding prefiguring ours when we finally cross over and all is completed. The kingdom has come.

❊

The diet here is very simple and frugal. Mainly it is just what is coming from the garden now: potatoes, squash, beans, with some beets, tomatoes, and cucumbers. Usually one dish, with some olives on the side. Three or four days a week are fast days—only one meal (though one can get a bite in the kitchen after Vespers) and no wine or oil. On feasts and Saturdays there are a couple of spoonfuls of koliva as dessert. No eggs ever, and fish only two times so far on the great feasts. It is quite a contrast from Aghios Panteleimonos.

Even at Stavronikita, which is quite a strict monastery, they have eggs regularly and fish and cheese frequently. The frugality here is not because they cannot afford more, for they are one of the monasteries that are well off. It is by choice. In fact, the younger monks take no wine, contenting themselves with water. Wine is served because it is in the typicon here and the old monks are used to it.

❊

The simple man does not mind seeming to be foolish in the eyes of the world that he may be wise in the sight of God.
— WILLIAM OF SAINT THIERRY, *Golden Epistle*, 49

❊

For the tree which gives knowledge of good and evil in paradise is in religious life the power to decide, and it is entrusted to the Spiritual Father, who judges all things while he himself is judged by no one. — *Golden Epistle*, 54

Here William is certainly close to Orthodox monastic practice on the role of the Spiritual Father.

Thursday, June 25

🙘 We are having a bit of rain—the first on this side of the Mountain since I arrived.

We did not have Liturgy this morning. All the functioning priests are away. There are at least ten priests in the community, but two of the old ones do not serve any longer and three are assigned to the houses in Athens, Thessaloniki, and Ormilia. Father Palamas is at studies. Father David went to Dionysiou for the feast, Father Dionysios has gone to Karyes to see Father Paisios. The Hegumen is off to Russia—there was much ringing of the bells after the Liturgy yesterday to see him off. Father Theologos has been away for some days now. At the Services the litanies and other parts said by the priest are simply omitted, so they are somewhat shorter.

There are lots of visitors. This morning there were too many for the boat so it had to return. Even before this group got off another twenty were arriving.

❉

I am with Joshua conquering the Holy Land these days. Something in me kind of reacts to putting whole peoples under the sword. Perhaps it is that part that is not yet illuminated by faith and the Spirit to see things God's way. The earth and all its fullness are his and he gives us a certain bit of it to use in his service. Life is his gift and he gives it to us for a time. For the Canaanites the time was up. Does it make much difference really if God calls time by Joshua's sword or a drunken driver or a cancerous cell? Not even a sparrow falls from heaven without the Father willing it. We can be sure whatever it be, it will be in his Providence. I wonder how he will call time for me, and when and where? But does it really matter? I had a young friend who was told he had a year to live. After the initial shock, he got used to the idea and pretty much forgot about it and went on living to the end in a quite normal way. We all know that the Lord is going to call time—we have just so many minutes on the boards of life to play our part in the drama of salvation. What we need more is that insight from the Spirit to grasp this fact in a real way and so play our part accordingly. Then the how, when, and where will fit in just perfectly. This is what we should pray for and desire—not to know how, when, and where, but to receive the Divine Light that we might understand what is going on.

❉

What a man must the Lord have been—a real *vir*—to clear the temple the way he did. The sellers were doing a good thing—making the necessities for sacrifice readily available to the worshippers. But Jesus cleared them out as "thieves." It was not what they were doing but their motive—not to help others but enrich themselves—a motive that so got hold of them that they robbed their customers, those whom they were supposedly serving. I am God's temple. As Saint Paul asked in 1 Corinthians 3:16: "Do you not know that you are God's temple?" I must not allow any trafficking. I do need to search the Scriptures for that insight that will fuel the fires of love and self-sacrifice. But I must take care not to sell such thoughts and insights or to use them to make others think more of me or to write them in books to make money. I must have that purity of heart, the Lord must so cleanse my temple, that I seek only him and share only to help others find him. Lord, give me a clean heart and a humble, serving love.

※

From my balcony I can see a number of paths up and down the mountain, threading through the olive trees and shrub oak. I find myself giving an undue amount of time to watching people make their way along these or the boats coming and going in the port. This is about the only activity on this utterly peaceful scene besides Father Myron's activities in the gardens on the terraces below. He has a wonderful garden, laid out with care, every space used. As one crop is reaped, the patch is turned over and another is planted. I especially like to watch him irrigate the garden. The flood of water speaks to me of grace, guided by the work of the monk (prayer) to where it is needed, so that the Lord can give the increase. I suppose I have to admit that all my interest in these bits of human activity are something of an escape from the solitude of being so constantly before God, with the total demand that that makes. Certainly, while I am here on the Mountain with God I cannot let the toiling of his pilgrim people up and down the ways of life and in and out of its ports be absent from my heart's concern. But with it there, my part these days is to be Mary's. And I must not let precious moments get lost in idle gazing.

※

Father Eliseos has gone to Karyes for a year to serve as secretary for Iera Kinotis.* Last year this community provided both secretary and undersecretary. The secretary is supposed to be a priest and at least thirty years old. Father Eliseos is neither. Here, too, the young are coming into their own. It is a real sacrifice for the community to let him go for a year. He is the Hegumen's first assistant. Father Serapion and Father Theologos take care of the administrative affairs.

Friday, June 26

〜 Today would be the Feast of Pope Eugene III at home (July 9). It is funny how some odd little incidents stick in one's mind. I remember twenty-two years ago today picking stones in the field north of the church under a very hot sun. Father Eugene was with us and we piled three straw hats on him as his tiara for the feast.

❄

Friday is washday. No one knows in which century the laundry here was built. It is outside the monastery gate where it can get the water coming down from the mountain. A bit of grit in the water makes it a better detergent. In the corner there is a very large black cauldron. Around three sides of the room are marble basins with holes in them to let out the water. Each monk does his own wash. A brother sets a fire under the cauldron right after lunch. Each one gets the number of clothespins he needs from the econome, clogs up the hole in the bottom of the basin with a bit of cloth, fills the basin with hot water drawn from the cauldron with a five-gallon can. Then the clothes are scrubbed with some heavy brown soap and set to soak during the siesta. After the siesta each one gives his clothes a good rubbing and rinsing and then carries them up the equivalent of about six stories to the roof where they are hung on a line. The sun is strong and hot, so they dry quickly. Before Apodeipnon, the finished product can be collected and the pins restored to the econome.

While I was about my laundry, two of the monks were transferring wood from the large pile outside the gate up to the bakery in the courtyard. They had little donkeys with big baskets strapped on each side. It was quite picturesque for someone from New York, but just part of everyday life here.

When you come from a rather fastidious culture, as do most Americans, to one that is less concerned about cleanliness and diet, you have the choice of adapting to local ways or spending an inordinate amount of time and attention on the details of life. If you plan to stay for a long time, the first is the only feasible solution. But it takes a bit to swallow down some of the dishes set before you, even when others around seem to be devouring them with delight. And the switch from the daily hot, sudsy shower to a cold-water spigot or a bucket of stream water is not the easiest, especially when it is not just for a weekend camping trip but represents a new way of life. In all this, one has to discern the lurking of inordinate self-love and what are simply cultural hang-ups that one has simply to admit and make the best of. Athos is changing, and some of the monks would probably say much too rapidly and for the worst, but there is now a complete telephone system, including intercoms in the big houses, some roads, buses, jeeps and tractors, running water, some flush toilets and showers, an occasional cassette player-recorder. Soon there will be electricity and the endless things that can come with it. Will this make a difference? From what I see among the monks in the monasteries open to these things, I think not, at least not in regard to the essentials. They treasure the tradition and have a good grasp of it. Accidentals are discerned as accidentals. Facilities facilitate taking care of everyday cares and leave one freer for the essentials. At least, that is the way I see it. However, I do not want to deny the fact that we can surround ourselves with too many facilities and become enslaved in our need for them. The American monk has to be careful of this. Besides the direct effects that the multiplication of "needs" can have on his life in the time and attention they demand, they can also affect his economy and make it necessary for him to concern himself about earning more money to obtain all these things. Man is quite incarnate and there is need for a good bit of discernment in how he is to live his sharing of the Divine Life in a human incarnational context.

This afternoon Father Dionysios told me about Father Demetrios, one of the parish priests near Trikala, where the community was located before. Father Demetrios, who reposed a year ago last January, had been given to the Lord since early age. He had a special devotion to the Archangels Michael and Gabriel, who had a small chapel near the town. He wanted to become a monk on Meteora, but the Angels told him to marry a girl of the village and told her mother to give the girl to him. He had five daughters, four of whom he married off. The fifth became a nun and he built a convent for her. His life was full of miracles and visions. When the communist guerrillas came in the late 1940s, he opposed them and won the enmity of the Bishops and others who were trying to work with them. One time the communists were pursuing Father Demetrios and he came to a great river, swollen by floodwater. He knelt in prayer and suddenly a beautiful young man appeared and whisked him over the torrent.

The monk asked the young man his name. "George"—and with that the Patron Saint of Greece disappeared. On another occasion, Father Demetrios had hiked a long distance to a small chapel of the same Saint to offer Liturgy. When he got there he found no water. He remonstrated with the Saint and immediately a spring gushed forth. And so his life proceeded.

Father Dionysios spoke also of the Bishop there, Bishop Dionysios, who reposed in 1970. He once hid an English soldier in his monastery during World War II, when the Axis occupied the country. The Germans found out and imprisoned Dionysios in Dachau concentration camp for three years, where he shared his meager clothes and food with other prisoners and spent his nights in the barracks transfigured in prayer. It is good to be so close to the Saints.

Father Dionysios directed a boys' school in Trikala for a year for the Bishop. Three of the young monks here at Simonos Petras were boys he had supervised at that school.

Father Ananias came to the Mountain in 1886—ninety years a monk! Although he is one hundred and ten, he wants to go to Athens to raise money to build a chapel for Saint Nikodimos near Karyes.

Father Kallistos, the oldest monk in this monastery—he is ninety-six—is having trouble with his eyes. He asked that they get him some glasses—the doctor would know what he needs—something to help him see distances well. When he heard that the Hegumen's father was in America, he felt sure he would be able to find what he needed there. Father Dionysios offered to take the old monk to Thessaloniki, but he could not see the need for it. I am sure the Holy Community will set up some health facilities at Karyes with eye doctors and other specialists once they get electricity.

Keep your mind free from colors, images, and forms; beware of the imagination in prayer—otherwise you may find that you have become a fantasist instead of a hesychast.

— SAINT GREGORY OF SINAI

So as not to fall into illusion while practicing inner prayer, do not permit yourself any concepts, images, or visions.

— SAINT NIL SORSKI

※

There are unfathomable depths within the heart. God is there with the angels, light and life are there, the kingdom and the apostles, the heavenly cities, and the treasures of grace: all things are there. — SAINT MACARIOS, *Homily*, 15

Saturday, June 27

I received a letter from Abbot Thomas. Father Basil's sister Lorraine died the night preceding his ordination. All the concern had been whether his *mother* would live for his ordination. His sister's death must have been an awful shock. God's why is very mysterious at times. I will offer the holy Liturgy today for Lorraine.

※

I have been reading through the Old Testament with real relish. One thing stands out very clearly—God's election. He chooses whom he wants, when he wants, and for what he wants. I have to get a good hold on that and let him have things his way. "Not as man sees does God see, because man sees the appearance but the Lord looks into the heart." Lord, look into my heart, but first put there what you want to see. Amen.

※

The Jesus Prayer helps us to see Christ in all men and all men in Christ.

Sunday, June 28

I like the way they do the Services. Usually one or a small group around the lectern does the reciting or singing. The rest are left free to follow along, moving with the theme of the prayer, carried as it were on the wings of the prayer of the Church, in a very simple prayer that can be very free and elevated. This is why they can have such long Services. Instead of everyone being expected to sing almost everything, as it is with us in the West, the strong singers can carry the larger part of the burden, yet even they get time to rest while others recite the Psalms and the like. Coming from the same tradition as Saint Benedict, they do the whole Psalter each week besides the Psalms, which are part of the daily basic structure of the Services. They divide the Psalter into twenty-eight sections. One section is done each day at Vespers, beginning at first Vespers for Sunday, and three are done at Orthros. This morning we had a typical Sunday Orthros and Liturgy with meal, lasting a little over five hours.

❀

Father Methodios, pastor of a small church in Athens and a spiritual son of the Hegumen, is with us and conducted the Liturgy today.

We will have an All-Night Vigil for the Holy Apostles Peter and Paul.

Monday, June 29

෴ As we celebrate the Feast of Saints Peter and Paul, I wonder how much our Orthodox brethren reflect on the fact that they are not in communion with the See of Peter. I suppose very little, just as we in the West advert very little to the fact that we are not in communion with the many sees to which Paul ministered and addressed his Epistles. And they are in communion with Peter's first see at Antioch. But as we celebrate the feast, my prayer centers on Church unity and the fulfillment of Christ's prayer that we all be one as he is one with the Father. The first litany prays for "peace in the whole world, the well-being of the holy Churches of God, and the union of all." In general, though, and in the other litanies, the prayer is specifically for "Orthodox Christians." In my heart I always add "and all others, too." I do not know if in the West we ever pray so exclusively for "Catholic Christians." I think we are "Catholic," not only in name and geographic extent, but in outlook, more and more. Orthodox often question our use of Byzantine liturgical prayer, but the Catholic rightly feels all these belong to him as a Catholic. His outreach to and use of methods of meditation, from Hindus and Zen Buddhists, are even more difficult for Orthodox to understand. And some Catholics find them difficult, too. But all things are ours and we are Christ's and Christ is God's. Anything that is good or true, in any way, is, to that extent, of Christ, and the Christian may claim it and use it in his service. In the sureness of his faith, the Catholic can share the goods enjoyed by others and not fear being deluded, because he has the faith as a sure guide. He need not necessarily use these things from other traditions. He has more than enough in his own tradition. But he may. He is free. And he cannot forget that his own tradition was formed with borrowings "baptized" from Jewish, Greek, Roman, and other traditions. In the end, though, the call seems to be to use less and less and abide in an ever-greater simplicity before the hidden Face of God, begging with all one's being: "Show us your Face, O Lord, and we shall be saved."

❋

I received in the mail today from Brother Jerome a copy of *Byzantine Daily Worship*, with the Services and Liturgy in English. I am sure it will help me to get even more out of the rich Services we enjoy here.

❋

I find myself asking what am I getting out of this retreat, but I realized today that that is the wrong question. This retreat is not for me, but for him. It is to give him, at least for this little while, the fullest attention and love that I can, freed as I am from many other cares and concerns that ordinarily clutter my life—a chance to live out a bit Mary's part in this house that looks to her as a special patron. Lord, help me to let go and rest quietly at your Feet in complete attention to you. And then my life will be refreshed and renewed.

❋

For the Orthodox, in the making of a monk there are three elements: the *profession*, which takes the form of a series of questions and answers in which the candidate declares his intentions; the *tonsure*, which signifies coming under the authority of the superior; and *receiving the monastic habit*, which means taking on a new way of life. Most commonly the rite is referred to as "tonsure"—the tonsure of a monk—though they might speak of "receiving the Great Schema" or "making profession," but most commonly it is "tonsure."

Obedience is central in the Orthodox idea of monasticism. It is the sure way to escape from self-will, to be open to the Divine Will, to attain to perfection. I think we in the West have made a mistake in dropping tonsure from our profession rites. We let it go, I think, out of a sense of authenticity, since we no longer wear the tonsure as we used to. But the Orthodox do not wear it either. At their rite, only four snips are taken from the top of the head in the form of a cross, and if the candidate's hair is long the locks are cut above the collar. But after that, his hair is never cut but allowed to grow fully. The significance of the rite is the thing. In the West we are weak on symbolism, but I think today we are grasping for more symbols, to enrich our lives and ceremonies. I would like to see us reintroduce tonsure at the profession, and perhaps do it the way the Orthodox do it, showing its meaning in relation to the Superior and the Gospel.

Tuesday, June 30

 As I read through the Books of Kings, I shake my head and wonder why king after king failed the Lord and lost out in the same way. Few seemed to learn from the mistakes of their predecessors. Then I take a look at my own life and see how I have failed over and over again in the same stupid ways and have failed to learn by my own mistakes. If I cannot learn by my own sad experience, with the fullness of the grace of Christ present, how can I expect those kings of old to learn from others? More the wonder is the unending patience of Christ with the likes of me. Praise him!

✻

My cell here is about eleven feet long and seven feet wide, not counting the window sill. The outer wall is about four feet thick, so the deep sill of the large window adds a lot to the seeming size of the room. There is a built-in stove about three feet square in one corner. Around the wall, except at the door and stove, there is a shelf at the level of about six feet, which can hold many books and things without detracting from the size of the room. This cell is typical of the monks' cell here. We judged such a small size inadequate when we were planning rooms at Spencer, but for the simplicity of life here— no need of wardrobe or big desk—it seems quite adequate.

❊

. Father Maximos brings me English-language periodicals (*Saint Vladimir Theological Quarterly*, *The Journal of the Moscow Patriarchate*, etc.) and books from the library. Last night I read an interesting article in the *Journal* (1975, no. 2) on the Presanctified Liturgy. It made it clear that daily Communion was the common practice of the early Church, urged by Saint Basil and others, to the extent that the people took the Consecrated Bread home to receive each day. Thus they frequently received under only one species. When they received in church they usually received the two species separately. The spoon only came in later. At the Presanctified Liturgy some Churches allowed the priest to consecrate the chalice, with the usual words to go with the Bread, but the more common practice was to dip the Bread in the cup and conceive of this as consecrating the wine.

❊

We had cheese at lunch today, now that the twenty-day fast in preparation for the Feast of Saints Peter and Paul is ended. I like the Greek feta, though it varies from place to place. What we had today tasted quite salty and was very strong.

❊

Last year they celebrated the Liturgy on the twenty-ninth down at the arsenas.* An American Benedictine from Mount Angel Abbey, in Oregon, Brother James, was being received into the Orthodox Church. He made his profession of faith at the end of the Vigil and was baptized in the sea before Liturgy.

❊

The building I now have my cell in is the newest of the buildings here, dating from the turn of the century. The Hegumen has the top floor, with living quarters, chapel, office, reception, library (he has a fine patristic and monastic collection), and kitchen. The older monks have the floor below his—the fourth floor—with Father Dionysios. There is a chapel there, too, dedicated to Saint Charalambos, the patron of the last Hegumen. There are actually only three old monks on that floor now. Father Kallistos, ninety-six years young; Father Simon, the old priest who keeps the Services going; and Father Evstratios, eighty-one. Father Evstratios gets around a good bit yet. Usually it is a novice or young monk who leads the Little Hours, but when Father Evstratios gets a chance, he likes to slip into the reader's stall and, holding the book at odd angles to catch the limited light filtering down from the small windows in the cupola, he fervently prays his way through the Service. Every once in a while he notices the grandfather clock in the liti has stopped. He will dutifully wind it and then, because he is a little man and his sight is not what it used to be, standing on tiptoe or almost shinnying up the side of the tall clock, he will rather unsuccessfully set the hands by feel. The clock will then tick away and run down till he notices it again.

I am on the third floor where one old monk lives, Father Chrysostomos. There is a special guest room where Saint Nectarios stayed, a couple of rooms for long-term guests like myself, a wardrobe from where I hear the treadle sewing machine at times, the infirmary where Father Myron dispenses medicine and care, the stationery room, a storeroom, a "coffee shop" where one can brew a cup of coffee, and a washroom with a shower. Below, on the second floor, many of the young monks have their cells. The first floor seems to be unused cells. It is on a level with the main gate of the monastery. But a stairway immediately goes down one more level to where the mules have their stables. Then the ground falls away to the vegetable terraces.

From the main gate a steep incline leads up to the courtyard which is as high as halfway up the fourth story of the new building. The katholikon is at this level, also the refectory, kitchen, bakery, and the econome's storerooms, the synodikon* or community meeting room, and some guest rooms. The floor above this has the reception and most of the guest rooms. It seems to be the custom on the Mountain to put the guests at the top of the house. Below the kitchen and refectory are more cells, another chapel, a library, storerooms, etc. The main buildings in their essential fabric date to the time of Saint Simon, in the fourteenth century. The thick walls built on the solid granite outcropping have withstood the repeated fires. It would be a fascinating job to draw a floor plan of this multilevel plant.

❀

The other long-term guest here now is Father Amphilochios from Crete, who is to spend a year here before going to the mission in Zaire to begin a monastery there.

❀

Archimandrite Aimilianos urged that while he is in Russia I visit the neighboring monastery, Grigoriou, to talk with the Hegumen there. Father David just came in to say he would be going over to Grigoriou tomorrow after the Liturgy, so I will probably go with him.

After supper I went to tell Father Dionysios I would be going over to Grigoriou tomorrow. We got into a very intense discussion on Church outlook. The Orthodox see themselves as Christ's little flock —the one, holy, catholic, apostolic Church who Christ is. They feel it is important to know clearly the boundaries of Christ's courtyard. Without denying the freedom of the Spirit, they see Christ working ecclesiastically only within the Orthodox Church. The Sacraments in other Churches are not valid, but, by economia,* some Orthodox Churches only require Chrismation at reception of converts and recognize Matrimony and, in various ways, Orders. They believe that if any man truly opens himself and seeks God's will, he will receive the Orthodox faith. The assumption that is present in this, that all other Christians in some way are not open or not seeking Christ's will, I find impossible to accept. I think we have to admit that not so many years ago Catholics were also very concerned in defining Christ's courtyard, but they did not take the same exclusive attitude toward Christ's working through their Sacraments. The Orthodox see the schism as caused by Rome's establishing new doctrines—*Filioque*, papal primacy—and thus seceding from the Church, and they believe history proves this is the case. As Catholics, of course, we see it as Constantinople and the others breaking off communion with the See of Peter.

I personally have not wanted to get involved in discussions of this sort because I feel poorly prepared for such things, and it is not the purpose of my being on the Holy Mountain. But I suppose it is inevitable that such discussions do arise at times.

Wednesday, July 1

It is the feast of two Roman un-mercenaries, Saints Cosmas and Damian. I remember well visiting their tombs and home church in Rome on their feast.

❄

Father David waited for the hottest part of the day and then wanted to walk instead of taking the boat, so we arrived at Grigoriou in early afternoon a bit done in—at least, I was. It is much warmer down here; the monastery is right on the water. It is a very well-kept monastery; all is bright and clean, bright flower beds and palms line the path to the gate. There are thirty-eight in the community, many of them young.

Father Georgios, the Hegumen, was a professor in the University of Athens. He taught for a year in the United States. In 1972 he became a novice at Pendeli. His teachings attracted young men and soon he had a following, but they did not want to become monks at Pendeli. So Father Georgios took over some buildings near Halkis and, with the young novices, began restoring them. In the early months of 1974 the Patriarch of Constantinople succumbed to pressure from the junta of the Colonels, and the elections of a number of Bishops which had taken place during the dictatorship were declared invalid. Fearing the new Bishop of Halkis might not respect their monastery and their monastic needs, the community—Father Georgios and eight young monks and novices—came to Simonos Petras. At that time Father Dionysios, the Hegumen at Grigoriou, a good monastery but not getting recruits, had been asking for some young monks from Simonos Petras. So after eleven days Father Georgios and his men came here. They liked it. The old monks liked them and soon chose Father Georgios as Hegumen.

Shortly after we arrived at Grigoriou we received the usual refreshments and then some lunch. Father David and I were given a room to share. He slept while I read. At one point the semantron sounded to call the monks to common work, bringing in wood. After Father

David awoke he started a discussion on the differences between our two Churches. He felt the *Filioque* made Christ more remote from us. I tried to assure him that, in both popular devotion and deeper spiritual experiences, Christ was very present and central for the Catholic. He thought, too, that the idea of deification was absent from our teaching. He had once studied Catholicism after his father became a Catholic and the parish priest who was instructing him never spoke of this to him. Again I tried to assure him. He asked what ecumenism meant for me. I told him that I saw it as an outreach of love to all fellow Christians, as affirming all that we have so mercifully received from the Lord and share in common, and as trying to be one as much as we can in response to Christ's prayer, and above all as trying to stand together before the Lord in complete openness so he can lead us all into oneness in the possession of the one faith.

We were joined by Father Symeon, the young convert from Peru. He had been studying in Greece, and under the influence of Father Georgios, the Hegumen, he became Orthodox and a monk. He is a very intense young man and was eager to discuss the theological differences between our Churches.

After Vespers Father Georgios greeted me warmly and after a fine supper we walked together by the sea. He has thirty-eight monks in all and since they do not have the outside commitments of Simonos Petras most are here. Most of the fifteen old monks are actively present in the choir or in the liti for the Services. It was very touching to see an old blind monk feel his way from icon to icon to venerate each. They have only one novice but a number of rasophores*—men who have received the habit but have not yet made profession. They are generally considered monks and may not marry. In this monastery, after one year as a novice, one receives the rason and after a couple of years the Great Schema. They do not use the Little Schema.

Contrary to what I had been previously told, Father Georgios is Spiritual Father to most of the community in the full sense, although he has given his blessing to some of the old monks to confess to a monk he brings in from New Skete. The young monks seem like a very sincere and lively group. The few I contacted were quite friendly. The Hegumen is a very impressive man, humble, gentle, but firm and wise. He asked many questions about my monastery. We talked about the role of the Spiritual Father.

When we broached the question of my staying a week or so he said while he would like it, the old monks were scandalized at the idea. He works closely with a council of eight Elders, as is the more common rule on the Holy Mountain. He had met with the Elders briefly after supper. The offenses of the Latins, past and present, make it difficult for them to accept at face value one coming out of simple love and good will. There is a Uniat Church in Athens and recently, contrary to the expressed wishes of the Orthodox, the Holy See named a Uniat bishop. They see the use of the Liturgy, Services, and clerical garb by the Greek Catholics as masquerading as Orthodox to deceive the people. They recall how half the Antiochian Orthodox returned to Rome, or, as they express it, how the Antiochian Patriarch lost half his flock. I tried to explain how the Catholic Church in no wise meant to masquerade or deceive but simply saw all Christian rites and traditions as having their proper place within the Catholic Church. It is unfortunate there is duplication of jurisdictions, but this is necessary as long as the Orthodox Bishops are not in union with the See of Peter. The older monks feel that the late Patriarch Athenagoras of Constantinople came under the influence of Rome and fell into error in his ecumenical outreach.

Because of the feelings of his older monks, the Hegumen felt it best I did not stay. At Vespers I had been asked to stay out on the porch of the katholikon.

Implied in what Father had said was something beautiful and something sad. The high value these men place on their faith is beautiful. But their fear and defensiveness, which warps in a way the full outflow of their love, is sad. It seemed they saw my presence as more "unitism." One young monk remarked, "He looks Orthodox on the outside. Why is he not Orthodox inside?" They somehow expect a Western monk to look different—he should not have a beard, perhaps, and should have his head shaved, etc. If he looks Orthodox, he is masquerading and seeking to deceive and mislead. Also I think the Hegumen implied that if he did receive me, he might lose the confidence of the older monks who would see him falling into the errors of Patriarch Athenagoras.

It is not perhaps the old monks only. At Vespers and Orthros the young priest made a careful point of not incensing me. However, the ecclesiastikos did in the usual way.

As I settled in our room, Father David asked me why I came to Mount Athos. He seems to feel I am searching and is making a more and more obvious effort to convert me. I tried to explain my need of a retreat and my choice of the Holy Mountain because of the vitality of monastic life and tradition here. But basically I came because it seemed to be what God wanted. Certainly the experience here helps me to enter into and appreciate the values of my own tradition better. Perhaps my simple perseverance in prayer and humility might help break down some of the walls. As I told Father Georgios, I do not want to discuss the theological issues. I do not feel particularly equipped for that. I want rather simply to be present in love and share an experience of God's Presence.

Thursday, July 2

It is the Feast of the Deposition of the Mantle of the Virgin. I arose a bit late as I did not want to be present for the Midnight Service, which is held in the liti. I assisted at Orthros from the porch. Then I slipped away over the mountain back to Simonos Petras, not wishing to cause any further embarrassment to my host. As the Lord said, if they will not receive you in one place, go on to another. I, perhaps, realize better now how the traditional Orthodox feel. I begin to realize it was somewhat audacious of me to decide to spend several months in their holy place. I think some of them feel this is being done against their will and there is nothing they can do about it. I am sorry if my presence is being misunderstood. I appreciate more the fullness of love at Simonos Petras. I am sure that they, as true Orthodox, share some of the feelings present at Grigoriou. But all have lovingly welcomed me. Love is kind, patient, bears all things. After lunch Father Maximos hastened to try to explain the attitude at Grigoriou and assured me it would not be the same when I visited Dionysiou.

❋

As I returned early it was still fairly cool, but making the ascent left me breathless and soaked with perspiration. I realize that a man of forty-five cannot quite do what a lad of nineteen can, but what concerned me more was my attitude. As a young monk I worked long hours in hot, humid weather, under the sun in the fields and late at night in the hot, stuffy barns, yet I seemed to take it in stride with my concern set on the Lord and his work. Now when I get hot and tired my concern seems to become too centered on myself, to the detriment of prayer and getting done what is to be done. I feel the pleasure principle so prevalent in our American society has gotten hold of me to some extent. My attitude is not that described by William of Saint Thierry when he spoke of manual labor in the *Golden Epistle*. I have let the body become too much of a weight on my spirit. How to regain freedom? As a sort of discipline, I will begin to skip breakfast, do some serious exercise, and cut down at other meals too. More important, I will try to attend more to the Lord in what I am doing for him than to how it is affecting me.

I think this insight and a clearer understanding of Orthodox feelings are good fruits that have come out of my visit to Grigoriou. Thank you, Lord.

Father Georgios, at Grigoriou, had pointed out that in the choice of a Hegumen the monks have to consider not only his quality as a spiritual man but also his ability to care for the administration of the temporal affairs. On Mount Athos he must also be a priest.

At Grigoriou early in this century a couple of wings of cut stone were added to the front of the original monastery, forming a second courtyard. The gate is in the new south wing. They have room for about thirty more monks there. They have just renovated one wing for the monks and are now making plans to move the guesthouse to the front wing. They do not want to get too big, though, so that the Hegumen can keep in personal contact with each of his monks.

In the valley between Simonos Petras and Grigoriou there are two sketes which cannot be seen from Simonos Petras because of the steepness of the mountain. The lower one, by a very attractive beach, is beautifully kept; everything looks newly painted. The gardens are handsomely laid out, with hearty tomato plants and other vegetables and a water tower. They also have many beehives, unlike any I have previously seen, lined up along each side of the path. They are round and seem to be made of bamboo and mud with paper sacks on top.

❋

Father Georgios: The whole monastic community is pneumatic, not just the Spiritual Father. He is the center of the focal point of the pneumatic community.

❋

After supper I met my new next-door neighbor, Nicholas Tzabellas, a lawyer who is studying for his exams to become a judge. He is a friend of Father Maximos. They studied together in England. Nicholas studied theology before doing law, so after we discussed canon law a bit, I found myself again engaged in a discussion of the differences between the Churches. Since Nicholas had studied in the West and visited New York, where he has a brother, he has a more open attitude than is generally common. He feels the two Churches must reach out toward each other. Because of the past latinizing history—Nicholas pointed especially to the deliberate absorption of the Greeks of Southern Italy, a question which he has studied—the Greeks tend to be suspicious and fearful of the Latins and put all they do in outreach in a bad light. He gave me one example: the medal Pope Paul VI gave to each of the Greek party of Patriarch Athenagoras in 1964, when they met in the Holy Land, showed a Greek and Latin priest kneeling before the newborn Saviour. The Greek offered a chalice; the Latin, a church. This the Greeks interpreted to mean that the Pope expected them to offer a chalice of tears for all their offenses while the Latins offered a church as a symbol that the Roman Church is truly the Church. I said it seemed very unlikely to me that at a moment when the Pope was reaching out in love he would have sought to convey such an attitude. The chalice undoubtedly symbolized our most sacred offering to the Lord —his own Eucharist. It shows though how careful we have to be and, humbly listening, try to prevent such misinterpretations and make every effort to make our true intentions as clear as possible.

Friday, July 3

 I am continually impressed by the number of very fine-looking young men at my table in the refectory. These are young men who look to the Hegumen as their Spiritual Father and may eventually join the community—as well as those who already have and are now novices. While they are here, they take a full part in the life, often singing or reciting at the Services. It is readily visible that there is a good variety of personality types, but a certain aliveness is a common denominator. I saw a similar group at Grigoriou and Stavronikita. This certainly speaks of something wonderful happening among Greek youth, at least in some segment of it, and a promising future for the Holy Mountain.

※

The monks here have been at work up on the mountain near the water source, putting in a cistern to prepare for a generator. Soon they will have electricity at Simonos Petras and without the noise of the diesel generator they have at Vatopedi.*

The Hegumen gave me a book from his library, which I read a bit of in the evening before going to sleep, and I am finding it very interesting: Michael Wauryh, *Initiatio Monastica in Liturgica Byzantina* (Pont. Institutum Orientalium Studiorum). Father Maximos gave me a couple of other books that look interesting: Vladimir Lossky, *In the Image and Likeness of God* (Saint Vladimir's, 1974); J. Meijer, C.SS.R., *A Successful Council of Union: A Theological Analysis of Photian Synod 879–880* (Analecta Vlatadon 23).

※

Essentially hesychasm [literally, silence] is a process of interior cleansing, of uprooting passions from within the depths of the soul, of purifying the heart and guarding the mind in order to prevent the re-entry of sinful thoughts which feed the passions and lead to actual sin. The practice of unceasing prayer—which the Scripture demands of us, is fulfilled by the use of the Jesus Prayer, "Lord, Jesus Christ, Son of God, have mercy on me a sinner," developed under the guidance of an Elder (staretz) (for obedience is both the beginning and consummation of all Christian spiritual labors). The Jesus Prayer fulfilled in obedience to an Elder is the central weapon in the interior struggle. — ARCHBISHOP ANTONY (MEDVEDEV), *The Young Elder: A Biography of Blessed Archimandrite Ambrose of Milkova* (Jordanville, 1974)

❀

Prelist = spiritual delusion, self deceit
Podvig = *askesis*, the form of spiritual struggle undertaken with the blessing of the Spiritual Father

❀

Love is the head, root, source, and mother of all good; without it everything else brings no benefit. It is the sign of the Lord's pupils, a distinguishing characteristic of God's servants, a sign of the Apostles. — SAINT JOHN CLIMACUS

❀

Try to confess not in general but in such a way as to experience shame; then it will be more beneficial.

❀

The monastery life progressed in the usual order: good and evil struggle in the common life and in each individual soul.

❀

Before Vespers Father Dionysios came in with a box of sweets. He looked very tired. He admitted he was not feeling well and had not slept the night before, yet he went down to one of the hermitages to offer Liturgy today and planned to do the same tomorrow. He pushes himself quite hard and always remains smilingly at the service of each and all. As usual, he was concerned that I might be neglected.

We talked a bit about the prayer or the life of the monk in the cell. A visitor from Germany had asked me: "Do the monks meditate in their cells?" Father Dionysios asked, "What is meditation?" I described briefly discursive meditation as it is found in the Cistercian tradition and then intuitive meditation and mantric meditation as found in the Far East. Father Dionysios said the monk in his cell sleeps, reads, makes prostrations, prays, and is simply present to God as God is to him, forgetting all the past, not planning the future, but being in the "now" with God which is the eschaton. The novice is led into this by the Gerontas. The Gerontas leads him not only by his words, but by his presence and by his absence and most of all by his prayer in the night when he is alone with God. Without the novice's being aware of it, the Gerontas mystically visits him with Christ, healing the soul, giving him light and grace.

❈

After supper a guest approached me, asking about the book I was using at Vespers. I sometimes follow the Services with Bishop Raya's *Byzantine Daily Worship* (Allendale, N.J.: Alleluia Press, 1969). He turned out to be Baron Guy Buysse from the Belgian embassy in Belgrade, Yugoslavia. This was his fourth visit to the Mount. Since his last visit he has converted from Roman Catholicism to Orthodoxy. Metropolitan Stilanos had urged him to stay in the Catholic Church. But he found a good Spiritual Father in Belgrade, where he has been for two years, Father Anderkey. For years he has been attracted to the Byzantine Liturgy and often went to Chevtogne, in Belgium. Now, constantly in the midst of Orthodox life and prayer in Belgrade, he found it too difficult to remain an outsider. Father Anderkey prepared a special profession of faith for him, very deliberately worded so he did not have to betray any of the beliefs he had been living by. He was especially attracted to Orthodoxy by the Liturgy and the fact that it retained the ancient forms and that dimension of mystery. He also was attracted by the emphasis placed on the role of the Holy Spirit in Christian life. I think we need to listen to men like the baron. What attracted him certainly is not absent from the Catholic tradition, but shows where we are weak in living out the fullness of our tradition. This should be one of the fruits of ecumenical sharing—to see better what we really are and have.

Saturday, July 4

☙ Tomorrow is the Feast of Saint Athanasios, the Founder of the first cenobium on the Holy Mountain. There will be a great celebration at Megisti Lavra. Father Simon and two of the young brothers are going to represent this community there. The Service, which will begin at sundown this evening, will last fourteen hours. Surprisingly, one gets a second wind or something. I have found it a very beautiful and uplifting experience, these long, night watches, and I am not tired when they are over. But I am just as happy staying quietly here at Simonos Petras this time, even though I was invited to go along.

❋

As I sit on the balcony I often watch monks and visitors make their way along the winding trail that crawls up our steep mountainside from the sea. At times they get lost beneath the olive trees or scrub oak or the outcroppings of granite, like little insects lost in the undergrowth. Lord, what is man that you are mindful of him? Yet as each one winds his way along, a loving Father has his eye upon him, even though no one in all creation is aware of his present movement through creation. And the traveler, as he moves along, may be aware only of himself—probably painfully so, with the exertion of the climb, the heat, perspiration, weariness. But if he is not centered on himself, but is making his ascent for the Lord and to the Lord, he is aware of the Father's love and that, even there in his hiddenness, he is a focal point of creation, lifting the whole of it up to God as he moves forward. And then his journey is a very meaningful and exciting one. His is the choice. And so it is through all life's ways and journeys. The choice is ours. We can lift up our hearts, expand our vision, and know the wonder of "filling up what is wanting in the Passion of Christ." Too often have I chosen the wrong one. Lord, have mercy.

❋

You know in monasticism there are many thorns, but what roses!

❋

The wisdom of directing a monastery is found in the ability to maintain a harmony of spiritual life and material life.

❋

In the monastery, refusing to judge one's neighbor is honored as the most indispensable virtue.

❋

Judging is worse than fornication.

❋

. . . an adhesive binding all the fathers and goats such as me, into one flock.

❋

As I was flossing my teeth today, part of a filling came out. I hope it does not create a problem. The thought of going to a dentist who does not have an electric drill is not particularly an exciting one. The allergy continues in spite of the pills, itchy little bumps all over.

Sunday, July 5

❧ I have been a month here at Simonos Petras. I do not know where the time goes. Each day disappears. I have a sort of fear that the whole retreat will just slip away without anything ever really happening. But then, what do I want to happen? Certainly I would be delighted if, in some very real way, the Lord would show me his Face, let me experience him.

But then he does, but in no sensational or dramatic way but in a very real constant Presence of peace and joy and love. I cannot be sufficiently grateful for what I have which is so much more than I could ever deserve. Yet I know the Lord is pleased at my constantly wanting more.

❋

After supper I was very pleasantly surprised when, one after the other, I was approached by two friends from the Oxford Orthodox-Cistercian Symposium. Father Palamas, a priest-monk of this community, who continues his doctoral studies at King's College, London, just arrived home for a visit of a month or so. Father Nicholas Gendle, a Dominican of Black Friars, is in Greece on a two-month study grant. Nicholas, who visited here five years ago, was very enthusiastic about the new life he has found here. We had coffee together with Father Maximos, who had studied with him in England.

Father Maximos returned from England only last January to become
a monk and has hopes of going back to finish his doctoral thesis.

Monday, July 6

⧄ I spent a good bit of time over breakfast talking with Nicholas Gendle and Father David. Then, when I retired to my balcony,
Nicholas Tzabellas came along and we talked for the rest of the
morning. I do not know how much profit comes from all this ecumenical discussion. I think prayer and presence does more. But I try
to listen and learn and share. There is a great difference between
these two Orthodox men. Tzabellas is a native Greek, a lifetime Orthodox, who has studied in England, is very open to other Churches,
and is strongly ecumenical. Father David is native English, has only
been in Greece a couple of years, is a convert, and is assertively an-
tiecumenical and eager to make converts. He is very kind and has
been very good to me, but he is clearly out to convert me, which
rather mars the freedom of our sharing. It is a delicate thing to
share, to give true witness to one's convictions and not be argumen-
tative or controversial. One really needs the Spirit and his precious
fruits of love, joy, peace, patience, kindness, and long suffering.

This afternoon, too, was fully occupied. It was a general work day.
First we brought in wood for the church stove for next winter. Two
laymen, who work for the monastery up in the forest, cut the trees
and brought them down. Then a nearby hermit, who makes his living with his power saw, cut them into little pieces. We had to load
them into baskets on donkeys and take them up to the church where
they are stored in a couple of bins outside the door. As we were
working, the monastery truck arrived (I believe it is the only real
truck on the Mountain) with cement and watermelons, which we
unloaded and stored. But the last melon we cut open and shared.
There is nothing quite so sweet as the first watermelon of the season.
One of the novices arrived with coffee, cold water, and Turkish
delight. The Greeks know how to add the touch of human culture
even to common work.

We returned to our firewood till Vespers. During the work I had a
chance to get acquainted with Father Theonas, a young deacon who
just returned from Thessaloniki. He was studying political science in

Athens the last time I visited the community. He was tonsured two years ago and is now studying theology at the University of Thessaloniki. For the last six months he has been assistant econome in Thessaloniki. He is happy to be home again, although he expressed a desire to visit England and the United States. I invited him to Spencer, saying we would profit much by a visit from some of the monks. "We would profit much by such a visit, too," he said in reply. Not many monks on the Mountain would say that, but here there is an unusual openness in their friendliness and love.

Father Palamas' attitude is different from that of Father Theonas. He is home for about a month but is eager to be back in London where he enjoys the academic scene. Like Father Kallistos Ware of Patmos, he will probably follow an academic career and spend only one month a year in his monastery here. The monks seem to have a real grasp of pluralism and be able to be happy in each other's joy, with no resentment or jealousy. During the afternoon some merely walked about and looked on, staying aloof from the work, dressed in their good robes. No pressure was put on them to join the others in their labor. They were fully free to be as they were.

The novices were working with Father Michael, the ecclesiastikos, making charcoal for the church. In the course of the afternoon I discovered all the novices speak English. Father Michael was lamenting that he could not speak with me in my own language.

I think this afternoon's kind of sharing is more fruitful than this morning's.

Tuesday, July 7

꿈 The assistant cantor, Father Gervasios, is painting the room next door. As he does, he fills the air with *Doxas* and *Kyries* with his rich melodious voice. What was it Saint Augustine said: "He who sings, prays twice." Father Gervasios truly prays as he works. And the joyful cascades of his prayer pour over into my room and lift me on their waves.

❈

The care of this large and old monastery is a very great task. Traditionally, the roof of the katholikon is covered with lead. For several days now two laymen have been working on the roof, pounding in new sheets of lead where needed and welding on smaller patches. They work from early morn until late at night, no doubt eager to get the job done and return to Greece and family. Another layman is rebuilding the stone wall along the path up to the monastery. He breaks apart the old one, resets all the stones in good order, and then puts a cement cover on the top. The sounds of these labors fill the air, as little noises carry far in the great silence of the Holy Mountain.

❋

I continue to read the Bible—the Old Testament in the morning, the New in the afternoon. I just finished reading the life of Archimandrite Ambrose of Milkova last night and feel I have found another heavenly friend and patron. He died young, in his thirties, of tuberculosis, but managed in a short life to go far in the way of monastic wisdom and love and left many grateful sons and daughters. He is called "the young Elder." May the Lord give us in our times many "young Elders" like him and those whom I have been meeting here on the Holy Mountain.

❋

How numerous have you made,
    O Lord, my God, your wondrous deeds!
And *in your plans for us*
    there is none to equal you;
Should I wish to declare or to tell them,
    they would be too many to recount.
                                    — Psalm 40:6

❋

In midafternoon Father David came along to say they would be making candles tomorrow and they would like me to join them—not so much to help as to have the opportunity to ask me questions about Spencer. I think this rather confirms my feeling yesterday—that more is effected by just working together, doing and being together, than by discussion. I am looking forward to his further sharing.

Wednesday, July 8

🕮 The fast day fare here is certainly simple enough. Lunch was bean soup, a cucumber, bread, and water. There is no scheduled supper, but those who feel the need can go to the kitchen for some of the soup left from dinner. Others prefer to go down to the garden to get a tomato or cucumber. I suppose there is always a good bit of left-over food because the cook can never tell how many visitors are going to drop in for lunch. Some days, like today, there is only one; other days there are twenty or thirty or more, so he has to have something ready. The waste must be considerable as they have no refrigeration to keep food over.

❄

As I try to pray I often find my mind leaping ahead, planning things I will do in the future, when I get home, etc. This is another form of self asserting itself, enjoying the imagined experience of being in control, mastering a situation, accomplishing, achieving, instead of living in the present moment before God, experiencing my own minuteness and incapacity, crying for the mercy and love of God. How true are the words Dom Edmund used to repeat to us: "The past and the future are only other forms of self; God is in the *now*." Each time I catch myself moving into this kind of self-indulgence, I have to let go and gently return to the present, where I stand in nakedness before God, an open cry for the healing shower of his merciful love. O Lord, be merciful to me a sinner.

❄

After lunch we went to work on the candles. But we just got started when it was decided we needed more wood to heat the wax. So we brought in wood, and while we were at it we made an afternoon of it, bringing it in for the kitchen and church as well.

❄

As I was sitting on the balcony this evening, I could experience from my perch a whole cross section of Athonite life. Far below at the port, Father Gelasios was fishing at the end of the pier surrounded by his cats, all hopefully waiting to enjoy what he might be lucky enough to catch. There were some pilgrims climbing up the trail. On the terrace garden Father Myron was hard at work, with young Father Joasaph standing nearby enjoying their conversation but keeping aloof from the work. Father Daniel was busy tying up the plants, keeping aloof from the conversation. Father Theonas, looking quite prim as he always does, was carefully making his way down the path to join them in the garden. Peter, the hired man, was leading a donkey toward the garden, laden with a couple of big sacks of ashes from the kitchen stove. Over on the porch of the cemetery chapel, Father Maximos was engaged in lively discussion with a couple of university friends. From the secretariat, on the top floor of the next building, I could hear Father Serapion's animated voice busy about the many details of administration. Above me Father Dionysios was pouring out the milk of human kindness for Father Evstratios, who delights me every time he says the Our Father at the Liturgy with all the serious simplicity of a first communicant. From the floor below came the joyful chants of Father Gervasios, the carpenter, as he finishes painting one of the monk's cells. Soon Father Michael appeared at the end of the balcony to ring the bell for Apodeipnon, the familiar Athonite melody:

1 – 1 – 1——1 – 2 – 3——1 – 2 – 3——1 – 2 – 1 – 2 – 1 – 2 – 3——1 – 2 –
3——1 – 2 – 3——1 – 2 – 1 – 2 – 1 – 2 – 3——1 – 1 – 1

And in and through and behind it all is the Christ presence of Father Aimilianos, the Father, the young Elder, the Hegumen, who centers the living bond of love in Christ. This is Simonos Petras, human, very human, and divine. This is the context I have been living in for a month—and it is good, very good. It is life according to the Gospels—it is peace.

Thursday, July 9

In the West today is the Feast of Saint Mary Magdalen (July 22), a special patron of this monastery and of my monastic life. On this feast day twenty-five years ago I received the habit. There were many novices at Spencer then, perhaps eighty. Very few of them are wearing the habit today. They are scattered far and wide. Perhaps some of them are already in the Kingdom. It will be good to

see them all there some day again. For now, I humbly thank the
Lord that I am still wearing the habit. Mercy upon mercy upon
mercy. Twenty-five years of unlimited mercy—and all the years that
went before, to prepare for it. How very far short I have fallen from
the full potential of the life the Lord has given me. He alone knows
and he alone can forgive. I can only ask pardon even as I say my
humble "Thank you, Lord." By your great mercy, may I die in the
habit and in a state more worthy of it than I am in now.

※

But I, like a green olive tree
    in the house of God,
Trust in the kindness of God
    forever and ever.
I will thank you always for what you have done,
    and proclaim the goodness of your Name
    before your faithful ones.
             — PSALM 52:10–11

※

We had a rather festive lunch: fried fish caught by Father Gelasios—the cats do not get everything—with prosphora* (because the
large number of guests had eaten up the week's bread supply), salad,
wine, and watermelon.

※

We will not celebrate Saint Mary Magdalen for thirteen more
days, of course, because we follow, as does all Athos, the old calendar, but already Father Nilos is shining the candelabra for the great
feast.

※

After lunch I went to help the candlemakers. They had begun
early in the morning and will be going two or three days. Six or seven
strands of string are cut twice the length of the candle, doubled over
to provide a loop at the top, twisted together, dipped in hot wax,
dried, and rolled tight. Then these wicks are hung by their loops
from small, round brackets that hold eight to twelve. The wax is
melted and poured into a tall (three feet), round can. The wicks are

then dipped into the wax three times, allowed to cool and harden, dipped three more times, etc., up to twenty-four dips to get the size candle wanted.

In the course of the afternoon we had a little celebration. Father David received word he had been "written out" of his monastery in The Hague and so could be "written in" here. Father Dionysios produced a box of candy to celebrate. A little later Father Gervasios arrived with rolls just out of the oven (he had to do a special baking—it is usually done on Saturday—since we ran short this week). Then someone brought watermelon.

Through it all the monks kept dipping. They hope to produce a full year's supply, some thousand candles—a lot of dipping.

Friday, July 10

ɚ Father Gervasios is painting all the cells around me. I suspect I will soon get moved into one of them so he can paint this one. They are actually in good shape, just some soot marks around the chimney openings.

Father Theologos and Father Palamas arrived back from a trip to Karyes. Father Dionysios left with Father Tikon for a day's visit at the Skete of Aghia Anna.* The Orthodox monks do a good bit of visiting. Almost every day we have one or more arrive here for a visit. Yesterday it was a little monk from Romania, the gardener of his monastery, who is visiting the Holy Mountain and then going to Jerusalem. He told us that monasticism is flourishing in Romania, spiritually and materially. Today we have two monks from Serbia.

❉

It is washday, so before Father Dionysios left he loaned me a robe so I could wash mine. Now people will be confused for sure, for I look completely like the natives except for the absence of the skouphos. Visitors do keep trying to speak to me when I am over by the church or refectory, but I try to avoid it as much as possible. They have come to experience the life here and speak with the Orthodox monks here, not with someone who, like themselves, has only an outsider's view, albeit I am privileged to share an especially intimate view, for which I am very grateful.

✻

When I told Father Michael, who has the responsibility of all the bells along with many other things, that in our monastery the novices take turns ringing the bells, he said he would willingly become Hegumen just to be able to make that change. For his consolation, though, I told him of another monastery where the same monk has been in charge of the bells for fifty-three years. Michael admired the stability but favored change so each monk could get an all around view of his monastery.

✻

The brothers always pray a couple of Services together, sometimes several. They feel the Service is too short if they do only one. I think I would agree that our Little Hours tend to be a bit on the short side. But I think ours have their purpose which I find helpful. That is why I do them here on my own. Unlike the principal Hours of praise and worship, Lauds and Vespers, which should have their fullness, the Little Hours, it seems to me, are moments of recall, when we drop everything else and give our complete attention to the Lord for a moment, as a help and support to making all our doings through the day prayer, done for him, and with him, and in him.

Saturday, July 11

❧ Another week gone! They sure go fast. But this week the Lord seemed, as it were, to be reaching out, calling me to deeper and more constant presence. Lord, help me to be more totally responsive.

✻

Today we are celebrating a special miracle of Saint Euphrasia and celebrating it in a rather big way, for we had a full Orthros omitting the cell prayer. Usually the monks arise an hour before going to the katholikon, but here they cut the cell prayer down to thirty minutes in the summer because the night is short. (Grigoriou omits it altogether in the summer.) But if the Service is going to be long, like today, they just omit it altogether. Today's is one of the special feasts of Orthodoxy. At Chalcedon, during the Fourth Ecumenical Council, after the Fathers had determined the True Faith, concerning the

two natures of Christ, one tome of orthodox teaching and one of heterodox were placed in the casket with the relics of Saint Euphrasia,
a fourth-century martyr. The next day the orthodox tome was found
in her hands and the heterodox under her feet. Some books make
this sound like the deciding factor which the Fathers used to determine the issue, but I would be unhappy to think that the Church,
gathered in Council under the Holy Spirit, needed miracles like this
to discern the True Faith. In actual fact, it seems to be at most a
sort of confirming event after the determination of the Fathers.

The Service was over four hours long. As a group of monks was
out working on the candles and there was a Liturgy in the cemetery
chapel, one of the novices, Andreas, did most of the singing. He has
a very good and strong voice, but I marveled how he continued for
over four hours with little respite. Andreas has been a novice for four
years. During the first three he was studying theology at Athens.
This last year he has stayed at the monastery. But last month he
went to Athens for his final exams and then for a two week visit to
Romanian and Bulgarian monasteries with his fellow graduates. His
is typical of the quality of novices now coming to the Holy Mountain. They are an impressive group.

I must confess I find it usually quite difficult to maintain any satis-
factory level of prayer presence consistently through such long Services. I gather the monks here do not worry too much about that.
They tend to come and go to some extent. Maybe I should try stepping out after a bit, for some fresh air and a drink of cold water to
keep the mind more alert and the heart more completely attentive.
And on my return to the church I can stop for a bit before the icon
of Mary and ask her help. She certainly was a woman of constant, intent prayer full of love. O Mother of love, pray for me.

❄

Before Vespers I stood on the balcony watching a storm sweep in
from the sea, clouds swirling around noble Athos, waves rolling in
against the stony shore, lightning streaking from cloud to cloud to
sea. It was a good preparation for Psalm 103 with which we begin
Vespers. And up the hill paths, hurrying to beat the storm, were the
hermits coming home to the cenobium for the Sunday Services. Father Eliseos arrived also, from Karyes, and Father Methodios from
Athens.

Sunday, July 12

 We had a visiting cantor, a layman, with a very powerful voice. The Services lasted longer than usual, somewhat over five hours. I have been having lots of thoughts of all kinds, good, bad, and indifferent. I begin to feel discouraged. I am so far, very far, from a true and full conversion to the ways of the Lord. Yet I have to ask myself, what is my real option in life? But how can I judge this? By the way I consistently act? Yet there are these alien thoughts and the awakening of old desires. But do we not have to expect this at times—the failures of human weakness? "The just man falls many times a day." "The man who says he has no sin is a liar." It is necessary to accept our state and the reality of being fallen men, struggling to lift up our head to Divine Mercy. And in the midst of the storm of thoughts, to look to our real choices. When I stop and reflect, I choose only God, to be to him, to live his holy will. That is what matters. And the constant, patient, humble striving with God's help to purify mind and heart: to avoid associations that recall the unwanted past, avoid idleness, turn to good reading, keep saving texts at hand and in the memory. And when I become aware of alien pulls, to strongly reject them, to positively choose the abiding Lord, to avoid all self-indulgence. The struggle is a lasting one, though, thank God, with its wonderful seasons of calm.

I received a letter from Abbot Thomas this morning informing me that my Aunt Marge died on June 26. I am happy I had gotten to see her in May. At that time she looked quite well. She had gotten into transcendental meditation (TM) some months ago and it meant a lot to her. I am glad the Lord gave her this gift of meditation during her last months. She left all she had to Christ's poor. I am sure this will was very pleasing to him. I prayed the Mass for her as soon as I received the letter. May she rest in peace.

There has been a heavy downpour that lasted through the night until late this morning—a real rain. Father Nicholas Gendle arrived around noon for an overnight-stay before leaving the Mountain. He had made the rounds of the Holy Mountain and was quite footsore. Father Michael repaired his sandal and I gave him some Vaseline for his feet. His tales of the different monasteries were well spiced. After supper we spoke with Father Palamas. Nicholas enjoys taking on an educated Orthodox in friendly debate.

⁂

The Jesus Prayer helps us to see Christ in all men and all men in Christ.

⁂

"The half was not told me." — 1 KINGS 10:7

⁂

"Then she gave the king one hundred and twenty gold talents, a very large quantity of spices, and precious stones. Never again did anyone bring such an abundance of spices . . ." — KINGS 10:10

The Queen of Sheba is the Church coming to Christ our King in the heavenly Jerusalem with adoration (gold) and suffering (spices) and all good deeds of the saints (gems)—no one brings such to him as she.

Monday, July 13

☙ The blend of the old and new sometimes strikes me as humorously incongruous here. When I went to the courtyard for the Midnight Office this morning I had to smile. There was Father Nilos pounding the semantron, with a large flashlight hanging around his neck casting wild shadows on the walls as he walked along. I wondered if, in his own little way, he was making history—the first monk to strike the semantron by flashlight!

In the West today it is the Feast of Saint Anne, the holy mother of the Mother of God (July 26). I have on my desk a small icon that shows Saint Anne seated on a great throne surrounded by King David and three other Forebears. In her lap sits a very adult Mary, complete with halo, and on Mary's lap is the young Jesus solemnly blessing us. It was on this feast in 1953 that I made my vows as a monk, was tonsured, and received the monastic cowl. It had been a very happy day. It was the last profession in the temporary barn-monastery at Spencer. It also brought a family visit, my brother Dale having just returned safe from the Korean front. It would be another four years before we would all be together again, for my priestly ordination.

At my profession Abbot Edmund told me to pray to Saint Anne that I be faithful to the interior life, the life of prayer. I have, almost every day. It was on a pilgrimage to her shrine at Sainte Anne de Beaupré, in Quebec, in 1950 that my vocation was confirmed. It was an unexpected coincidence that I made my profession on her feast and she has continued to watch over me. I certainly can never be grateful enough for the graces of these years.

In spite of all the involvement in activities, the life of prayer has remained primary. The beautiful gift of this retreat is the latest grace in this line. May it lead to greater fidelity, a more constant, delicate sensitivity to the presence and movement of the most Holy Spirit who must in all things be my prayer.

❀

As I move along these days, I sometimes feel a bit disappointed that I am not getting more lights, more insight. Today I found this rather reassuring passage in William of Saint Thierry:

> Now this is the life of God of which we spoke a little while before, not so much an advance in reason as an attachment of the affections to perfection in wisdom. For the fact that a man relishes these things makes him wise and it is because he has become one spirit with God that he is spiritual. And this is the perfection of a man in this life. — *Golden Epistle*, 287

> He is always sought in order that He may be found with greater pleasure and is found with the utmost pleasure in order that He may be sought the more diligently. — *Golden Epistle*, 295

❀

I think I have to ask myself constantly, Do I really want to be a monk? Then I have to be *monos*—alone—with God alone. That means the letting go of everything and everyone else. Here comes the paradox of Mark 10:30. When I give up things and even loved ones for Christ's sake, I receive a hundredfold even in this life! And that happens even quite literally. Certainly it has in my life. Why? So that I might give up even more. It leads to more and more purity of heart, a more and more total choice of God. When he has given me all, in the way that I really experience it as my own—is this the meaning of Saint Benedict's vision, seeing the whole world in a single ray of light?—and I still freely give it all up for him and then I am truly a monk—*monos*—alone, yet possessing all. To want to be a monk and yet to want to hang on to things, people, my own will, is to want a fiction, to want to make my life a fiction. It is to choose to live in dichotomy, in tension, to give up all hope of deep peace, of true happiness. If I really need to hang on to people, to things, then I had best stop hanging on to the idea of being a monk.

❈

Papa Simonos is a beautiful old man and much loved. To him has fallen the role of handing on a heritage. All the other old monks have gone to the outlying dependencies or are not able to be that much with it. But he is at everything, ready to show the young monks how it has always been done at Simonos Petras. I am sure that when he entered thirty-five years ago he never foresaw such a role, but his quiet fidelity through the years prepared him for it. Even before the first bell in the morning I hear him out on the balcony above busy about his prayers. It is a beautiful thing to see *tradition* so palpably at work. In the West I do not think we look enough to our seniors or listen enough to them to receive the living tradition. Then, after they are gone, we find ourselves searching through archives trying to get hold of what happened!

Tuesday, July 14

Today we celebrated, with considerable solemnity, the Feast of Saint Nikodimos of the Holy Mountain. He was a monk of Dionysiou but spent most of his life in a kellion near Karyes doing scholarly work. He did a complete edition of Saint Gregory Palamas, which was destroyed in a fire before it got published. He did a collection of the Sacred Canons with commentary, and commentaries on parts of the Liturgy. His best-known and most significant work is the

Philokalia, which Paisios Velichkovsky translated into Slavonic. Thus it got to Russia and led to the great spiritual flowering there during the last century. Saint Nikodimos died in 1809 and was canonized in the 1930s. He has a special significance for the community here because Archimandrite Aimilianos looks to him as his Spiritual Father, having kept close to him through his writings since he was ten years old. I got a copy of the *Philokalia* and read some of it before Vespers.

❋

I am painfully surprised at how weak the Orthodox position is as it is set forth by many to me. This is no doubt the reason for the defensiveness I find here. The monks argue that teaching authority cannot be in one person (the Pope) or even in the Bishops as a whole, but lies in the consensus of the faithful. A Council is not recognized as ecumenical until it is accepted by all the faithful as such. Quite logically, then, the Orthodox recognize only the first seven Church Councils. But here is the great weakness of this position. If the faithful are the holders of inerrancy and the vast majority of Christians in the world hold the truth to be with the Roman Catholics, then how can the Orthodox hold that their small number are possessors of the True Faith? They argue consonance with the Scriptures and the Fathers. But it is precisely here that we need teaching authority, because the Scriptures and the Fathers need to be interpreted and are interpreted in diverse ways. The Orthodox are selective as to which Fathers they will listen to and how they will interpret them. On what authority? Why does Saint Basil carry more weight than Saint Augustine? One is left in the end without a sure basis, only a later tradition influenced much by polemics with the West. Great stress is laid on the differences, in an effort to safeguard an identity and justify a separateness.

I do not think this is a total picture, but it is the picture presented to me by some who are in fact very devoted Christians, oftentimes very kind, and, I trust, very pleasing to the Lord. Yet they certainly have a perception of things that is very different from mine. For them it is impossible to please the Lord outside the True Faith. Therefore most who are called "Christians" are not in fact Christians; their Sacraments are not true Sacraments, they have no grace, they cannot be saved or in any way please God. Before ecumenism can make any real progress, there has to grow a widespread good will and desire for unity at the cost of the sacrifice of separate identity. That is not to deny the fact that there must be within the unity great pluralism, truly national Churches. The Roman Catholic Church has taken the first steps toward preparing the way for union in its present move toward national, hierarchical self-determination. This has to grow and work out its true relation to the papacy. Then it will be ready to enter into communion with the other Churches. The Orthodox, too, are facing a challenge which, if successfully met, can greatly help them in the move toward union. And that challenge is the development of an American Orthodox Church, a Japanese Orthodox Church, and also an African one. If Orthodoxy can successfully express itself outside of what is the former Byzantine world and integrate itself in new cultures and peoples, it is on its way to becoming more truly catholic and able to be with other Christians in a catholic orthodoxy and an orthodox catholicity.

Generalizations—yes. Challenges—I hope. We must not come to the prayer for Church unity with our own preconceived ideas of how the Father is going to bring it about. But we must come with a true, sincere longing and desire for the fulfillment of the Lord's prayer: that we be one, even as he is with the Father.

I am reading an interesting study on the Photian Synod of 879–880. It was a Council of union that succeeded largely because both leaders realized that East and West saw things differently to some degree, had to express things differently, had to give way a bit —and yet all this did not stand in the way of true Christian unity. Pope John VIII let Patriarch Photius rewrite the papal letters and directives to the Council in a way that the East could accept. The Pope also let certain things go, so that all could enjoy communion in the awareness of a central unity in Christ. The *largeness* of Pope John and the *understanding* of Photius and the *common will for unity*—these are the virtues we need today in our leaders and in our members.

✼

I spent most of the afternoon sitting on the porch of the cemetery chapel praying for Aunt Marge. As one looks north from there, there is only one vast expanse of sea drifting into the horizon. Gentle breezes trace their paths across its placid surface; occasionally, very

occasionally, a boat. As the boat passes off the scene, its wake soon
follows it and all trace is gone. So is man's life on earth—passing,
with little trace long remaining. Here at Simonos Petras a monk lies
in a marked grave for three years. Then he is dug up and his bones
join the large anonymous pile in the charnel house.

From time to time the silence is broken by the braying of the donkey pasturing somewhere down the mountainside. He seems in his
aloneness and lostness to want to affirm for the world his existence.
But quickly the sound dies in the hills and is forgotten. (I wonder if
my writing is not just so much of the same type of braying.) It is
only that which we store where moths and rust are excluded that will
endure. Happily, Marge made such enduring provision when she
wrote her will leaving everything she had to Christ's poor.

As I gaze out into the emptiness, it is very easy to pass into the
emptiness that is all fullness. I am glad Marge found wordless, image-
less meditation in those last months of her life. I am sure it was a
great grace for her. It is too bad she had to go to the Vedic tradition
to find it, but good that she could. I fear that we Christian ministers
are going to have much for which to answer. We have a tremendously rich and full heritage but we do not enter it ourselves and do
not allow others to enter. If our people have to go to Hindu and Zen
masters to learn meditation, it is our fault. We neither practice nor
teach as we ought. Lord, have mercy on us.

❋

I got off a note today to Abbot Edmund to thank him for those
graces I have received through him: for the monastic habit and profession and many others. May the Lord fill these last years of this
saintly old monk with great blessings and peace. He teaches us more
now by his living example than ever he did by his eloquent and powerful words.

Wednesday, July 15

⮑ Today is the Feast of Saint Kyrikos. It is one of the feasts
that betray the Orthodox sense of humor, something like that of the
Old Testament writers who delighted when the evil man dug a trap
and then fell into it himself. Saint Kyrikos' father had already died

for the Faith. When Kyrikos was three his mother was called before the persecuting authorities. The magistrate hurled all sorts of threats at her as she stood there with little Kyrikos in her arms; he vituperated Christ and his holy religion. Whereupon the precocious child spat in the face of the magistrate. The enraged man grabbed the child and dashed him to the ground, killing him, and then dispatched his mother.

We celebrated the feast with some solemnity, as the monks here possess the foot of the little Martyr. Also it is the name day of the present guestmaster. As I felicitated him, I was tempted to ask if he received the name because of his childlike innocence or because he could spit well.

❊

At lunch, after pouring myself a glass of wine, I managed to knock the pitcher over and spill the wine across the table into one of the novices' lap. I must say, he took it quite in stride and things passed without too much of a stir. I sometimes wonder what the novices think of the big, bearded monk from the West who shares their table. They certainly are good to me in every respect. I sense at times their own ups and downs, as they give themselves very generously to what is not an easy life. As Andreas said the other day: "I must be ready for all." Like novices in the West, they get all sorts of jobs dumped on them, are at the beck and call of all, and do a great deal of the reciting and singing in the choir, being the most regular after Father Simon in attendance. A group of novices such as they certainly give a monastery a promising future.

❊

I like the almost blunt forthrightness of the Fathers. Saint Antony begins his text on saintly life saying:

> The intelligent are not those who have studied the sayings and writing of the wise men of old [and he would probably be too humble to include himself among them, yet willingly apply what he says to his own sayings and writings] but those who . . . avoid what is evil and harms the soul and care for and practice what is good and profits the soul, greatly thanking God. It is these alone who should properly be called intelligent.

In other words, if you do not avoid what is evil and care for what is good, you are just plain stupid.

Today is my forty-fifth birthday. Again, much for which to thank God—the precious gift of life and all he has added to it in spite of my constant infidelity and irresponsiveness. May he have mercy, be thanked, and accomplish in me all his wants. I guess on such a day one inevitably asks oneself where he stands and what lies ahead. Is this a terminal year or just a halfway mark? Father Bernard is over ninety; Father Ananias, a hundred and ten. Yet Father Alberic was younger than I when he reposed, as was my own father, from whom I received this gift of life. I will write to Mom to thank her again for this gift. She is seventy now and has her collection of ailments. Yet she keeps going in her peaceful way of love and service, a woman, I am sure, very pleasing to God.

To escape the four things that hinder the mind in the quest of virtue:
1. Bad habits.
2. Sensible goods.
3. A clouded mind.
4. Evil spirits.
We need:
1. To turn to God for help.
2. To constantly feed the mind with knowledge—so to know the greater good of the first cause.
3. To mortify the flesh: fasting, vigils, sleeping on the ground, rough clothes as needed, exhausting labors.
— BLESSED THEODORE, *Theoretikon*, 15–16

❉

. . . that most insatiable thing—care.

Thursday, July 16

❧ I spent the morning in ecumenical discussion with Father Maximos and Nicholas Tzabellas, the lawyer from Athens. I have also been reading the book by Vladimir Lossky which Father Maximos gave me. One thing occurs to me. The Orthodox do not seem to grasp when we of the West are speaking analogically. In this case, we realize the reality is more unlike what we are saying than like. In this we are closer to their apophatism than they realize. But they tend to take us as making univocal affirmations. This underlines a more basic problem. We tend to interpret what the other says in our own way and then attack or respond to that—sometimes pretty much straw men. We need to really listen and let the other interpret himself until we finally clearly hear him. Another problem, which I find in Lossky and also generally, is the tendency to identify Western teaching with Thomas Aquinas or the scholastics. Few Westerners would accept this. The scholastics are only a school of theology and not the official teaching of the Western Catholic Church. More basic yet, though, is the need to really have that mind and heart of Christ for wanting union, to emphasize likeness and accept all the diversity we legitimately can within union, to foster basic good will and love for each other, rejoicing in each other's joy and richness. This is what John VIII and Photius did, what John XXIII and Athenagoras did. This is the heart of ecumenism—love, prayer, openness to the Spirit of Love. Doing the truth in love.

In ecumenical sharing I am not interested in polemic, in argument —no one can ever be argued into faith. It is God's gift. But I want to share the diverse insights in faith that my brother has received, so that my own response to the precious gift of Revelation which we share can be fuller and richer. When his insight seems to contradict mine—the Catholic teaching—so that I cannot hold it, I will respect the difference and not be closed to the oblique light it can throw nor to the possibility that the contradiction may be only in words or be resolved on some higher level. Let us, though, always accentuate what we share in common and, above all, deeply love one another in Christ our Lord. He certainly loves us all.

Father Dionysios and Father Tikon went to the Skete of Aghia Anna to see Father Chrysanthos. He once was a monk of Simonos Petras. In time he became a prominent confessor in Athens and gathered a community of young monks around him in a monastery in the hills above the city. He also has a household at Aghia Anna where a few young monks live with him and paint icons. He spends some time with them and hopes to die on the Mount. He is about eighty-four now. As Father Dionysios and Father Tikon got off the boat, he was at the door of his house, a long distance up the hill, yet he said to his disciples, "Two monks come now from Simonos Petras to see us." He shared many beautiful thoughts with the two of them for over three hours. Then a fisherman brought them home.

Some of the monks from here have gone to Konstamonitou. Father David, who was formerly here, will be ordained deacon on Sunday by the Archbishop of Vlatadon* (formerly of Australia). The Archbishop will then come here to celebrate the Feast of Saint Mary Magdalen and ordain here. Father Justin here is making sort of a retreat in preparation for receiving both the diaconate and priesthood. He is the community's representative at Karyes.

The monks are very busy up on the hill preparing the foundation for the electric generator. I am amazed how they made their way up the narrow, rugged mountain trail not only with cement and gravel and lumber for forms but even with a big cement mixer. Some of the monks here work very hard, especially young Father Aimilianos, who rides a donkey like a Western cowboy. The sight of him up on the forms, pushing concrete, or running home barefoot in his short robe because his boots got too full of cement brings back scenes from our own happy, hard-working days on construction at Spencer Abbey.

This afternoon the Lord put on a magnificent spectacle. And I had a box seat on the porch of the cemetery chapel. An electric storm marched majestically across the bay, shooting lightning bolts at each step, sending rolls of thunder ahead on the swirling winds, as thunderheads made their steady approach on mighty Athos and sheets of rain calmed the darkened waters. The freshness of newly washed air gave it a delicious smell and taste as it swept across my observation deck. And through it all, filtering down from the monastery, was the melodious strong voice of Father Gervasios as he hammered away in the kitchen. It made the Psalms rise to my lips:

Give to the LORD, you sons of God,
    give to the LORD glory and praise.

Give to the Lord the glory due his Name;
    Adore the Lord . . .
The voice of the Lord is over the waters,
    the God of glory thunders,
    the Lord, over the waters.
The voice of the Lord is mighty;
    the voice of the Lord is majestic.
The voice of the Lord strikes fiery flames;
    the voice of the Lord shakes the desert,
    the Lord shakes the wilderness of [Athos].
The Lord is enthroned above the flood,
    the Lord is enthroned as king forever.
May the Lord give strength to his people,
    May the Lord bless his people with peace!
          —PSALM 29:1–5, 7, 8, 10–11

Bless the Lord, O my soul!
    O Lord, my God, you are great indeed!
You are clothed with majesty and glory,
    robed in light as with a cloak.
You have spread out the heavens like a tent-cloth;
    you have constructed your palace upon the waters.
You make the clouds your chariot;
    you travel on the wings of the wind.
You make the winds your messengers,
    and flaming fire your ministers.
          —PSALM 104:1–4

❉

After supper a falling sun smiled on the beautiful fresh scene. The few clouds floating past the summit of Mount Athos looked too perfect to be real, as though they were painted in, except for the real shadows they cast on the Mountain. Then one gently encircled the highest peaks and gradually clothed them in its fleece till they were lost in God.

But all this is a lot of thoughts—thoughts and images. How I want to plunge into the very center of the storm, to that eye of absolute stillness, wrapped in the sounds of silence, knowing only the Presence.

I have thoughts, thoughts, and more thoughts. All my impurities rise to the surface—my lack of openness, my attachments, my lack of docility. After twenty-five years and I still have not begun to grasp the fundamental attitude of a monk. My will and mind goes rushing ahead with its stupid imaginings and plans: on the way home I will stop in Rome to get the Holy Father's blessing. Of course, while there I will have to call on Father Athos and Father Gabriel and see how they are making out. Then there is Father Richardson, who wanted to know more about Centering. And Father Ansgar, the novice master at Tre Fontane.* I should call at the General House, though everyone from there will all be in the United States for the meeting of the Consilium. And there is Father Bill Crowley, who did the workshop in New Orleans. I should see how he is doing. And Richard Kamm, the sculptor I met here, who asked me to look him up when I got to Rome. And Sister wanted me to see Archbishop Van Lierde. Et cetera, et cetera. That's me, ever involved and getting involved. Should I just accept it and go ahead with as much peace and presence as I can? Or should I take a radical stand on it? Cut it all out? Fly right over Rome and every other place and go only where I absolutely have to? What does the Lord really want? How does one come to the freedom of complete openness and detachment? Is it by struggling with these things head on or is it by just letting it all go and being to God? As I was grappling with this, quietly there came the deep peaceful realization that God is my Father and that he would take care of everything. Great peace followed. He has care for every hair on my head—and they are fewer and fewer, so he should have more time for these problems!

❊

After my walk this evening, as I got back to the monastery gate, Charalambos was there with Father Amphilochios and Father Michael. He was trying on Father Amphilochios' rason: "I should be getting ready." (Charalambos should be tonsured soon.) Novices are the same everywhere.

Friday, July 17

☙ It is washday and my wash is soaking while I write this. Last night I finished reading Johann Meijer's *A Successful Council of Union,* staying up late to do it. (I was pretty tired through the morning Services, but I found—if it is not a profanation to think this way—that the prostrations with the cell prayers are excellent "getting-up exercises." Before I started doing them, I was having trouble keeping awake sometimes during the long night Services. Much of it is done by a single reading voice while the rest of us sit or stand in the darkened church. But since I have been doing the prostrations, even when I am tired, I do not have trouble with sleep.) It is a very good study. Meijer bends over backward to be ecumenical but does not go too far. The points that should be considered he makes well. Cannot both Churches accept the ninth-century Photian Synod as an Ecumenical Council? There certainly are Orthodox today who do. Pope John VIII certainly accepted it. If we adopted the prevailing attitude of the supreme importance of unity, would we not find that we can absorb a good bit more difference of outlook and understanding than we do? I agree especially with his closing paragraph:

> Return to a common path does not mean betrayal of our history and tradition, but demands confidence and repentance: confidence in the other Christian, in his faith, in his good will, in the holiness and spirit which lives in him because of his Baptism; repentance for onesidedness, for the pride which hurt the other. It means obedience to the Word of God, prayer that both sides remain faithful, and become united.

I think that Catholics have largely adopted these attitudes, though we certainly could pray more and with more longing, according to the heart of Christ. More Orthodox are moving in this direction, but many, even very good men here on the Mountain, cannot accept them. For them there is no true Baptism outside Orthodoxy, no presence of the Spirit, no True Faith. If one is not Orthodox, it is because of bad will—he is not really open to the Word of God. And as far as they can see, all the hurt has been suffered on their side. I am sorry to say this, but I know many of the monks on the Mountain will insist that this is the right attitude. Thank God, not all. And in practice, kindness and civility almost always prevail; more often, true Christian charity.

Even a respectable scholar and man of some spiritual depth like Lossky can end an article ("The Procession of the Holy Spirit in Orthodox Trinitarian Doctrine," Chapter 4 in *In the Image and Likeness of God*) saying:

> Reconciliation will be possible . . . at that moment, when the West, which has been frozen for so long in dogmatic isolation, ceases to consider Byzantine theology as an absurd innovation and recognizes that it only expressed the truths of tradition. . . . The Greeks have ceased to be Greeks in becoming sons of the Church. That is why they have been able to give to the Christian faith its imperishable theological armory. May the Latins in their turn cease to be wholly Latins in their theology!

A rather "one-sided" view, to say the least. But we should not forget that Lossky wrote this in the 1940s and approved it for final publication before his death in 1958. In the grace of Vatican II and with the leadership of Patriarch Athenagoras he might well have changed that. May he rest in peace and enjoy that supernal Vision in which he will see the Fullness of which he so earnestly studied and wrote.

But I am writing too much and getting too involved in this kind of thinking and discussion now, considering the primary purpose for which I am here. So I'd better be more cautious in this regard. Lord, guide me.

And I had better go get my wash done!

❈

. . . open wide your mouth, and I will fill it. . . .
. . . I would feed [you] with the best of wheat,
and with honey from the rock I would fill . . .
— PSALM 81:11, 17

Saturday, July 18

⤳ Today is the Feast of Saint Aimilianos. Unfortunately, the Hegumen is not yet home from Russia. And young Father Aimilianos is too busy working on the generator to take time to celebrate. They hope to have electricity very soon. The main concern is to get refrigeration, for so much food has to be thrown away in the summer. The plant they are building will potentially produce enough electricity for all the monasteries on this side of the Mountain. A like one could be installed at Megisti Lavra for the other side. The Greek government recently offered to bring in electricity to the whole Mountain at the cost of $600,000. But with these two small plants using water power, the monks can produce their own electricity and not have to continually pay the government for it.

Blessed Theodore of Edessa says: "The cloud of cares is made up of evaporations from the principal passions—love of pleasure, love of money, and love of glory, so that a man free from them is a stranger, too, to cares." How tremendously true that is! And it seems good to me whenever I am taken away from myself by thought or desires to stop and see which one of these three is at work. Gradually, then, with God's help, I can perhaps be freed from them and have only one care—to be to him.

THE FEAST

Megisti Lavra

⤳ Father Dionysios invited me to go with a group after Liturgy tomorrow to Konstamonitou for the Feast of the Prophet Elijah and the ordination of Father David. A boat will come from Daphni to take us there.

❋

We had Services yesterday in Saint George's chapel downstairs since Father Nilos took all the stall platforms out of the katholikon to scrub the floors. When they prepare for a feast, they really prepare for it. Everything in the church is shining like new. And now the monks are moving to other parts of the monastery and outside, too, scrubbing, mopping, sweeping. Dozens of sheets and blankets are on the drying line so there will be plenty of linen for the many guests coming. Another truckload of watermelon arrived this morning, so we will have plenty of that, too.

❋

Is it possible to think a man leads a divine life, in accordance with the Word of God, if he lives without a guide, pandering to himself and obeying his own self-will? Of course not. To such monks Saint John Climacus says: "Know that you are attempting a short but hard way which has only one road leading into error."

Sunday, July 19

⤳ Right after lunch (I still find it difficult to call a meal at 8:30 A.M. "lunch") those of us who were going to Konstamonitou boarded the truck and drove to Daphni—unfortunately just missing the boat. Father Theologos welcomed us at Simonos Petras' other port which is just next to Daphni and from where they ship their lumber. We got the two o'clock boat. The monks of Konstamonitou had a train of donkeys waiting at their port to take us up into the hills to the monastery.

It is a wonderful, warm, loving, joyful little community. Their out-

of-the-way placement and lack of art works leaves them almost totally undisturbed by tourists or guests, except for the most devout—
few, in any case. The community, which has always been very fervent, was dying off because no one was coming to enter—the disad-
vantage of its hiddenness. Two monks died in 1974 and two more in
1975, leaving only eleven. They appealed to Simonos Petras for rein-
forcements. Six were sent. The old Hegumen resigned so that one of
the new ones could be elected. They chose Father Galliton. His son,
Father Athanasios, a hieromonk and last year's secretary for the Holy
Community, was also one of the six. His daughter, Mother Nicodime, is Hegumena* (Abbess) in Ormilia, and his wife, a novice
there. His son-in-law is being ordained priest today at Thessaloniki.
He also has a nephew at Simonos Petras. He is a most gracious,
warm person. Needless to say, we received a very warm welcome.
After visiting the katholikon and venerating the icons, we received
the usual refreshments. After supper there was a formal reception of
the Metropolitan of Vlatadon, Archbishop Ezechiel, and more refreshments. The dozen or more monks from Simonos Petras swelled
the ranks of the local community. For all, it was a most happy reun-
ion and most of the night was spent in sharing. I met two Americans, a medical student at Athens from Montgomery, Georgia, and a
theological student from Pittsburgh. There are a number of young
boys here, too. Andreas, age fourteen, from Crete—Father Samuel's
brother—is to receive the order of Reader tomorrow.

Monday, July 20

🕮 Feast of the Prophet Elijah—patron of our Byzantine chapel
at Spencer. I was also invited for this feast at the Skete of the
Prophet—Propheti Iliou—but I could not be both there and here.

※

Services started here at about 4:15. The Archbishop made his
entry at 4:45 and immediately gave Father David the order of
Reader. Just before the Liturgy, some hours later, he ordained him
subdeacon, after giving Andreas the lectorate. The little fellow
looked like a picture, in his rason and skouphos. At the end of the
ordination to the Subdiaconate, David washed the Archbishop's

hands. After the Archbishop dried his hands he put the towel over David's head. For the next hour and a half, while the Liturgy progressed, David stood with the towel over his head and the pitcher and basin in his hands, first before the icon of Christ and then before that of Mary, to meditate deeply on the meaning of Diaconate —service—and to prepare for it by intimate prayer.

The ordination to deacon took place just before the Communion Service. Most impressive was the part where two deacons—Father Tikon and Father Theonas—led Father David three times around the altar to kiss each corner. For the actual ordination David knelt next to the Archbishop before the altar—with the Eucharist, ready to be served, standing on it—while the Archbishop placed his hand on David's head and said the ordination prayer.

The one sad part for me was when Father David came forth with the Eucharist inviting communicants. No one in the whole crowded church came forward—not even the boy ordained to be Lector. By that time we had been six hours at prayer and celebration, with tremendous singing and five chandeliers swinging around the corona—a great and beautiful Liturgy—but no one felt ready to receive our Lord in Communion. It is here where we have to make a real effort to step out of our own outlook and try to appreciate another attitude of reverence mixed with familiarity. The scene in the katholikon at that time was seemingly holy chaos. While the priests and deacons were receiving Communion behind the screen and the cantors were chanting beautiful Communion hymns, some monks were running around pulling down chandeliers or carrying long sticks to put out the dozens of candles lit for the Service. Other monks and lay people were going in many directions venerating the icons, some were sitting in the stalls conversing, others were settled deeply in their stalls evidently enjoying intimate prayer (or sleep). It is a chaotic scene to Western eyes. To the Orthodox it is the acceptable thing, and in and through it all the Lord is being responded to according to the grace and gift of each one present.

After the Liturgy we went to the cemetery for the reading of the indulgences, or absolutions for the dead, from the Patriarch of Constantinople. The graves here are unusual. There are about eight graves with stone sides, each about three feet deep. The body can simply be laid in the bottom. A ledge in the stone allows for placing boards over the body. Then it is filled with dirt. This makes it very easy to dig up the body three years hence and place the bones in the charnel house under the cemetery chapel. One recently opened grave had the Great Schema of the exhumed monk still lying in the pile of dirt. Again, it called for an effort to appreciate and respect the customs of others. Perhaps there is some sort of implicit affirmation here that after three years a monk should surely be fully purified. However, the responses to my questions about Orthodox belief concerning the state of the soul after death have been variant and unclear. The monks seem to hold that those who are not ready to enter beatitude wait in some neutral state till the great judgment, but little is known about the state. Prayers help, probably at the judgment, perhaps even for those who died in serious sin. There do seem to be various schools of thought, some of which are substantially the same as Catholic teaching. But I find that Orthodox believers, even those who specialized in theology at a university, have very strange and limited ideas of Catholic teaching. Purgatory seems to be for them the place Catholics created for the dead to complete the penance the priest gave them in confession, which they failed to complete while alive. I sometimes get the impression, as Orthodox explain what they think is false Catholic teaching, that Catholic teaching has been distorted by some Orthodox teachers so that it can be easily refuted. This comes back again to the need for us to really listen and let the other really make clear to us what he believes and to respond to that, rather than to our interpretation of what he believes. Often there is nothing to respond to—we agree.

❈

After a good dinner and a rest we started down to the port. Quite a sight, with the Archbishop leading the procession astride his great white mule. Mule travel is not the best. It was very warm and humid, insects were abundant, and the mules take their time, scrambling over rough spots, etc. But the ride through the mountains and down to the port had its beauty. A special boat was waiting—then the Land-Rover at Simonos Petras' port. Another reception for the Archbishop, Vespers, and supper. After supper Archimandrite Aimilianos arrived back from Russia.

Tuesday, July 21

൜ I have been on the Mountain for two months today. Time
has passed very quickly.

The Service this morning was somewhat a repetition of yesterday's, but done a bit more simply, as Father Justin received the orders of Reader, Subdeacon, and Deacon. Father David presented
him. I was happy to see a number of his brothers come forward for
Communion when he brought out the Chalice. The governor was
here from Karyes for the Service and lunch.

Archbishop Ezechiel was twenty-two years in the United States
(as Rector at Holy Cross in Boston and as Bishop in Boston and
Chicago) before going to Australia for sixteen years. He knows the
New England area, and also our Order as he has read some of
Thomas Merton.

At Little Vespers two young boys were tonsured as Readers.

※

The daily cross:

The vertical   — following Christ to heaven.

The horizontal — my own tendencies and desires.

I can escape the cross by not following Christ, forgetting his call,
dropping the vertical out of my life. But the horizontal has no destination; only ultimate frustration—that is hell.

To carry the cross daily—consciously choose to be a Christian.

Wednesday, July 22

൜ The great and holy Feast of Saint Mary Magdalen—and indeed a full-scale Mount Athos feast. Over a hundred, perhaps a hundred and fifty, guests, many of them monks, crowded the monastery
and the relatively small katholikon.

The Services began shortly after nine last night. We left church
only shortly before nine this morning. Then it was for a brief reception (the Archbishop graciously asked for me in particular to be with
him at this—and they had to fetch me from my cell where I had

gone for a few minutes' breather). A festive ritual meal (Father Basil did wonders in the table he spread both yesterday and today). The refectory was jammed; some had to wait until second table. (They had even special tableware and dishes for the occasion.) And then back to the katholikon in procession for a final Service.

This was one of the fullest and most beautiful celebrations, as well as the longest, I have shared on Mount Athos. When the Greeks created their Liturgy they sublimated the fullness of their great dramatic tradition. The whirling chandeliers . . . the deacons with chests of incense on their shoulders, passing through the dancing candlelight in their rich brocades, censers going in all directions! Six deacons and fifteen priests assisted the Metropolitan and another Bishop from Constantinople.

There is something incredibly exciting about great chandeliers swinging through the air, with their dozens of living tongues of fire reaching out to bring every icon into the heavenly dance and inviting all of us earthbound ones to join them in our hearts. But then there is something poignantly sad as they slow down, adopt monotonous patterns, and finally come to a halt and are extinguished. It is the story of man. Of God's wonderful plans for him and man's frustration of them. But after a dark, quiet hour of psalmody, suddenly the chandeliers are all illumined and set to swinging again amid hundreds of Alleluias. Christ, our Light, has come. He has risen and ascended on high, leading captivity to full freedom, leading the heavenly dance. And there is Mary Magdalen, out of whom he cast seven devils, at the center of this night's dance. What hope for us sinners! (The Eastern Christians clearly separate the three Marys: Mary Magdalen, Mary of Bethany, and the sinful woman who washed Jesus' feet. Mary Magdalen, though possessed for a time, is thought of as a virgin, an innocent victim of the devil. I must confess I am inclined to prefer the Western idea of putting the three together—though there is probably not too much basis for it. I like to think of this Myrrh-Bearer-Equal-to-the-Apostles, to whom the Lord first appeared, as a repentant sinner, like most of us, who found the fullness of contemplative love.)

❊

The ordination to the Priesthood was very simple and similar to the ordination to the Diaconate. After the great entrance, two deacons turned Father Justin over to two priests who presented him to the Archbishop (Orthodox practice allows a Bishop to ordain only one priest and one deacon a day). The Archbishop blessed him and spoke to him. Then Father was led three times around the altar, kissing each corner as he went. Finally he knelt at the side of the Archbishop in front of the altar. The Archbishop placed his hand on the Father's head and said the ordination prayer while everyone else prostrated himself and quietly sang the *Kyrie*. Father Justin was then vested amid the shouting and singing of "*Axios!*" (he is worthy). Immediately after the epiclesis* the Archbishop took the Lamb (the Consecrated Bread) from the diskos and placed it in the hands of Father Justin who held it—becoming a diskos himself, as it were—meditating on what had been committed to him, until time for the elevation and breaking of the Bread. I like these contemplative moments in the ordination ritual.

Happily a number of the community came forward to receive Communion. It meant a great sacrifice for them to prepare, for yesterday while all were enjoying the feast, they had to be content with fast-day food: boiled potatoes and tomatoes (no fish, wine, oil, cheese, etc., allowed). Certainly one of the factors that cuts down on Communion is the custom—I do not think it is a strict law; where more frequent Communion is being introduced it is being cut back and the priests do not seem to observe it—of fasting three days before. We in the West have perhaps gone too far in disregarding fasting or any other special preparation for Communion. We can, of course, appeal to the practice of the first Christians and even the Last Supper, but, still, we would do well to prepare more fully and even incarnationally for the Eucharist. When Pope Paul VI relaxed the law of fasting for Roman Catholics, we were still encouraged to fast from midnight if possible. But we do not seem to give it much thought now.

❋

After supper the Hegumen gathered the community together in the synodikon to begin relating his experiences in Russia. We started with coffee and sweets as usual. He is a vivid speaker. The ecclesiastikos went out to ring the bell for Apodeipnon and the priest of the week went to sing it, but the Hegumen went on. It looked as if we were going to have another All-Night Vigil! And I do not think any one would have minded it. (The Hegumen took the opportunity of the gathering to tell the brethren to put their watches ahead one hour. Although by Byzantine time, twelve midnight is when the sun goes down, in practice the monks here change their watches only about once a month.)

The Hegumen wove into his talk a brief history of Russia, its geography (the shortest flight of their journey was from Athens to Moscow; all the flights inside the country were longer), and its social climate. He saw Orthodoxy as the cohesive force in the vast country with its mixture of races. This even made possible the acceptance of socialism. Church and state were always close in Russia, he said. The rulers, the peoples' saints. But the czars made "mistakes" and alienated the people. The Hegumen found the people relatively immobile and Moscow a city of silence. Tourists made Leningrad more lively. Russia, he said, is a country that has tried to deny its heritage or at least some have tried to make it do so. The endokia* of Iviron with the icon of the Portatissa* used to stand where Red Square now stands empty. The godless forces have been more successful in the outlying regions where the people are fewer and scattered; churches and institutions have generally been closed out. But in the cities, and especially at the monasteries, the Faith is very lively. The government has made laws limiting the numbers in monasteries, but many of them have forty to eighty novices, some as young as ten years of age. The monasteries are vital centers of life, with Liturgies, Services, Sacraments all day long—fifty to ninety Baptisms a day in one monastery.

Everywhere the visitors went great crowds crushed them. They needed constant police help to move about. The Hegumens had to keep their arms constantly extended so that the faithful could grasp their hands and kiss them. Many were weeping. Even late at night, when leaving a reception, they would find the crowds waiting and it would take half an hour to reach their cars.

The visitors were given abundant rubles to buy what they wanted, but little could be found to buy. I was amused as the Hegumen related his search for cassettes and batteries for his tape recorder. In Russia only foreigners have such things. After searching many stores, he found only second-hand cassettes with very short tapes. The officials were also—I guess—amused by this concern. They finally produced three cartons of batteries for the searching visitors. Promis-

ing to speak more tomorrow or soon, the Hegumen invited questions
and received a few sensitive ones:

Someone asked, What about persecution?

The Hegumen replied that Christians have to be ready to suffer
for their faith. Outside the great population areas, faith in some
places has been almost wiped out of the people's lives. But in the
cities the people stand strong. When the government tries to close a
church, the people crowd around it to protect it, ready to die for it.
The Church Services are attended equally by men and women,
young and old, with more men on the feasts. The priests and prelates
go about in religious garb and are everywhere met with reverence. In
stores, airports, theaters, etc., they are put at the head of the lines by
the people. In religious practice in Russia there is little difference between a monk and a devout layman. (That is true in Greece, too. I
am delighted to see how the lay visitors can enter right into the Services here and even take turns in leading the singing and doing the
reading.)

The Bishop from the Ecumenical Patriarchate, Bishop Germanos,
asked of Moscow's pretension to being the "third Rome."

The Hegumen replied that this was a thing of the past, gone with
the czars. Metropolitan Nikodim of Leningrad said that the Russian
Church recognizes that it is the fifth of the Orthodox sees.

Another asked about the Russian Orthodox allowing Roman
Catholics to receive Holy Communion.

Again, the Hegumen said that Metropolitan Nikodim assured the
visitors that this was only taking place in areas where it had been
going on for centuries, and only when there is a shortage of Catholic
clergy. It has been allowed in these places by economia and is not allowed elsewhere.

The Hegumen also developed some of the differences between the
Greek and Russian Churches, as well as their likenesses.

Thursday, July 23

❧ Today is celebrated as the "coming back" of yesterday's
feast. I like this idea—a chance to celebrate a feast more quietly and
deeply, after all the excitement is over. We have it a bit in the oc-

taves* of the great feasts, but this one-day carry-over for more particular feasts is very good.

Most of the visitors have finally gone, and all is quiet again.

※

At two in the afternoon we gathered in the synodikon for coffee and the Hegumen continued to answer questions about his Russian trip. Many of the questions the monks asked were the same we at Spencer would ask—about the different ways the monks there do things. The Holy Community had officially declined an invitation from Moscow, so the party went unofficially. It would have been bad not to have gone, the Hegumen felt. They were helped a good bit by having in their party the Hegumen of the Russian monastery, Aghios Panteleimonos, Archimandrite Avel. He had gone to school with Metropolitan Nikodim of Leningrad and lived in his home. The Hegumen spoke very highly of Father Avel. The latter had been tonsured at nineteen and was a very zealous missionary, always dreaming of one day coming to the Holy Mountain, a dream realized when he was appointed Hegumen of Aghios Panteleimonos. He had tonsured many monks and nuns secretly in Russia. Everywhere there he was received with special veneration. The monks at Athios Panteleimonos hope to receive ten more from Russia before their feast next Monday, and forty before the end of the year. Father Aimilianos was a bit skeptical as to how successful they would be in redeveloping Aghios Panteleimonos with formed Russian monks. He thought they might succeed better with laymen. Many Russian laymen want to come to the Mountain, but the problem is getting visas. The life of the Russian monk is much closer to that of the lay people, differing most notably in not eating meat and not smoking. (I was surprised that during their visit to Russia the Athonite monks ate the "fish of Vatopedi"—Vatopedi is the one monastery that allows meat on the Mountain.) The monastic life on Athos is the most severe in Orthodoxy (though it is not all that austere by Trappist standards). From my own brief visit to Aghios Panteleimonos, I can vouch for the fact that the Russians there do have a less austere life than the other houses on the Holy Mountain that I have visited.

The Athonite visitors were not able to get into much serious dialogue with their hosts in Russia. Only the Metropolitan of Leningrad was willing to talk about the persecution and the existence of torture. The Soviet Department for Religious Affairs makes the decisions about opening and closing churches, appointing Bishops, etc., and the department is made up wholly of atheists. Bishops are considered public servants. Patriarch Pimen of Moscow said nothing, only smiled sweetly. There was some discussion about the Pan-Orthodox Synod while they were visiting. Some wanted an agenda, others not. Some were for changing canons, others were opposed to any change and held that only an Ecumenical Council could change them, even the most minor ones about fasting, etc. The Russians wanted jurisdiction to be discussed, since Constantinople claims all the "barbarian world" (which includes the United States and Japan), whereas Russia has recognized autocephalous metropolia for America and Japan and wants a Pan-Orthodox typicon and ritual for these countries, rather than a continuing plurality of Orthodox Churches and jurisdictions. Father Aimilianos explained a little how Orthodox Synods do not go by vote but must come to consensus and identify with tradition.

He spoke with much humor about some of the delegation's practical difficulties on their trip: trying to exchange money, getting taxis, waiting for baggage, trying to buy things, coping with crowds, eating thirty-course banquets, etc.

The faithful, he said, were very generous to the Church in Russia in spite of the high cost of living—though common food and clothes are not too expensive. Unable to do much else with the money it receives, the Church is converting it into gold ornamentation for the altars, shrines, etc., which perhaps at some distant date can be cashed in.

He stressed that Communion is given to Catholics by Orthodox only when Catholics are in danger of death, and this is a real response in love. (I must say, this does not square with what Metropolitan Nikodim told a priest friend of mine. Indeed, he permitted this Catholic priest to concelebrate with him at the theological academy in Leningrad.)

The Hegumen feels that the Greek Orthodox are stronger in the theoretical but the Russian are stronger in the practice, in that feel and sense of Orthodoxy, and that the Slav nations are an important complement to Greece.

When one of the monks asked about some of them going to Russia for a year, the Hegumen spoke of the two theological schools.

The one at Moscow is more conservative and primitive; the only out-siders there are Serbs. The one at Leningrad, while holding fast to tradition, is more open to new ideas in today's world; there are about eighty foreign students there.

The monks asked about establishing a metokion (dependent house) in Russia. Considering the entrance problems there, the He-gumen said, it might be easier to set up one in Romania and then move on from there. I felt like urging the monks to think first of the United States. A number of them speak English. There would be no entrance problems. There is no Greek Orthodox monastery that I know of in the United States. And I am sure they would find many candidates among the American youth.

We concluded with the semantron for Vespers at five o'clock.

※

Prayer is the fruit of joy and thanksgiving . . .
— SAINT NILOS OF SINAI

Friday, July 24

In the West today is the great and holy Feast of the Transfiguration of our Lord and Saviour Jesus Christ, the Son of God (August 6), the patronal feast of Mount Athos. A chapel of the Transfiguration stands on the summit.

※

There are two fourteen-year-olds sharing the room across from me —the brother of one of the monks and the son of an employee in an-other monastery. Their conduct heightens my question of the wis-dom of having young boys stay in the monastery. They carry on until quite late, making it difficult for others to sleep. Then they sleep late and do not attend the morning Services or Liturgy. I do not know what they do during the day besides hanging around the monks at work or swimming off the pier. It is a sort of vacation for them. And probably it fits in more with an Orthodox cenobium than it would in a Catholic one.

In some respects I am questioning the development of these two months. On the whole they have been quite peaceful and prayerful.

But they have also been very interesting. There has been a certain amount of stimulating theological dialogue. There has been much more monastic sharing, experiencing another expression of our common monastic heritage. But has all this stimulation and interest somewhat undermined the primary purpose of my coming—for a time of retreat, of spiritual deepening? I think the question arises because our Cistercian ideal tends to find this deepness and intimacy with God in silent, solitary prayer. The Orthodox sees this as a hesychast ideal, which they greatly reverence but somewhat reserve to the hermit or the sketes. One of the two monasteries that tend in this hesychast direction on the Holy Mountain is characterized as being influenced by the West—the Hegumen studied in Paris, was a pastor in Belgium, and has some monks from the West—and the other as being too regimented—indeed, it is like a Trappist monastery, though the Hegumen is wholly Athonite in his background and a strong Palamite. The thing that stands out in the Orthodox cenobium—and perhaps this is the thing the Lord is trying to get me to understand more fully—is that cenobitic* life is a shared life, of men looking together to a great and lofty ideal but fully accepting their humanity and that of their brothers and guests as they strive together toward it. Undoubtedly here it is colored by the strong family spirit present among all Greeks. Love and a father are the cohesive forces and the source of order and co-ordination. A young Greek-American theologian here for the feast frequently spoke of the need for more democracy in the Church. So I wonder if a lot of the particular color does not come from the culture. Yet the ideal is certainly totally valid and freeing and is something worth experiencing.

After Vespers we gathered in the synodikon for coffee with the Hegumen. I like the way he conducts his meetings. There is a leisurely opening over coffee. The men are given a chance to raise questions, etc., and there is always a bit of pleasant repartee. At the end of his talk he asks for questions or objections and allows a time of quiet while the men reflect on what he has said. There are usually some questions. Then the Hegumen might make some announcements or there might be further light exchange.

This evening the Hegumen compared Russian Orthodoxy with Greek. He had previously reflected on Latin influences on the

Church in the Ukraine which made it somewhat different from the Church in the rest of the country. The kinds of anecdotes he chose to use to indicate the Russian Orthodox spirit said in themselves something of the spirit of Orthodoxy. There it was in the marks of holiness in young and old, their devotion, the nimbus of glory around them. Cemeteries received special attention, both the modern ones with their statuary, which he appreciated, and the ancient caves of the monks that became burial catacombs. There was some exchange this evening about the possibility of having catacombs here and not having to exhume the bodies and mix the bones all together.

The special mark of the Russian Christian seemed, to the Hegumen, to be that of a cross-bearer, one who shares in the Passion of Christ and awaits the Resurrection. The Greek Orthodox, when the cross comes, prays for immediate deliverance. The Russian prays to be able to bear the cross well. He is very conscious of his sinfulness and, at the same moment, of Christ's healing grace, and he is happy to bear the cross with him. Another note in all this is the Russian's vivid sense of the Presence of God come very close in Christ. This sustains him in his cross-bearing. He turns to his Spiritual Father, or Staretz, as a Christ Person and a bond with the Church—in all things. In Greece one might go to his Spiritual Father to express his spiritual aspirations and to confess. The Russian goes to his Staretz in all things and expects him to obtain from God all he needs. It is told of Saint John of Kronstadt that he placed a stack of letters from his spiritual children before the Lord and asked for answers to all their needs, and at that moment God cured all the ills mentioned in the letters. Saint John's shrine is closed now, as is that of Saint Seraphim, although the latter's incorrupt body has been hidden in the catacombs. The Russians' sense of Presence comes out very much in the churches where crowd follows crowd to attend the successive Services and receive the Eucharist, to go forth strengthened. The people always stand in the churches and sing with great fervor and vigor, and all—young and old—join in the singing, which is done in four parts.

The Hegumen took the opportunity this evening to exhort his monks on church Services: just as one must rise from his bed and open his eyes before going to the katholikon, so they should open their spiritual eyes, so they can truly see God present and go to the church with eagerness to be in his Presence and glorify and praise him. Otherwise, they should not go to the church. And in church their whole being should be to the Lord in praise—no sleeping or being taken up with things surrounding them or thought of work, etc.

After the talk the Hegumen announced that he would be leaving in ten days for Constantinople. While the visit to Russia was a visit to the Orthodox spirit, the visit to Constantinople is to a mother, as it were, one who is widowed and in prison, and needs this sign of her son's love and affection. So he is happy to go. He urged his sons to be good while he was away, leading lives intent upon magnifying God. His paternal heart would be grieved if they did wrong while he was gone and he was not here to absolve them. Although he had been away almost a month, he was happy to see how good they have been; it shone in their faces (and there is more than a little truth in that).

When he returned, he said, he hoped to have the other deacons ordained priests and more deacons made, including a permanent deacon, for they will always need one. He remarked on how poor they were at the moment in regard to priests, especially priests who could sing. This caused some pleasant exchanges. Also there were suggestions about who might be the permanent deacon. When one brother was named, it was remarked by another that he was always getting headaches and would leave in the middle of the Service to get an aspirin!

There is a wonderful brotherly spirit among the monks, and even the novices feel free to join right in. The Apodeipnon bell had rung long before, but no one went to the katholikon. So old Father Simon did it alone and then came to bring the key to the ecclesiastikos after having locked up the church. There was a bit of jesting about this, which the dear old monk took in stride. When the Hegumen encouraged them to sing more fully in church (they already do a very good job of it as far as I can judge—certainly they produce a lot more volume per man than we do at Spencer), like the Russians, one of the youngsters suggested they might do better if they ate like the Russians. It is a very happy, loving community to be in the midst of. When men take the Gospel seriously and try to live it together, the result is inevitably joy and peace even when the cross is very present.

Saturday, July 25

꙳ Today is the Feast of Saint Anne. It caught me a bit by surprise because it is the twenty-sixth in the West. If I had been aware of it earlier yesterday, I might have taken the 11:00 boat to the Skete of Aghia Anna for the Agripnia there. The Hegumen celebrated the Liturgy with Father Justin and there was a general Communion.

꙳

It is quite cool. We had rain last night. I am wearing a coat and hat and using two blankets at night.

I have been reading—I give very little time to reading; perhaps I should do more—Saint Antony's *One Hundred and Seventy Texts of Saintly Life*. Some of them are very rich indeed:

47. By his Word, God called into being various kinds of animal for our use—some to be used as food, others for our service. But man God created to be a witness and grateful interpreter of his works . . .

We begin Vespers every day with Psalm 103. It is a wonderful thing. The Psalm speaks at length of God's Providence and then breaks into praise and glorification. We need to be reminded daily of his great and loving care. And, above all, we need to glorify and praise him. We are weak on that in the West. Perhaps it is because of our rationalism. We tend to try to reduce everything, even God and what we know of him and his creation, to rational concepts, something we can get hold of, possess, and use. But anything that our small minds can master is very small indeed, certainly only a caricature of God and his wonderful doings, and not capable of drawing from us that wonder that falls down in admiration and rises up in praise. We need to take time to stop thinking and analyzing and just be, and be open, and let the reality of his works and his deifying Presence pour in upon us. Then our whole being will respond in adoration, praise, and awe.

We go on to Psalm 140—the first lamplighting song—where our prayer rises to the Lord with the evening incense. The verse there that has been striking me especially these days is: "May a just man chasten me with justice and reprove me." What a blessing it is to have someone in our lives who cares enough for us that he actively helps us to stay on the straight and narrow. This is part of the role of the Spiritual Father. It is something one can hope to receive from his brothers when he joins a Christian community—what Aquinas calls the "alms" of fraternal correction. It is something worth praying for and seeking. A tremendous help to progress; I might say, an almost absolute need if one hopes to avoid all self-delusion and to progress steadily in the ways of Christian holiness.

He who winks at a fault causes trouble, but he who frankly reproves promotes peace. — PROVERBS 10:10

". . . It is by way of admonition that he chastises those who are close to him." — JUDITH 8:27

Lord, on this Feast of Saint Anne, with all my heart and as much love as I can muster, I renew my vows as a monk. With the help of your grace and by your mercy, I promise to strive to live more fully in obedience and according to the monastic traditions of my community and Order, seeking ever greater stability of mind and heart as well as body. I humble myself before you for having failed in many ways to live according to the deeper meaning and spirit of my vows during the preceding years. I ask your forgiveness and the forgiveness of all whom I have hurt in doing this. And I ask you in your great and compassionate mercy to make up for my failures, forgive all my offenses and help me as your son and servant and loved one to begin to be more faithful to you in all respects. I thank you, Lord, for your abiding love and mercy.

". . . the things you decide on come forward and say, 'Here we are!' " — JUDITH 9:6

Sunday, July 26

❧ Father David gave me a book to read: *Athos, the Holy Mountain*, written by Sydney Loch, a Scottish Protestant, who lived near the border of the Holy Mountain for many years. The book was published by Molho in Thessaloniki in 1957 and reprinted in 1971. It is interestingly written, with a number of photos of varying quality. The treatment is sympathetic, a bit patronizing, and highlights the Athonite "characters" as such books usually do. He shared some of the Hegumen's insights in comparing the Greek and Slav:

> The Slav devotion inclined to be by way of the heart, the Greek by way of the mind. The Slav understood reverence, dignity, music. The Greek sometimes became a little at home in his Services. But the Russian owed his religion to the Greek.

I think I am more of a Slav—of the heart. That is why I do not find all the discussion so fruitful, but more the living. And that is more where true Orthodoxy lies. And indeed, all true orthodox Christianity. It is a religion of love. Yes, true love has to be based on true faith and understanding. But this knowledge is the springboard for love, which goes far beyond it. Even Aquinas held that.

Loch goes on to add two sentences which I find to be quite true:

> Strange that the individualistic Greek has proved so conservative in his Church, which has remained unchanged for more than fifteen hundred years. He finds this a matter of pride.

Actually there is probably more change and development than even the unbiased outsider—scholar and friend though he be—perceives. But the attitude and conviction is prevalent.

The great difference between the early 1950s which Loch speaks of and today lies in the pessimism that prevailed then and the hopeful optimism that is beginning to prevail today. As the hierarchy has gone into a sort of eclipse, monasticism is emerging. Athos is readily acknowledged as the heart of Orthodoxy. Many young Greek priests and laymen are coming on pilgrimage and some are staying. Yet perhaps the most prevailing current in Greece is toward secularism, and those Orthodox who cannot conceive of Orthodoxy outside of a

Byzantine culture created by Church and religion see the future in very dark colors.

❈

I have been struggling with a good bit of tiredness and sleepiness since the feast and the trip to Konstamonitou. I guess as one gets older he loses more and more of his flexibility and an upset in schedule takes more out of him. We are also getting up an hour earlier now which takes some getting used to. The weather, too, has been heavy. We have had the first succession of cloudy days since I came to the Mountain.

Monday, July 27

୧ Today is the Feast of Saint Panteleimon. Four of the monks have gone to the Russiko* for the feast. Here it has been celebrated with much solemnity. For some reason, this fourth-century Martyr is very popular on the Holy Mountain. Most monasteries have his icon in the katholikon and possess a relic of him. Why he is so popular is, I guess, one of those mysteries of Divine Election. God chooses whom he wants for what he wants. Saint Panteleimon was not necessarily the holiest or greatest of the martyrs of those days. But God has chosen him to be specially honored through the centuries in Orthodox churches, and in honoring him, men and women come to magnify God more in his wonderful works and find inspiration to die to self and to live to God, especially in the living martyrdom that monastic life should be.

❈

I was thinking especially today of Father Panteleimon and his community in Boston, a bit of Athos in America.

❈

The Gerontas invited me up for coffee and we spent some hours in conversation. One of the first things I spoke of was the possibility of his coming to America to start a Greek Orthodox monastery. Providence has given him many sons who speak English; there will be less difficulty entering our country than there would be entering Romania or Russia; there is no Greek Orthodox monastery yet in the United States; and the Church very much needs this kind of presence. It would be most important that the monks who come have a solid grip on their tradition and are very careful in screening candidates. The Gerontas spoke of many difficulties. He said he thought such a monastery would attract many disaffected Catholics and Protestants. He asked what I would think of their accepting Catholics and making them Orthodox. I replied that there must always be careful discernment of the spirit. He said that at times there is no time for this. He has to deal with the person who is, here and now, convinced he should become Orthodox. It is not possible to say what the future will bring. To refuse them might lead to disaster in their lives. They may be making a mistake, but we come to God by the full use of our freedom and by making mistakes and even by sinning.

I agreed on the importance of the freedom. That is why, when a person comes to me wanting to convert to Catholicism, I tell him of my conviction that we have in Roman Catholicism the True Faith and the source of unity intended by Christ and that I would be very happy to welcome him as a brother Catholic, but I challenge him first to explore his own religious tradition to the full and, if he still finds it lacking, then to come back with freedom and sureness to embrace Catholicism. I have met some converts to Orthodoxy on the Mountain who were very defensive and gave me the impression of having to justify their conversion to me. This is not good. One should be in full possession of what he believes, to be able to freely share it, and to openly hear other views and positions without feeling threatened.

For the Gerontas freedom is absolutely basic. If a candidate comes to him wishing to enter the monastery and does not have psychological freedom, he will send him back to his people—to share what he has experienced of God and hopefully to grow into freedom—or to another monastery where a more structured life might not be built on such freedom. But, still, the man will not find full joy and happiness without this freedom. One is to be led by the Spiritual Father into spiritual freedom.

I asked the Elder to say more about this, how he helped a man to come into this freedom.

First, the Gerontas replied, he tries to help him to realize in his mind and sense in his heart that God the Father loves him and that

Christ has redeemed him from his sin and bondage. He must come to accept himself as a sinner, as a human being. Then he must be freed from all his own doings and achieving, realizing nothing is gained by these but that it is all God's doing. Then he is guided into self-denial, not to achieve for himself so much as to express to God his will, his desire, and his openness to receive the redemption and freedom from Christ. He is thus cleansed and open to receive the Holy Spirit, who will continue to guide him into the mystic experience of the light from Christ's Face. Then he will have the complete freedom—spiritual freedom—that makes one free to be the servant of Christ, in complete servitude. At this point the Spiritual Father steps to the corner and rejoices and worships what the Lord is doing in his son.

I further asked how the Elder helped the beginner with prayer in the cell. Did he give him a rule of prayer or a method? Did he prescribe certain reading?

The Gerontas replied that the monk has to be left to face God. The Spiritual Father's role is to encourage, to stand between the monk and God as mediator—this is his main role—and not get between God and the monk. He is to help the monk in discernment so that he will not take sensible feelings or imagination as being the work of the Spirit and miss the true movement or leading of the Spirit. A beginner is given a rule of prayer and some help, but he quickly goes beyond this. Leaving the world by entering the monastery, he has no reason to go back to it in thought or imagination. If he does, he can lose all. He quickly quiets down and finds the interior silence so he can hear God. For a young Greek coming to the strict, secluded life of the Mountain, the Elder said, this happens rather quickly. It seems to me we find it more of a task in the West. But perhaps not all the modern young Greeks are so successful. Perhaps, too, the Spiritual Fathers of the West do not take their role seriously enough. They do not pray and groan before God through the night for their sons and visit them in a mystic way with Christ to help them. For many in the West, spiritual paternity is mostly spiritual direction—an exercise of power—rather than a realization of helplessness and being before God in need. The Gerontas stressed that the prayer of the Spiritual Father is the most important part of spiritual paternity and of helping his sons to freedom. Sons have to be left to exercise their freedom, even to do what the Spiritual Father thinks is not good—to make mistakes and to sin. Through all this they will grow and come back to God.

In connection with this, the Gerontas said, if one or more of his monks came to him wanting to go to America, he would bless them. God has to take the lead. If they wish to go to study or travel or work, he will let them. But they must be free and open. That is essential.

We moved into a discussion of the ecumenical movement. The Orthodox see it largely as unilateral. They feel no need or desire for it. They have the fullness that the Church always had. The West tended to make too much of the response of Patriarch Athenagoras, the Hegumen said. The Orthodox respect their Patriarch. They hear with varying interest of his doings, but it does not really touch them. Some might reprimand him, but out of reverence most will pass over his failings in silence. The Catholics have to realize that Orthodoxy is not organized or centralized and is not met in a few chosen leaders or scholars. The Orthodox do not think of union but of communion with other believers of the same Faith.

The Uniat Churches remain a stumbling block. The Orthodox believe they cannot have the same true spirit of Orthodoxy and are therefore masquerading as Orthodox to lure the faithful away. This the Orthodox believe is worse than past attempts at forceful union and latinizing. I tried to explain Rome's dilemma in finding Orthodox Greeks and other Orthodox who want to be in union with Rome. I agreed that to force them to latinize is wholly undesirable. And since corporate communion is not yet possible, some provision has to be made for these people.

The Hegumen felt that progress toward communion can be made only when Catholics stop thinking of the East as a territory, a place, or a segment to be incorporated into their Catholic world and see Orthodoxy as she sees herself—as the source and origin of the West's Faith and of the Western Church's own past. When the Catholic Church stops and takes a good inner look at her own past and is renewed in the light of that, then there can be hope of something.

The Hegumen pointed to my visit as perhaps exemplifying what he was saying. His own monks, knowing my goodness and respecting him, are happy to have me. Others on the Holy Mountain do not readily understand, not knowing my intentions, but out of respect for the Hegumen say nothing. One simple monk expressed their sen-

sitivity. He said he was surprised I was not yet baptized as an Orthodox and thought I should be baptized or sent away. The only union
many here can conceive of is Catholics simply becoming Orthodox.
My presence is well-received in this community, the Hegumen said,
because, from being among the first in my own monastery, I accept
to be the last here. I have left my own community, Services, works,
spiritual sons, everything, and come as one seeking to learn and not
trying to teach. If the Catholic Church approached Orthodoxy in
this way, it would be received with the same good will, respect, and
love.

I thought this was a very good parallel. I have come to the brethren here, conscious that we have a common past and tradition. I can
see here our earlier selves as monks and see how the one tradition has
developed in different ways. I think we have to recognize that monasticism, both East and West, has developed—and hopefully the development of both, though different, is legitimate. The same is true on
the ecclesial level. Both Churches have developed. Most Orthodox,
though, do not readily acknowledge any development but claim that
all is exactly as it always was and see all development in the West as
deviation. The concept of the development of doctrine, with which
the Catholic Church herself has had to struggle over in recent decades, remains a crucial issue. The ecumenical path is surely, by
human vision, a long, difficult one, stretching far into the future. But
with God, all things are possible. We all can agree on that. And the
most important thing is prayer, with fasting and humbling ourselves
before God and men. God will only hear prayer from a sincere heart,
one that really shares the concern of Christ's heart for all his flock.
Without this concern our prayer for union is only words. We must
first take all into our own heart and suffer over the hurts and wounds
and limitations and weaknesses and sins, even as we rejoice and
thank God for the good will that is present. The monk who wanted
me to be baptized spoke out of a faith-filled love, according to the
ardor of his own faith conviction and the vision he had. A Westerner might be tempted to label it as prejudice or narrowness, but if
he did, he would be missing the reality that was present, a beautiful
reality, even if partial.

I seem to get caught up in these ecumenical discussions, but the
Greek functions much at this level in his faith and love. Yet, as an
Orthodox, he will readily affirm that the experiential level is the im-

portant thing and ultimately mystic experience. At that level we are all surely very much one. My daily life here is mostly at that level, and so it is a beautiful experience of oneness in respectful and sincere love. Thanks be to God. *Doxa si, o Theos, doxa si.*

I expressed again to the Hegumen my desire to do some work, but he passed it off lightly as "unnecessary," with a word of thanks for help on the work in the past. Work here does not seem to hold the same place in the life as it does for Cistercians, though some do a great deal of it and miss Services and Liturgy for it. It is more of a working out of individual vocations.

❋

Around two in the afternoon, Andreas, one of the novices, came to ask if I wanted something to eat. Andreas has just finished theology at the University of Athens (equivalent to college in America, though giving a diploma rather than a bachelor's degree). He is intent upon becoming a monk now but thinks in the future he would be happy if the Gerontas would bless his going to England or America to study theology. He likes to think and to sing, and if he thinks as well as he sings, he will be a great theologian. But I am happy he is first intent upon becoming a monk. As a true monk, he will be an even more integral theologian—a theologian in the traditional sense as was Saint John the Divine, Saint Gregory Nazianzen, and Saint Symeon, whom the Orthodox call "theologians."

Andreas' kindness is typical. Yesterday John, a candidate from Athens, who is in the cell next to mine, came along after his nap to offer to make me a cup of coffee. On baking days Father Gervasios' first baking includes a batch of fist-size rolls. As soon as they are out of the oven, he is off to where the brothers are working with an armful of them. If I should not be at work with them, often enough someone will be sent to my cell with the hot, fresh bread. When they are sharing sweets in the hegumenate, some will usually find their way to my cell. The librarian brings in any newly arrived books or periodicals he thinks might interest me. And Father Dionysios might arrive in the middle of any afternoon with a tray of coffee and sweets. Thoughtful kindness is a trade-mark of this truly Christian community.

❋

After supper I usually take a walk up to the crest of the hill where the road turns and begins its long, slow descent to the port of Daphni. Up there I have a small, stone bench in the shadows of the last spur, for the sun is still hot even as it is setting. Here I do some of my daily reflecting, before the awesome granite pinnacles of the Holy Mountain. Across the deep valley tumbling to the sea I can get the full picture of Simonos Petras that distance provides. And I can, at the same time, get a distanced view of my life—so empty, yet so full, wanting more and more, yet peaceful and deeply content, beaten down by my constant sin and failure yet filled with the joy of being loved, healed, and uplifted by an immensely loving God and Saviour. Saint Bernard speaks of our being at the feet of God—one foot is justice, the other, mercy. We must take care to embrace both, lest justice alone cause us to despair or mercy alone cause us to grow careless. There is a lot of practical wisdom in that.

Looking up at the summit of the Holy Mountain I have been speculating about ascending to it for the Feast of the Transfiguration. There is a small chapel there, visible as a white speck on clear days, where a hearty group of monks and pilgrims celebrate an All-Night Vigil for the Feast. It is usually quite cold even though very warm down below. I do not know if I am up to the climb. Nor am I sure of the value of it. The *Imitation of Christ* says that those who go on pilgrimages rarely become saints. We—I am prone to escape from inner solitude, the face of my own pretty wretched mess and the Face of the living God, by changing the exterior scene. Even sitting quietly on my balcony I find myself inordinately attracted to watching the little activity that occurs on our peaceful scene: the arrival of the daily boat, skiffs going up and down the coast, the fishing vessels or tourist launches going by, the guests struggling up and down our steep ascent, the work in the vegetable terraces. Even in the quiet evening, on the crest, the myriad display of colorful stones crushed from the rich mountain granite and marble to establish the road, attracts my greedy eye. My possessiveness wants to start scooping them up and is checked only by the painful realization that everything I collect will have to be carried away on my shoulder over rough mountain paths. After a few steep ascents under the burning sun, one gives a light load a high priority. All this makes me appreciate more and more, on a very existential level, the value of that free-dom of passionlessness, freedom from curiosity, from possessiveness, the freedom of the true adorer who can see each thing in its God Presence and go on adoring without distraction. With such God con-sciousness, unity consciousness, all is peaceful, unending, deepening prayer.

※

Today is the anniversary of my Baptism, an event I am inclined to call the most significant in my life. Its significance is the more fully perceived as I understand, little by little, more and more, what it means to be baptized into the Lord Jesus, to be a son of God not only in name but in inner transformation, to be an heir destined to glory, to be dead to sin—in spite of the struggles—and alive to God, to be indwelt by the most blessed and adorable Trinity. All praise, glory, and thanksgiving!

Tuesday, July 28

In the West it is the Feast of Saint Lawrence (August 10). And I think of our Father Laurence at Spencer and pray Mass for him. And Father Lawrence of New Skete and his little community. We were with them on this feast two years ago for the tonsure of Brothers Job and Isaac. How I wish all of them could have the won-derful grace I am receiving, being here on the Holy Mountain for these months.

※

Here it is the Feast of Saint Paul of Xenophontou,* founder of the Monastery of Aghiou Pavlou—so boatloads of monks and pil-grims have gone by to the feast there.

※

One of the guests left in the guest book a "Poem to Athos":

As I sit here and listen to the Petras church bell *ringing*
To call these monks to worship,
I can only think, though they believe in God and truth,

That unless they accept Christ, as their personal Savior,
They will in the flames of hell be *singing*.
— FROM A BELIEVER

He added a saving footnote: "But let me add, the monks on the
Holy Mountain are fine people, and ones to be respected. This world
could use more of this kind."

Yes, we all have our different perspectives, even those of us who
have faith in Christ, the Son of God, love him, and are dedicated to
being his followers and disciples. He sure leads a mottled flock. May
we all come together to eternal life! Our Orthodox brothers seem to
have a pretty dim view of how many are going to make it up the narrow way. Our "believer" is perhaps more open but still quite limiting. I wonder if we do not put awful human limitations on our loving and all-powerful God's universal and salvific will. Christ did die
for all! Praise him!

❋

Peter, the very dedicated hired man, who sees little of his family
on the mainland, is turning out the last of the potatoes on the terrace. The summer squash is done. Now we are into cabbage,
cauliflower, and an abundance of tomatoes, along with the ever-
present beans. One becomes very aware of nature's moves here. The
figs are plumping out, the grapes softening, walnuts are for the gathering; the mulberries are about done, the blackberries just coming in.
The gorse is pretty much all gone, but other flowers have come,
though not in such wondrous profusion. The rich blues and greens of
the sea are the setting for it all. It is a place of tireless beauty. Praise
the Maker!

❋

Sydney Loch, in the final pages of his book (still a manuscript
when he died in 1954 and edited and published three years later by
his wife), has some prophetic words:

. . . something intelligent monks constantly underline, that the
ailing community can only be restored to health by men of education, conviction, and good will taking the habit. Newcomers with
the gift of leadership and purpose must be found to take the age-
old vows of stability, obedience, poverty and chastity. But in this

motor-boat age [!] is it possible to find numbers of men whose fullest way of self-expression in the world is to be found by withdrawing from it.

Looking over the Mountain today, and indeed even America, we can say: "Yes."

❋

After supper we peeled potatoes and then went to the synodikon to hear a tape made by the Hegumen in the course of his Russian journey, recounting all he was experiencing. At the Monastery of Saint Sergius in Moscow he found that there were as many as ten Liturgies a day, with five priests distributing Communion. Perhaps the Russians receive with greater frequency than do the Greeks. That monastery kept forty confessors available and busy from dawn till dark.

As we were listening the bells began ringing—Archbishop Ezechiel was arriving for an overnight stop en route to Karyes. He had with him a Greek-American student, Soteri, from Hellenic College in Boston. Soteri had completed three years there and had received a blessing to spend a year in Greece to learn Greek. Since the Archbishop speaks English, Soteri is very fortunate to be able to be with him in Thessaloniki.

❋

After lunch I met two Lutheran seminarians who had walked over from Grigoriou for a brief visit. We talked while we helped young Father Aimilianos cut and thread pipe for the generating system. They are having more difficulty harnessing the water supply than they expected. The two Lutheran visitors are at a five-year seminary where they live in a brotherhood and celebrate the daily Office in common. They are being prepared for the missions. When they complete the seminary, they can make commitments of obedience and even celibacy in the brotherhood and go to missions in South America, Africa, or India. One of them, Albricht Benz, is already determined to go to India. He is very interested in learning more about the way of prayer in the *Philokalia* and was inquiring about spending a month here next summer for that purpose. The other seminarian's name was Wolfgang Fromm.

❋

We need truly and absolutely to accept the vow of poverty: to seek no rule, but rather anarchy, the anarchic life of fools for Christ's sake; to seek no monastic enclosure, but the complete absence of even the subtlest barrier which separates the heart from the world and its wounds.

— MOTHER MARIA SKOBSTSOBA (1891–1945)

Wednesday, July 29

The Archbishop celebrated the Liturgy and left shortly after in the Land-Rover for Karyes with eight other guests. Father Nicholas from the Kellion of Saint Nicholas, arrived last night to take up the life here. He is attracted by the greater openness of this community. Father David arrived back after visiting Grigoriou after the feast at Aghios Panteleimonos. He had a Dutch boy with him whom he met at the feast. The two Lutherans also returned.

❄

In the last of his *Hundred and Seventy Texts on Saintly Life* Saint Antony tells how we can fulfill the Lord's precept to pray always even while we sleep:

When you lie down on your bed, remember with thanksgiving the blessings and Providence of God. Thereupon, filled with this good thought, you will rejoice in the spirit and the sleep of the body will mean sobriety of the soul; the closing of your eyes, a true knowledge of God; and your silence, brimming with the good feeling, will wholeheartedly and with all its strength glorify Almighty God, giving him from the heart praise that rises on high.

Whether awake or asleep, it is more by being than by thoughts or words, that our creaturely lives can worship and glorify the all Holy Trinity.

Thursday, July 30

I am wandering through the Book of Proverbs these days. Some of them are not too relevant to my present need—to say the least!—but some are real gems. I was struck this morning especially by this one: "He who covers up a misdeed fosters friendship,/but he who gossips about it separates friends" (17:9).

It does not, of course, mean conniving at a brother's wrongdoing. It goes on to say: "He who condones the wicked, he who condemns the just,/are both an abomination to the LORD" (17:15). It seems to me that when we see our brother doing something wrong, there are two we should speak to, and sometimes a third, rarely a fourth. We should speak first to God, asking for understanding, love, mercy, and the graces our brother needs. Then we should speak to our brother: "A single reprimand does more for a man of intelligence than a hundred lashes for a fool" (17:10). The alms of fraternal correction is real. But we should approach with great humility. When we listen to our brother, we may discover there is no wrongdoing—we misunderstood. If our brother does not listen to us, is not open, the situation may warrant speaking to him before a couple of other brothers, as the Gospel says. If we are not sure how to handle this situation or if we are finding our peace disturbed by it, we may need to speak to our own Spiritual Father to sort things out and to see better how we should respond to the situation. Finally, in some rare cases, our own good or that of others may demand we speak to the Church, to the Superior, but we would do well to seek counsel before making this decision. In all, we need to keep in mind the following proverb: "He who spares his words is truly wise,/and he who is chary of speech is a man of intelligence" (17:27). And for the consolation of some of us, the wise man ends his chapter with these words: "Even a fool, if he keeps silent, is considered wise;/if he closes his lips, intelligent" (17:28).

❈

After lunch I went to see Father Dionysios. He told me that the Hegumen would leave for Constantinople tomorrow and he on the next day. Then he surprised me by inviting me to go with him Saturday to the nuns at Ormilia. I expressed my preference to stay quietly here on the Mountain for some time yet. He said he would speak to the Hegumen about it. So I am in a bit of limbo now, not knowing if I can stay quietly here or have to move on to do some visiting. In any case, I place all very peacefully in the Hands of the Lord.

ORMILIA

A Skete

꧁ Sitting on the hill this evening I was reflecting on my time here and what the Lord has been showing me. My being in the last place, off in a corner of the katholikon, or sitting among the novices, kind of puts things in their true perspective. For I have hardly begun to be a monk, to have a monk's or even a Christian's outlook. I am still so awfully centered on self. The pleasure principle is very strong in me. How much comfort or discomfort a thing will cause me weighs too much in my judgment. I regret the thought of moving on from here because I am "comfortable" here: I have carved out my regime and am set up in my little ways. It is cool here. I have a good cell. There are adequate facilities for keeping clean, etc. If I have to move on, I will have to rough it perhaps—hot trails, less comfortable monasteries, less privacy and ease, etc. Of course, in this case I can argue that the stability in a quiet and peaceful place is more helpful to my retreat. And that is true. But this is just an example of my proneness to be too aware of the comfort angle. I could fast more here. I could watch more in prayer. I could check my curiosity more. I could be more diligent at reading. More important is the need to find a new center in God. The *Kyrie eleison* and *Doxa* are not coming from my whole being. What, practically, shall I do? Beg more the Lord's help and try to be more faithful as an expression of my desire to receive that grace from him which alone can give insight and heart to truly cry *Eleison* and *Doxa si*.

❉

A novice arrived today. George is only fourteen. He has been a novice since he was ten. He continues at home and school and spends a month in the monastery in the summer. There also arrived a young Frenchman, a friend of Père Plàcide, the superior of our Byzantine monastery at Aubazine, in southwestern France, who is going to spend a month with the monks.

❉

Pray not to this end, that your own desires be fulfilled. You can be sure they do not fully accord with the will of God.

❀

Undistracted prayer is the highest act of the mind.

Friday, July 31

☙ It is washday and Father Theonas has loaned me a robe to wear while I wash mine. The Hegumen sent down a melon—it looks like a banana melon.

❀

Withdrawal from the world consists in not occupying your mind with the world. — ISAAC THE SYRIAN

❀

It does little good to come to Athos or any other monastery if one is still going to keep his mind and imagination full of the world and its doings.

❀

I spoke briefly to the Hegumen just before he left. He invited me to meet him tomorrow with Father Dionysios to go to Ormilia for the Feast of the Dormition on Sunday and the tonsure of three nuns.

The brothers are expressing their farewells with much kindness. Father Maximos took me to see the library and what he is doing there to classify their older holdings. He has a big job ahead of him. They hope to build up a good collection and to provide more ample and suitable space for it. The Hegumen has a good patristic and monastic library in the hegumenate. Certainly there is enough solid food to keep the monks going.

❀

I spoke with one of the Spiritual Fathers from another monastery for a time today. He feels that we can all use the early Fathers and the Apothegmata,* but later there is a great difference between Orthodox and Western spirit. The Fathers are interpreted and lived differently in the West. He suggested Dorotheus of Gaza, John and

Barsanuphios, and Saint John Climacus, with explanation, for beginners.

Talking with Father Aimilianos I think I saw a little more clearly into one of the areas of question or challenge for us at home. As a community we are deeply united at the level of Christian reality—love in Christ and for one another. Also, as a community of prayer. Yet we feel the need of a more pronounced experience of unity. We realize that doing things together is not in itself the answer. This could just be superficial or forced. We need to realize a distinctive way of living the Christian message of love and a life of prayer, *to be one at the level of a particular Christian spirit.*

Obviously, for us, this would be the Cistercian spirit. Techniques such as Zen, Yoga, TM, as techniques, can be employed in a Cistercian way. But Orthodox or Eastern spirituality, as a distinctive spirituality, cannot be *one* with Cistercian spirituality. Patristic and monastic spirituality needs to be integrated into our lives in a Cistercian way. A "spirit" is something undefinable. Since our tradition has to some extent been broken—in the East the later Fathers are one with the earlier Fathers; in the West, Franciscan, Jesuit, and Carmelite spirituality replaced monastic and Cistercian spirituality—it has to be bridged. We need to contact our Fathers as living and absorb by contact this spirit. We need to contact those they drew from and absorb as they did. When the community as a whole has this distinctive monastic Cistercian spirit, unity will be sensed on another level and more connaturally express itself in doing particular things, living a particular way. The more we get hold of this, the more we will experience and enjoy our unity, the more we will have hold of our identity.

It is not a question of who we are, but who we are to become. Life is given to us to grow and become. We should never be satisfied, but always want more. We are called to the full maturity in Christ. But Christ is such a giant that each of us can live but an aspect of his greatness. In discerning vocation we seek to discern our aspect. Deciding to profess monastic life in a Cistercian abbey we are responding to our personal discernment that we are to live and grow that particular aspect of the Christ life—a life apart, on the mountain in prayer. This is our way to full maturity in Christ.

❊

Now will I praise those godly men,
    our ancestors, each in his own time:
The abounding glory of the Most High's portion,
    his own part, since the days of old. . . .
Yet these . . . were godly men
    whose virtues have not been forgotten;
Their wealth remains in their families,
    their heritage with their descendants;
Through God's covenant with them their family endures,
    their posterity, for their sake.
And for all time their progeny will endure,
    their glory will never be blotted out;
Their bodies are peacefully laid away,
    but their name lives on and on.
At gatherings their wisdom is retold,
    and the assembly proclaims their praise.
                    — SIRACH (ECCLESIASTICUS) 44:1–2, 10–15

Saturday, August 1 / 14

☙ After lunch I had an opportunity to speak with Father
Nikodimos, the icon painter, who lives in the hermitage of Saint
John the Evangelist.

He stressed very strongly the need to be in touch with the sources,
or rather, with the source, the Fathers—Saints Basil, John Chrysostom, Gregory the Theologian, Gregory Palamas, Nikodimos—to
drink of this source. Father Nikodimos lamented that there are few
today who live out of the fullness of this source.

To make an icon, one must first come to a dispassionateness, a purity, so that the Saint can guide every stroke of the painting. It is all
to be pure prayer. One cannot paint a Saint except if he live the
same kind of life as the Saint. There needs to be technique, method,
but neither too much nor too little. Technique can never produce a
true icon.

Father Tikon told us that, as a beginner, he is only copying the
works of others. It is better to begin that way. But this copying, too,
must be pure prayer. The Gerontas insisted that in the icon there is

not only the presence of the Saint but the grace of God. For such a coming, the painter should prepare with a "Lent." Ordinarily the face is the last thing painted. Then one experiences the presence. Father Tikon added that the faith of the believer has a part in bringing about the presence.

Father Nikodimos urged me to stay longer on the Holy Mountain, here at the source, the tradition, even if there are few today who live it fully with power.

❀

At one o'clock we drove down to Daphni and caught the two o'clock boat: Father Dionysios on his way to Constantinople, Father Theonas to prepare for exams in Thessaloniki, Father Joasaph to take his entrance exam at the university, the young Father Aimilianos to get pieces for the water system in Thessaloniki, Father Palamas en route to the Pan-Orthodox Theological Conference in Athens, and myself. It was a strange feeling, one marked with a certain pain and sorrow, a sense of loss and a bit of repugnance, to leave the Holy Land and return to the "world." The Holy Mountain is a true "native land" for all monks. After being immersed in it for these months, the first view of the burgeoning tourist section of Ouranoupoulis made me very conscious of how alien is a pleasure-seeking, distracted way of life to the monk. I can appreciate why the monks generally are so reluctant to leave the Mountain. When I was leaving Simonos Petras, the monks were very warm in their farewells, really conveying a sense of how welcome I was to return and stay longer with them. But my invitations to them to come to America were generally responded to with an affirmation that it would be hard to leave the Mountain.

At Ouranoupolis, while the monks went to get a taxi, I stepped into the fifteenth-century tower near the jetty. This tower was an outpost for the Athonite Monastery of Vatopedi until 1922. When the government took the land to settle refugees from Asia Minor, Sydney Loch and his wife were asked to come and help. The Lochs made this tower their home. Sydney died in 1954. His widow published his book on Athos posthumously and continues to live in the tower, always ready to offer the passing monk a cup of tea or one of her Turkish kittens. While we chatted, the newest of these kittens played in my lap. The taxi was soon loaded and ready to go.

As we drove down the road, lined with flowers on both sides, we

could see the sea on both sides and Athos' peak in the distance. Soon
we climbed into the hills, knobby ones like those around Gethsemane* but with the rich red soil of Conyers.* Often there was little
sign of life or civilization except for the road and the accompanying
electric lines serving Ouranoupolis and the phone lines that reach
even beyond to the Holy Mountain. Other times we would go speed-
ing down the main street of a town, a frightening experience for pe-
destrians and passengers alike. We passed through Stagira and saw
the statue marking Aristotle's birthplace. Father Theonas remarked
that Aristotle is not studied much today—a little in philosophy;
Plato is more popular.

One of the young monks was hungry so he bought some cookies,
which we all helped him to eat. Another was not feeling too well, so
he asked his brother's shoulder and was soon sleeping. Father Joasaph, one of the better singers, started the Psalms of Vespers and Father Theonas joined in. After a while we turned back toward the sea
and ten minutes away from it we arrived at Vatopedi's former metokion, now Simonos Petras', just outside the village of Vatopedion:
the Convent of the Annunciation. We were warmly welcomed by
the sisters and after the usual refreshments we were shown to our
room—the basement of the building formerly lodging the hired help.

We had a quick supper and joined the sisters who had already
begun the Great Vespers. Their chapel is small, perhaps twenty by
thirty feet, with the iconostasis* carved by young Aimilianos at one
end. With thirty sisters and ten novices and even more guests
squeezed in, it was a cozy celebration. There were no stalls in which
to rest weary bodies a bit as the Vigil went on. The sisters found
chairs for us, but I think we were too embarrassed to sit when all the
others were standing. The Service was done more simply than on the
Mountain and we finished at 10:45, in time to get some sleep before
the four-thirty Liturgy and tonsure.

※

On the Mountain today was the beginning of the fourteen-day
Lent to prepare for the Feast of the Dormition. We completed it in
a two-hour boat ride, passing from the old calendar to the new. Sadly,
too, we missed the great and glorious Feast of the Transfiguration. I
really regret this. Although it is at the heart of the Palamite controversy, it remains for all monks—East and West—the great feast of
their vocation. We have been granted what Peter babbled—to build

tents on the heights and remain in the nimbus of the Taboric light and let it work in us its deifying work.

❋

This is a wonderful, youthful community. The Hegumena, Mother Nicodime, is the daughter of the Hegumen of Konstamonitou and Father Athanasios' sister. Her mother is one of her novices. Mother Nicodime looks like her brother, has the same attractive features, and is also blessed with the same beautiful and powerful voice. She is very much the figure of an abbess—taller than the rest, with pastoral staff in hand, graciously receiving the profound bows of all—even the monks kiss her hand. Like a Hegumen, there is a special invocation for the Hegumena in each litany chanted. As Sister Maxime, her second, later stressed, it is so important that there be a oneness between the Mother of the community and the Spiritual Father. Here this is complete for she also is his daughter.

Sunday, August 15

THE GLORIOUS FEAST OF THE DORMITION OF THE VIRGIN

The hope of getting some sleep was illusionary. When you get four or five monks together in a room they are like schoolboys on holiday. Everything short of a pillow fight! And I have found that true with monks older than the youths at this feast. Though I must confess, I rather enjoy seeing the playful fellowship. Certainly it is more attractive than the rather staid relations I have met in some communities in the West. The brothers are fully at ease with each other and happy, free, young men more interested in each other than in sleep. They had just settled down and dozed a bit when sister knocked at the door, and the fun started again as they struggled to get up.

It was a splendid night as we crossed the yard. One sister made her way along, pounding on the semantron. Another stood ready at the bells with an admiring crowd of youngsters around her. From all sides people were coming out of the shadows and, in the radiance of the light coming down from the high entrance, making their way up the ramps and stairs to enter the building.

Places with chairs were reserved for us. Others were crowded in. Most had to stay in the halls till Communion time. The Liturgy started at 4:30. The profession took place after the little entrance before the readings. It was identical to that of the monks. The habit, too, is the same except there is no skouphos and the veil is worn directly on the head. Even this small chapel was not free of the plague of nuns with tape recorders and flash cameras. (Recording and photographing certainly is a twentieth-century ministry in the Church and probably brings grace to many—but it mars the beautiful services.) When we finished the Services, the nuns had laid a festive meal for over a hundred and fifty—all that their refectory could manage—and still they had to send some away. I was delighted to see almost all the crowd receive Holy Communion.

❀

I spent most of the day sharing with Sister Augustine, Sister Maxime, and others. We visited all parts of the monastery: garden, external chapel, hegumenate, icon studio, etc., and were constantly plied with the rich pastries of Greece which guests had brought in great abundance. The sisters raise all the vegetables they need for table and have a small olive orchard. The icons and vestments they make and sell are their main source of income. Their schedule is the same as that of the monks at Simonos Petras. Like nuns the world over, they try to keep up with the monks, probably surpass them, and add the indefinable feminine touch which is so welcome. When the nuns came here, the place was virtually a shambles. They have worked their way toward making it quite livable and plan a new monastery behind and a chapel on the hill. Then there will be a school for girls in the area and missionaries for Nigeria. But first of all, a guesthouse for the steady flow coming to them.

❀

In his talk in the refectory, after sharing some of his rich experience in Russia, Archimandrite Aimilianos spoke about his first acquaintance with the newly professed nun, as a little girl. Almost all the community are from one section of Trikala and have known the Gerontas since childhood. As children they played "nun" and chose the present Hegumena as their Superior.

The Hegumen is strong on monastic vocations being fostered from the earliest years. Young Father Aimilianos, his namesake, was the only child of elderly parents shepherding back in the hills. He had never seen another child to play with until he went to school at six years of age and then went as a tough little scrapper. A few years later the Hegumen visited the school and saw him in the midst of a brawl. The Hegumen placed his hand on the boy's head and a new spirit came into the boy. From that time young Aimilianos stayed with the Gerontas, wholeheartedly seeking to follow Christ. Now, at nineteen, he has the Great Schema and is a very happy monk.

As the Hegumen continued his talk, he told of the cross and the joy of monastic life, that wonderful paradox every monk and nun knows who gives him- or herself to the life. Often others see the cross —all the monk or nun gives up—but also they see the evident joy, and they cannot understand. Such a life has to be lived. Until it is, even for the monk and nun it is a paradox; then it becomes a mystery of love.

Vespers, with the tonsure of two more sisters, was celebrated in the chapel outside the monastery. It is hardly bigger than the chapel inside but had the advantage of windows on both sides, allowing some air to circulate among the crowd. Most of the very large crowd had to be content to listen at the windows and doors. One of the sisters tonsured, Sister Gorgonia, is the sister of the chaplain here, Father Grigorios, and has a sister already in this community. Together they had the joy of clothing her. She has another brother at Simonos Petras, Father Tikon. Their oldest brother is married, but he said if he had not been the oldest, he, too, would have been a monk.

Tonsure is similar to the ordination Service but more elaborate. There is a full clothing. As the Hegumen pointed out in his talk at the banquet that followed (I am amazed at his vigor; he gave five long animated talks in the course of the day, each one very rich in content), the Lord completely clothed his new spouse for her new life, even down to her sandals. It is the same for a monk or a nun. In ordination to Priesthood or Diaconate, only the vestments are put on, over the habit—it is only an accidental change. The monastic profession is a complete change. In Orthodoxy the monk or nun will never again appear in public except in the habit.

※

At the supper talk the Hegumen developed the theme of monk as *monos* (alone)—one who stands alone before God and lets God come in and take the throne of his heart, until he finally takes full possession. The monk feels close to the saints because he is already in their way. That is why he commemorates them so frequently and with such devotion. And they inspire in him ever greater fidelity.

※

The Hegumen spoke of the monk being alone before God. But practically speaking, Orthodox monks seem to be comfortable in being constantly with others. Since we left Simonos Petras we have been constantly together, six in a room, with the sisters in and out—normal family living in a country and society where big families live in small houses or apartments. I felt the need of a little time alone with the Lord and wanted to pray the Mass on this great feast. I expressed this desire to Sister Augustine. With that wonderful *savoir-faire* of a woman, she arrived at our room around 4:30 with three other sisters and took the other five off for a little "picnic," leaving me a quiet hour with the Lord.

Monday, August 16

ᶜᵕᔰ Another rather chatty night with the boys and then Services and Liturgy at 3:30 this morning.

There is a young doctor here, a novice of Simonos Petras, who has just finished his medical studies at Athens. Since the program in medical school in Greece is almost totally academic, he feels the need of a couple of years of practice before settling on the Holy Mountain. It will be a great blessing for the community to have a doctor. I hope, though, he does not have to minister to the whole Mountain or he will be a very busy monk indeed. He probably should specialize in geriatrics, although he will have lots of young confreres at Simonos Petras to look after.

❈

I am experiencing something of the climate of obedience within which the Greek monk lives and grows. Obedience is very fundamental for them. The Lord truly stands in their midst in the Hegumen. Doing what he wants, when he wants, in the way he wants it— that's it. For the rest, the monk's work is prayer and he does that in all he does. The monks I am with are to go to Thessaloniki for their respective tasks, but they will go when the Hegumen gives the nod. Till then, one studies, another sleeps, and a third finds a hoe and helps irrigate the corn. Whether they will go today or tomorrow, by car or bus—that is of no concern to them. One of the monks who has studied in the West for some years and is more aggressive arranged things for himself and left last night. But he functions differently from the rest.

❈

Behold, as the eyes of servants
    are on the hands of their masters,
As the eyes of a maid
    are on the hands of her mistress
So are our eyes on the LORD, our God . . .
           — PSALM 123:2

❈

It is interesting to watch the Hegumena in the midst of her nuns in church or refectory. A glance, the rise of an eyebrow, a finger movement sets sisters into action! The Psalm is literally lived. It is very freeing when one need not plan but can live in obedience. Following Christ's each sign or nod, one can wholeheartedly love and serve him. It is a way of faith and presupposes that one has really died to self, given up one's own will save the essential will to love and serve the Beloved in all things. It is a very free, joyful, peaceful life.

❈

I spent a while with the Gerontas and the Gerontissa* this afternoon. I asked about the delicate balance of roles of the two in the monastery. The Hegumen insisted that in the Greek tradition each monastery is fully autonomous. The Hegumen is there with his community to help *only* to the extent the Hegumena asks. If he or a bishop steps into the life of the sisterhood, it means in fact that he does not really want the sisterhood. It must have its own identity. The Hegumena has all the rights and duties and privileges of a Hegumen. In the administration of her monastery she has full autonomy and responsibility. The Hegumena assured me that I had kept a place in their hearts since my visit three years ago.

I also spoke with Father Dionysios' cousin, Sister Epiphania, and Sister Militia, a doctor of chemistry from Yugoslavia, now a novice studying theology. Father Grigorios, who is as gracious as his brother, Father Tikon, and proud of their village, Trikala, nursery of monasticism (fourteen monks at Simonos Petras are from there and almost all the nuns at Ormilia), said he likes his assignment as chaplain because he has the Liturgy every day and he has much solitude and peace in his hermitage out behind the hill. But he does not find much time to paint icons. Sister Aimiliane is teaching him. At the moment she is doing a series of fourteen icons, two by three, for the price of five hundred dollars each. She always has more orders than she can handle.

✼

The Name of the Son of God is great and immense. It is this Name which sustains the entire world. — HERMAS

✼

The spirit becomes *monos* through the Memory of Christ (the constant use of the Prayer). — MAXIMOS OF KAVSOKALYVIA

Tuesday, August 17

☙ We left the convent in the truck of the friend of the nuns and drove to Nea Triglia to get the bus to Thessaloniki. There I went with Father Theonas to his home—a royal welcome and a good long night's sleep.

✼

I called Apostolos Karpozilos, and after coffee we visited a few of the most significant old churches of Thessaloniki. His wife, Martha, studied for six years in Connecticut and is now librarian at the

American College. We enjoyed a good lunch together and then I got
the bus for Ouranoupolis.

I had been trying to decide Sunday night what to do. When I
woke up Monday it was clear in my mind that I should return to the
Mountain for the Feast of the Transfiguration. The Gerontas was
pleased with this, and he also urged me to visit Patmos* and then return to Simonos Petras. I feel like the Lord is trying to teach me to
move quietly along with him and not make elaborate plans, but take
things as they come. This is something I need very much to learn.

As the bus passed into the mountains, night came upon us. Only a
hundred feet or so of the darkness was pierced by the shaft of light
from the bus's headlights as we bounced along the ascents and de-
scents. We never saw too far ahead of us. In the Greek buses, up
over the driver's head, is an icon of Mary, Mother of God—the
Panaghia*—with a light before it. Sometimes drivers add many others,
and prayer cords too. But always the Panaghia. It is good to move
along life's dark, winding path under her, in the light of her lamp.

It was a slow trip. After sunset, in each village, large numbers of
people were out strolling in groups of two, three, four, or more. How
much better and more truly human to be walking under the trees in
the cool of the evening, arm in arm with a friend—like Adam and
God in Paradise—rather than sitting home as a passive spectator before the "boob tube," as so many do today. We arrived at Ouranoupolis after ten but Mrs. Loch's door was still open. I chatted with
her while one of her friends, Mrs. Hanson, found me a place nearby
for the night; then Mrs. Hanson took me there.

If your prayer seeks only after justice and the Kingdom of God—
that is to say, after virtue and true spiritual knowledge—then all
else will be given to you besides.

If your mind still looks around at the time of prayer, then it does
not yet pray as a monk. You are no better than a man of affairs engaged in a kind of landscape gardening.

THE LIGHT OF TABOR

Koutloumousiou

Wednesday, August 18 / 5

❧ I am more and more taken up with the Transfiguration. It is perhaps all too significant of the way man functions that the very radiating Light of Christ—all goodness, holiness, and love—has become the very matter of division and controversy among those who call him Master and lay claim to being his disciples. Lord, help us all see the true light, *and quickly.*

❋

Mrs. Loch's maid had breakfast for me. Then it was a boat to Daphni, a bus to Karyes, and a short walk to the Monastery of Koutloumousiou* where they celebrate the Transfiguration as their patronal feast. There were mobs at Daphni and Karyes. But the crowd on hand at the monastery for the feast is the largest I have seen on the Mountain, and half or more are monks. Father David and Father Kyrikos are here from Simonos Petras, and Father Justin, too. Father Ephraim, a visiting Hegumen, who was to preside at the feast, welcomed me kindly and we were soon sitting down to a meal. Then I got some sleep and went off to the Protaton, for First Vespers.

As they sang again Psalm 103, I pondered on God's care, down to details. He had me meet Mrs. Loch so I had someone to welcome me at Ouranoupolis last night and provide for my needs. This morning I began worrying a bit because there were two boatloads going out to Daphni and the bus to Karyes could not take all and we were coming in last. But the bus did not open its doors until just as I reached it, so I even had a seat. I wanted to see the governor about my plans and, lo, there he was walking across the square just as I arrived in the center of town. But he told me to come later, so I went to Koutloumousiou, where I arrived just in time to meet the Hegumen and have lunch. Yet I found myself worrying again a couple of hours later in the governor's office and cut off a very interesting conversation with Professor Deno Geanakoplos from Yale, because I feared being late for supper at Koutloumousiou or being locked out.

The result: stomach pains from worry and rush and a wait for supper; and I also learned that when there is an Agripnia, the gates stay open all night. If I could just relax in my Father's loving Hands, do fully what I am doing, and move with what he permits, with full confidence that for those who love God all things work to the good.

⁂

Peter, James, and John had to follow the Lord to the top of Tabor or they would not have seen the Vision. I am sure they wondered where they were going, and what was up. But the Lord could not have really answered them with words. Their following him was rewarded. Then words became babble. Lord, lead me to the beyond-words and give me the good sense and wisdom to follow you there without question.

Thursday, August 6

The Vigil began at nine last night and, with a short breather before Liturgy, ended at 10:30 this morning, followed by reception and ritual meal. It was the longest for me so far. Metropolitan Dionysios from Ierissos presided at the Liturgy, with a couple visiting Hegumens. One priest was ordained.

There was one unhappy incident. At the end of Orthros a monk approached me and, learning I was not Orthodox, ordered me from the katholikon. The ecclesiastikos came to my rescue. About a half an hour later, when the ecclesiastikos was gone, the monk returned to the attack. Father David sought to answer him and soon there was a knot of five or six monks in the middle of the katholikon having a heated discussion. I thought it best during the Liturgy to stay out in the liti.

However, the sequel to this was a happy one. At Vespers the Elder insisted that I occupy the stall in church next to him, and our zealous friend came to say a few kind words with a warm smile. After supper he was even more profuse in his kindness, while still encouraging me to become Orthodox.—"Do not let the sun go down on your wrath."

⁂

Koutloumousiou is a large monastery very near Karyes, so many travelers come here. At the millennium of the founding of the monastic republic, in 1963, the civil government fixed up the guesthouse. It is large, bright, and clean, with sinks in every room and showers. Soon the dwindling community found itself almost wholly taken up with hospitality. So some slipped away to sketes, leaving only four old monks at the monastery. In response to an appeal, an Elder, Father Joseph, with his seven disciples came from their skete. One of the disciples, Father Grigorios, was elected the Hegumen since Father Joseph was not a priest. (Athonite laws require that the Hegumen be a priest.)

The community set a policy of closing the monastery gate from noon to four so the monks could have some quiet during the day and accepting only ten guests at night. They have been renovating the rest of the building—a big job—it is going to look very well. With the new young men, others are being attracted, and thus there is another promising house on the Holy Mountain.

In the courtyard there is a handsome, large holy-water fountain in a portico. At the end of Orthros, before the light of day became strong, there was a procession there, with candles and relics, to bless water for the feast. It was a very impressive ceremony.

The Protos* and Delegates came from Karyes for Vespers, and at the end there was a candle service and blessing of koliva in honor of the Radiant Light of Tabor. And another reception and festal meal. This time there were almost only monks present and it was less formal, with lots of good cheer. Before we left the trapedza* the monks were singing, finishing off the mountains of watermelon and decanters of wine, and sharing the koliva.

AROUND THE
MOUNTAIN

Chilandari

Friday, August 7

〜 I am once again on pilgrimage, it seems. I would prefer by far to stay in one place, but things are not quite working out that way. I trust that the Lord is behind it all. Maybe he is teaching me by this to love stability all the more. I do hope that when I finally get home it will be for good. I am also growing in feeling for the monastic guest and his needs. If I am ever guestmaster—and I hope the Lord spares me from that demanding service—I hope I will be a better one for having had the experience I have had as a monastic guest in so many monasteries under such diverse circumstances. After Service and Liturgy this morning we had another festive meal which was over by nine. I started out on foot for Stavronikita. The tractor and cart taking a group of visiting monks back to Philotheou passed me. I was hoping they might offer me a lift and even invite me to Philotheou, but they did not. It is a very good community but not very open to non-Orthodox.

I arrived at Stavronikita in late morning and was kindly received. Soon we were at lunch, fast-day fare, for it is the Lent of the Virgin* on Athos now.

❋

I sit in a fairly dark room with no external windows. Outside is one of the most beautiful views on Athos. Yet I prefer to be here for the moment. Perhaps it reflects more my own reality. All that beauty does tell something of God. Yet, in fact, God is nothing like it. In the darkness of my soul he dwells, and I wait for the dark ray of that resplendent Divine Light so to possess my mind that nothing else will be able to take me from his Presence. Being here a lonely wayfarer, far away from community and friends and home, among people who speak a strange language and see me as one more of a horde of not-too-welcome visitors (I paint the picture rather black), leaves me more truly in face of what life is. Settled at home in familiar surroundings, among loved ones' care, it is too easy to forget we are strangers and exiles on earth. We tend to feather our nests too comfortably and forget we are meant to be constantly flying toward the heights. Maybe this is one of the reasons our Fathers so stressed a spartan simplicity in our monasteries—the bare, impersonal accommodation that the traveler finds in a one-night stand, with no reserves in the closet to keep him grounded there. We must be constantly seeking, searching, longing for, wanting, pressing on to full possession and revelation of that which can only be possessed in this life in darkness and desire—painful but sweet and much to be desired. This darkness is more beautiful than all the glory of soaring Athos. And we can find it by simply doing as the Lord said and closing our door and being with the Father in secret. It is something we can do even in a crowded bus or in any other place that life's pilgrimage takes us, if we want. The quiet of our monastery, our monastic cell, our own room, is a blessing, but of no use unless we want to and do close the door of inner cell, too.

❄

> The soul from love of the Lord has lost her wits: she sits in silence, with no wish to speak, and looks upon the world with mazed eyes, having no desire for it and seeing it not. And people do not know that she is contemplating her beloved Lord, that the world has been left behind and is forgotten, for there is no sweetness therein. —FATHER SILOUAN

Saturday, August 8

I arose shortly after two this morning and assisted at the Service and Liturgy, which ended around six. We guests were given tea, bread, jam, and olives. Several guests and one of the novices took the early boat toward Ierissos. I was moving on to Iviron. I spoke briefly with the Hegumen, Father Vasileios. He gave me a carved icon of the Virgin as she appears on the iconostasis in the Protaton in Karyes. I asked his blessing, and as I went to kneel, he pulled me up and embraced me warmly giving me the triple kiss.

The early morning walk along the sea was good, though rugged in spots. When I reached Iviron, a group of tourists was just leaving to go up to Philotheou. At Iviron I asked to see Father Athanasios. I was informed that I could not see him until three. Indeed most of the monastery seem to have turned in for the day. The young monk offered to lock my bag away and suggested I might like to go on up to Philotheou.

The ascent of what is a fairly good road was yet quite difficult under the warm, now quite hot, sun. When I arrived at Philotheou I asked to see the Hegumen, Father Ephraim, a spiritual son of Father Joseph the Hesychast. Father Ephraim has a reputation for being one of the most skillful Fathers in leading monks into a deep experience of the Jesus Prayer. I was told that he did not leave his cell until two, so that it would be impossible to see him before that time. It was also uncertain whether he would see me even then, for he was disinclined to speak with heterodox believers. At first I thought to wait in any case, and Father Macarios, the very kind guestmaster, gave me a room in which to rest. He also provided me with a copy of *The Art of Prayer*. After about an hour he took me to see the katholikon. Philotheou is now one of the largest communities on the Holy Mountain, and the many young monks were very busy at work restoring the old monastery. The interior of the church is very rich indeed, but it would require a very sensitive skill to bring out some of the ancient beauty of the frescoes. Afterward Father Macarios gave me a very fine dinner. However, he recommended that I not wait to see Father Ephraim. Though the community is very young, it has very strong Orthodox views. Non-Orthodox are not allowed to enter the katholikon for Services but must stay out on the porch or in the liti. Father Macarios is perhaps a bit more open than most monks here, for he studied for a year on a scholarship at the American College in Thessaloniki in order to perfect his English.

As another young pilgrim was about to go down to Karakallou,* I descended to the sea with him and briefly visited the katholikon there. But as is the case in many of the monasteries, at this hottest time of the day one finds no monks abroad. I left the pilgrim there and walked back along the sea to Iviron. On the way I passed the large port which Philotheou uses to ship out its lumber. It is one of the most developed private ports in the Mountain.

When I reached Iviron I found Father Athanasios, sitting in the warm afternoon sun, at the side of the katholikon with a group of other old monks. He is quite deaf now and was not interested in trying to pursue conversation. Some of the other older monks started making fun of me because of my evident lack of success in communicating with Father Athanasios. On the whole, the welcome was not a particularly gracious one, unlike those I had experienced in almost all the other monasteries. And so I retrieved my bag from where the young monk had locked it away and went down to the pier to take the boat which was about to leave for the Megisti Lavra.

The boat was quite filled with pilgrims, priests, monks, older laymen coming to work on the Mountain, and some tourists, mostly young Germans. As we got off the boat the Greek police collected our passports and loaded us onto the back of a large truck to drive us up to the monastery. It seems that things are somewhat officially organized here because of the large number of foreign tourists, who seem to be attracted to this particular monastery so renowned for its frescoes and its library. When we arrived a monk took us in hand and guided us around the monastery. In the library we were shown a fourth-century manuscript of Saint Paul's Epistles and an almost contemporary monograph of Saint Basil's Liturgy and many other ancient texts. As it was now growing dark, it was difficult to really appreciate the rich frescoes of the katholikon and the trapedza. We all venerated the relics of Saint Athanasios, the Founder of the monastery, in the little chapel attached to the katholikon. At the end of the tour our passports were returned to us and we were taken to a basement room for a frugal supper of pasta, olives, bread, and water.

The sleeping accommodations at Megisti Lavra, in large open dormitories, are among the poorest that I have encountered on the Holy Mountain. This is undoubtedly due to the great number of people who come to the monastery. Almost every night the monks have to receive fifty to sixty new guests. They are also terribly short-handed. One young brother has to try to cope with the whole guesthouse situation by himself. He is friendly and cheerful, though, and does the best he can. The atmosphere is far from the quiet, peaceful, and prayerful atmosphere which I had encountered in Simonos Petras or Stavronikita. This is probably because the group not only includes a large number of tourists but also a good number of men who are coming to the Mountain to work. Megisti Lavra seems to be the port of entry for the workers coming to all parts of the north side of the Mountain. I tried to settle down and get some sleep but with little success.

❄

I am glad I returned to the Holy Mountain for the Feast of the Transfiguration and its octave. It is the feast for monks. And the Lord in his goodness is letting rays of that Divine Light flow gently into my soul with its painful healing and its healing pain. We monks are fools who have taken Peter's babble seriously. We are the fools who stay on the Mountain even after the Vision fades, and we have heard of crucifixion and death, even after the Apostles have descended to their important labors. We stay though others do not understand and even mock, certain that in his time, if we are really doing what we stayed to do, he who defended Mary at Bethany will speak out in our behalf.

Here on the Mountain the monks frequently read that Gospel—Mary has chosen the best part. Tabor, Athos, Mary's garden, the place for Mary's work. "He who does the will of my Father in heaven, he is my brother, my sister, *my mother*"—he is forming Christ within himself, in others, in the world, in the fullness. The period of gestation is long, quiet, sometimes painful, always exciting, if truly waiting. For hope is the vibrant, inner tension that holds us at his Feet to receive each life-bearing word that it might be seeded for eternal life. "Lord, it is good to be here"—but the here is not so much a place, even this very holy place, but a state of attentive hope filled with yearning love which is already in some way a fruition.

Sunday, August 9

☙ The semantron sounded at eleven o'clock last evening. I was happy to hear it, as it was proving a sleepless night. The Services continued until about eight o'clock this morning. Megisti Lavra is known for the length of its Services. I think the things that struck me most strongly were the noble faces of the monks, bearded, wrinkled, with bushy eyebrows, outlined in candlelight as they sang on and on, old men with strong and good voices. Opposite me there was a very old monk, who stayed the whole night in his stall praying the Jesus Prayer in a semiaudible voice. Sometimes he would stand bolt upright, other times he would hang from the arms of the stall and slip his tired feet out of his shoes and put them on the footrest, but the Prayer, the ceaseless Prayer, went on. There are relatively few

young men here, and in all it is probably a community of twenty or
so.

When we came out of the katholikon an old monk shared the
koliva with all of us with a great deal of joy and enthusiasm. In a
cenobitic monastery the community would now have gone to the
refectory for the festal meal, but since this is an idiorrhythmic community, the monks go off and eat by themselves in their cells. The
guestmaster said there would be a meal for the guests in a couple of
hours, as the boat would not be coming until noon, or even an hour
or two after that, to take us around the eastern end of the peninsula.

I was not tired after the Service. That is one of the things that has
rather surprised me here on the Mountain; the long Services seem to
have a certain rhythm to them, a time of quiet and a time of deep
prayer that renew and refresh one not only spiritually but also physically. One can come out from them without a sense of fatigue but
rather of having been well rested. So I decided not to wait for the
boat, but to walk to Kavsokalyvia. I had been told that the walk
around the end of the peninsula to the skete was beautiful. After a
couple of hours I reached the large Romanian Skete of Prodromou.*
I was told that there were ten or so monks there, although a few
younger ones have recently come from Romania. But there were
none in sight. It was that time of day when the monks are hidden
away in their cells. So after a coffee in the guesthouse, I went on toward Kavsokalyvia. An old Greek pilgrim who had been at Prodromou joined me.

To walk across the end of the peninsula is a unique experience. It
took us about six hours to reach our destination. The sun was very
hot. The way thrilling—very rugged. My shoes came completely to
pieces. We walked precariously across the face of rock slides that
plunged two or three hundred feet into the immense green and blue
sea. The water is very, very clear and its color varies, with streaks of
green running through vast pools of blue.

After we passed the roughest part we came into a region where
there are several sketes. We stopped at the first one for water and
Father Methodios welcomed us warmly. He is the old monk who
lives alone, having left one of the big monasteries because of his
health. He had an excellent vegetable garden in which he was busily
laboring when we arrived. He brought us, besides fresh, cool, clear
water from his spring, some fresh figs from one of his trees—very

sweet. Athos is, indeed, at this time of the year, a bit of paradise—everywhere there are trees of olives and figs, apples and peaches, vines of grapes and berries, and all sorts of vegetables in the gardens. Father Methodios had a great smile, showing only one upper tooth and one lower (not meeting). He showed us his chapel and climbed up to take down from a shelf the skulls of his three predecessors in this skete, including his Spiritual Father, Methodios the Senior. Father had come to the Mountain in 1931. As my companion lit a cigarette, Father Methodios indicated he would enjoy a smoke, too. As we parted, a supply of cigarettes was left with him as well as a small offering.

We went on to the next skete where we also made a brief visit. Father Nectarios was the senior priest there. He went about getting things for us, while his disciple, Father Joachim, a younger monk, chatted with us on a delightful terrace that looked out over the sea. My good companion and he talked about Catholics and had a friendly argument. It seemed that the old pilgrim was trying to get the monks to challenge this Catholic monk. But my kind hosts were only for showing kindness. We were served water, ouzo, and peaches and figs from the trees.

As we started off again, my Greek companion excused himself and went on alone—I think he was embarrassed to find himself with a Catholic and a little chagrined at what had taken place at the last skete. But when I arrived at Kavsokalyvia, I found him again on the path because he had lost his way and arrived at precisely the same moment as myself.

I asked for Father Antonios, about whom I had heard a great deal. As it turned out, he and his companion, Father John, were functioning as guestmasters this year. Father Antonios speaks very good English and is known for his open heart and open mind. Father John has been on the Holy Mountain for fifty-three years, since he was fourteen years of age; Father Antonios, for thirty-five years. They have never left the Holy Mountain. Father Antonios kept exclaiming how happy they were, and he radiated that happiness indeed. They gave us a very good supper during which my traveling companion got into conversation about Catholics again. Father Antonios asserted that Catholics, Orthodox, Protestants—we were all the same, all Christians. Holy families, he said, are formed everywhere. He is truly Christlike in his love and joy, but, I must say, known to be something of an exception on the Mountain in his openness to non-Orthodox Christians.

There are about forty houses in this skete and about only forty-five monks now. The Services are celebrated in the chapel of each house. On Saturday and Sunday and feasts the monks come together for the Liturgy in the kyriakon.* On a great feast they have an All-Night Vigil together there. In various households there are icon painters and wood carvers. Each house has its own garden. The monks take turns caring for the guests. The others help support the guestmasters and pray for them, since there are no Services in the guesthouse.

Kavsokalyvia is a very peaceful and remote spot. The monks here seem to appreciate that peace as giving them a good opportunity to live a deeper life of prayer.

❋

If you would retain prayer you must love those who offend against you and pray for them until your soul is reconciled with them, and then the Lord will give you prayer without ceasing, for he gives prayer to those who pray for their enemies. The man who loves his enemies soon comes to know the Lord in the Holy Spirit. But the man who does not love his enemies is to be pitied, for he is a torment to himself and to others and does not know the Lord.

— FATHER SILOUAN

❋

A monk is a man who is separated from all and who is in harmony with all.

A monk is a man who considers himself one with all men because he constantly sees himself in every man. — EVAGRIUS PONTICUS

Monday, August 10

During the night it began to rain. The sea is very rough. There will probably be no boats today. It is cold and I have caught a cold. There is, of course, no heat or electricity, nor hot water. The open dorms are primitive—no sheets or else very soiled ones.

We rose late (that is, in comparison to what I have ordinarily been doing) and then I went down to Father Antonios' house where he and Father John paint icons. Father said he would send me an icon of the Holy Mother of God and also one of the Christ of Daphni for our Byzantine chapel in Spencer. He gave me gifts of incense, pictures of icons he has painted, beads and crosses. He also gave me gifts to bring back to Father George Maloney at the Russian Center at Fordham, whom he considers his very good friend. We all went together then back up to the guesthouse where Father Antonios prepared a very good meal for me before I started off over the Mountain to the Skete of Aghia Anna.

It was quite a climb, but very beautiful. My shoes had been badly damaged yesterday so I was now wearing sandals, but it seemed to work out fairly well. The rain had cooled things off and much of the inland path which I had chosen was shaded by large trees. I arrived at Aghia Anna in early afternoon.

The welcome was warm and hearty and the usual refreshments were quickly served. Leaving my bag at the guesthouse, I made my way up to the house of Father Theodoretos. Father Kallistos Ware had spoken of him as a "courteous zealot." He lives in the house with his Elder. The two of them make incense in order to support themselves. Father Theodoretos told me that fifteen of the sixty houses in the skete are zealot and that the monks in those households do not go to the kyriakon to celebrate the Liturgy with the others, but gather for their own Liturgy in one of the zealot households. There are in all about eighty-five monks in the skete. We discussed Church unity for which Father Theodoretos, as a well informed theologian, has a very true concern. He is convinced the way to unity is by all of us returning to the true sources. We touched on pluralism, which was an idea foreign to him but recognized in the Eastern Churches up to a point. We spoke also of the need of patriarchates in the New World. It was, all in all, a very pleasant visit and I departed with a gift of some of his incense.

I then went down to the house of Father Ilios. A very happy monk guided me down, Father Klimes. He had been in the Greek Army fighting the Communist guerrillas in 1948 when all but two of the sixty in his company were killed in an ambush. He then left immediately for Athos. He told me other stories of his earlier life and of many favors that had been granted him through Saint Anne. We found Father Ilios was not at home, and so we walked back to the guesthouse, past a house and chapel built by a Patriarch who retired to this skete in the eighteenth century. The guestmaster gave me a bed, apologizing for such a poor accommodation, saying that he was not able to do better because of the many guests. The boats had stopped running because of the weather and many from different parts of this end of the Mountain had hiked to the skete in order to get the early morning boat. We had a very substantial supper of pasta with some shellfish, bread, and water. After supper the guestmaster gave me a very beautiful carved cross done by Father Paul of Kavsokalyvia. The universal love and primacy of love radiating from Father Antonios remain with me as the strongest impressions of the day.

❈

Grace hides its presence within the baptized, waiting for the soul's desire. When the whole man turns himself wholly to the Lord, then in an inutterable experience he reveals his Presence in the heart. . . .

❈

When we close every outlet to the mind by the recollection of God, it imperiously demands something to satisfy its need of activity. We must then give it the Lord Jesus, as the sole occupation that fully answers its need. . . . — DIADOCHUS OF PHOTICE

Tuesday, August 11

꙰ I arose around four this morning, washed, and prayed by myself on the terrace, since there are no Services available to the guests in the sketes. At six the guestmaster took me to the kyriakon to venerate the icon of Saint Anne. Saint Anne has always been someone very special in my life. When I was searching to know my vocation, I went on a pilgrimage to her shrine at Sainte Anne de Beaupré in Canada where they have a major relic of her. In a singular way, my vocation was made clear. And by those strange and wonderful ways of Providence, Saint Anne's instrumentality in my vocation was made manifest when three years later I was called to make my profession on her feast. On that day Abbot Edmund told me to pray constantly to Saint Anne that I might be faithful to prayer and the interior life. And through the years I have tried to do that. At Spencer we have in the transept an altar dedicated to Saint Anne, which I pass many times a day as I go in and out of the church. That is the time when I again and again commend myself to her maternal care. As I venerated the ancient and beautiful icon of the Holy Mother of the Mother of God today at Aghia Anna, I renewed my commitment to a life of prayer and interiority.

❋

The guests were served some coffee and then made the difficult descent to the pier to get the seven o'clock boat. I got off at Dionysiou taking the opportunity to finally visit the monastery about which Father Maximos spoke so highly.

The welcome which I received certainly did not belie the claims of Father Maximos at Simonos Petras. The Liturgy was being celebrated in a small chapel and I joined the monks there. It was truly a beautiful Service, led by a very old monk with a great long white beard. There was something transcendent about him as he prayed before the icon of Christ. We then went to the refectory and had a very good meal with the monks. There is something quite different in a well-run and fervent cenobitic monastery from what one finds in idiorrhythmic monasteries and even in the sketes.

The guestmaster assigned all the guests rooms. Then I was invited by three young Greeks to go with them to visit the nearby Monastery of Aghiou Pavlou. There an old monk welcomed us at the gate while we enjoyed their water and the purple grapes that hung in great clusters from the arbors over the entranceway. Up in the guesthouse Father Theodoros, a monk from Jordanville,* served us the usual refreshments. He then arranged for us to see the katholikon and venerate the relics. However, one of the priests came along and said as a heretic I could not go into the holy place and venerate the relics with the others. But Father Paul, a bright, smiling, friendly young monk, who had charge of the relics, said he would bring them out so that I could venerate them there and he brought out one after the other: the leg and the foot of Saint Gregory the Theologian, a large relic of Saint Basil, and many others.

Before leaving Aghiou Pavlou we chatted with the old monk at the gate. He had been a soldier in a military revolt in 1936, and when it failed, he came to Mount Athos. He spoke of Christ and the devil and of Mary of the Desert, of the Deifying Light and evil worldly entertainment. I think he would have happily gone on sharing with us for the rest of the day, if we did not have to break away to get back to Dionysiou. We helped ourselves to more of the monastery's wonderful grapes and made our way over the rugged but beautiful trail along the sea.

There is a fine group of young monks at Dionysiou under the guidance of a magnificent Spiritual Father who has served the community in this capacity for nearly forty years. Father Gabriel first came to the Holy Mountain in 1908. He is very strong in his Orthodoxy and deep in his spirituality and has tried to share this more widely through the publication of a small magazine.

The Vespers were very well chanted and were followed by an excellent meal. After supper the guests were taken to the library to see some of their manuscripts. The oldest was a sixth-century Gospel of Saint Luke. There was a very old scroll of the Liturgy of Saint Basil and some beautiful manuscripts from the thirteenth and fourteenth centuries and some incunabula. In all, they possess over nine hundred manuscripts and the Golden Bull by which the monastery was constituted in 1375 by Alexis Comnenus III, Emperor of Trebizond.

I asked to speak with Father Gabriel but was told that he was away at Thessaloniki. The monks were very friendly and showed a certain reverence toward me as a hieromonk—but some of them, as is frequently the case, kind of froze when they discovered I was a Catholic. I am usually initially taken to be Orthodox because I venerate the icons, and the monks somehow think this is something which Catholics would not do.

There are about thirty-five monks at Dionysiou and also at Aghiou Pavlou. Father Andreas is the Hegumen at Aghiou Pavlou; he is also Spiritual Father of some of the monks there, but others look to Father Joseph in New Skete, which belongs to Aghiou Pavlou.

❄

By waiting and by calm you shall be
    saved,
    in quiet and in trust your strength
    lies.
But this you did not wish.
            — ISAIAH 30:15

✿

I have to really want God, union with him in Christ, and nothing
else—otherwise, my heart is divided and my attention is drawn off in
pursuit of other things. Not even "for his sake" can I pursue other
things, until he truly indicates he wants them; then, by his grace, the
effort and concern spent on them are wholly integrated into my pursuit of him, a part of my union with him. This is purity of heart.
This is being *monos*—a monk, one-minded.

Can I accept this—to let everything go and walk in the full freedom of obedience? At Liturgy the Lord said:

> "Not every one can accept this teaching, only those to whom it is
> given to do so. . . . Let him accept this teaching who can."
>   — MATTHEW 19:11, 12

At Sext:

> "Anyone who hears my words and puts them into practice is like
> the wise man who built his house on rock." — MATTHEW 7:24

At None:

> The Lord withholds no good thing
>   from those who walk in sincerity.
> O Lord of hosts,
>   happy the men who trust in you!
>   — PSALM 84:12–13

✿

Lord, thank you for this light, grace, invitation, freedom. I need
seek nothing but you and all else will follow.

Wednesday, August 12

🙖 The Midnight Service started about two this morning and
concluded with Orthros at about four-thirty. In this monastery they
have a rather long break after Orthros and did not begin Liturgy
until seven. They served coffee to the guests a little after six and then
we went down to get the boat to Daphni. At Daphni I took the bus
up to Karyes and then started to walk down to the north side of the
Mountain. As I went along I was joined by Father Nikodimos, a

young novice, recently converted from a worldly life and full of enthusiasm. He has been on the Mountain for a year and a half and lives in a kellion at Karyes. He is an icon painter and said he would send me some icons. He emphasized strongly the primacy of love. And, while he was sure of some Catholic errors such as papal infallibility and Baptism by pouring, he believed if we really live a spiritual life we will all be saved and come to the truth.

I got the 9:45 boat at the arsenas of Zographou and walked up to the monastery. It was an easy walk of forty-five minutes or so. The young brother in the guesthouse welcomed me with great kindness and served me dinner immediately (bean soup, tomatoes, bread, and water).

As I sat down to my meal he asked me again: "Are you not a Catholic?" When I told him I was, he said to me with some surprise: "Then how is it that you make the Sign of the Cross the Orthodox way?" As he understood it, Catholics always make the Sign of the Cross with four fingers because they believe there are four persons in the Trinity. I have heard this before in connection with the controversy concerning the *Filioque*. It seems that, according to some of the Greek theologians, when the Western Christians postulate that the Holy Spirit proceeds from the Father and the Son as a common principle, they then affirm the existence of a fourth person in the Trinity, the common principle of the Holy Spirit. I am sure this very simple brother was not too conversant with the theology behind it but only knew the commonly held ideas about what Catholics believe.

As I continued my meal, he set about making a komvoschinion. One of our brothers at home had asked me to learn how to make such a prayer cord. But as I watched the brother making the intricate knots, I quite readily conceded that it was something beyond what I could learn with a simple lesson. There are twenty-one knots within each knot on the cord and these are done by rather intricately working the black wool around three fingers and finally using a pick to bring them into a solid little knot.

After lunch I found that the sacristan, another quite young monk, was working in the katholikon. And so I had an opportunity to venerate the icons and see the beautiful frescoes. This is a Bulgarian monastery and the number of monks is rapidly diminishing. Yet it has a reputation for being a fervent community, with a good Hegumen.

After the brief visit to the katholikon, I continued on my way toward Chilandari.

※

Chilandari is something different. You can tell it as you approach the monastery, walking along a gravel road with fields on each side enclosed with barbed wire on cement posts. The flavor here is very different from that of the rest of the Mountain. Nearest to the mainland, it is most influenced by it. The clock in the guesthouse not only works but also tells civil time. And right next to it is a mailbox. Chilandari also had a phone to the mainland long before the other monasteries. It has a good fire-protection system and an installation all ready for the coming electricity. Extensive renovation is going on. Usually the monastery has few guests as it is somewhat inaccessible, but at the moment there is a pilgrim group from Yugoslavia present. It was an idiorrhythmic community until very recently, but always fervent and doing the Services very well. There are young monks here and the welcome is warm and gracious.

※

Bishop Germanos, from the patriarchate of Constantinople, is here also, having come after presiding at the Feast of the Transfiguration at Pantokratoros. I had lunch with him and the Pro-Hegumen,* Father Nicanor. Before lunch I had talked awhile with the Bishop. He is exceedingly simple and genteel. He struggled to use what little English he has. In 1967 he spent four months with the Franciscans in London and then six months in Oxford at Saint Stephen's House taking some special courses to learn English. There was a certain pathos as he told me: "I did the three courses: beginners, intermediate, proficient. But I passed only the first and got the certificate. I did not pass the other two nor get the certificates. If I had passed them, I would do the English correspondence for the Patriarch."

The Bishop must have been in his late forties or early fifties when he went to England to learn English so he could do the Patriarch's correspondence. I tried to imagine what those months of fruitless study and the return to Constantinople, a failure, must have cost him. Yet we see, I am sure, some of the fruit of it in the humble gentleness and joy which so marks this Bishop. How different his life and his growth in Christ might have been if he had succeeded. The Lord is behind our failures, to make them his kind of success. Ever at the heart's center of Christianity is a cross, a Crucified, a failure, who alone is the truly successful One, and in his success, we all can know success, even when we continually fail miserably.

I am fortunate in being here with these pilgrims. They are a group of workers who formed a choir in Yugoslavia to sing in church on Sundays and feasts. Their singing is magnificent—worthy of the katholikon here, which is one of the largest on Athos—full of light, wonderfully fresh frescoes, good icons, and much gilt work. After the late lunch the group feted us with a repertoire of Serbian folk songs.

I spoke for a while with a monk here, Father Ananias, who left Yugoslavia in 1945 at the time of the Communist takeover and spent ten years in England before coming to the Holy Mountain. Then I spoke with Father Gabriel, here five years from Yugoslavia; he has a good sense of humor. (All the monks here are friendly and cheerful. They return from time to time to Yugoslavia for visits.)

Father Chrysostomos, who speaks excellent English, took me through the new fireproof library building where the collection of icons, manuscripts, and old printed books are well presented. There are twelve hundred manuscripts and five thousand old books, mostly liturgical, Scripture, and patristic. It is a model for Mount Athos, though it will be even better when the monastery gets electricity. There are special places for scholars to work and the monks here welcome them when they come to the Holy Mountain. It is here that Father Kallistos Ware, Professor Sherrard, and G. E. H. Palmer are doing the work on the new edition and translation of the *Philokalia*.

The Orthodox Serbs are very ecumenical. Along with the Catholic Serbs, they knew five centuries of "slavery" (as they put it) under the Turks. But they enjoy religious freedom now. They have all the priests they need in Yugoslavia, and if the monasteries are not getting vocations, it is not because of oppression by the Yugoslav government but lack of attraction for the young.

The food at Chilandari is abundant and well prepared. One is constantly offered more. Unlike other cenobia the guests eat in a separate refectory above the monks. And the Pro-Hegumen eats with the guests. At supper he presided, as the Bishop had left. He toasted "all

our American friends" and "that we might all be one in faith, as
Christ wanted—one in the face of the enemies of Christ."

Thursday, August 13

☙ I have passed many hours in the katholikon in the long
Services and quiet hours in my room trying to pray. I ask myself,
what is it all about? What can a poor little creature say or do before
God? I feel so trapped in myself. I want to go out of myself and be
centered in God. But this is ecstasy—his gift. I can only lean towards
him in desire and love. And this, too, is gift. If I can only transcend
all the pulls of passion and sense and even intellect—and be to him.
I find a great desire in myself to have clear ideas and insights, to experience in some sensible or conceptual way strong convictions of
conversion towards him. But, in fact, it is much more subtle than
that. That is still seeking self—wanting the satisfaction of knowing
that I am making progress or accomplishing something. Instead, it is
more a quiet "leaning," which gradually sets the direction—as trees
are shaped and bent by prevailing winds—until all is toward him
even in the midst of doings and sharings and weary being. May the
Lord be the "north" of my compass needle and exercise a constant
force upon me until I rest constantly at "N."

It rained all night with much lightning and it continues today.
The pilgrims sang Liturgy and then left for the early boat, after
lighting many candles and taking bottles of holy water.

✲

A young German student, Wolfgang, came late last night. We
talked for some time and climbed to the top of the tower. Then we
visited with different monks from Yugoslavia. Father Justin, the
baker, and Father Simon both came here via France. Father Symeon,
one of the council of Elders, came in 1957 with Father Arsenias
from England, where they had taken refuge after fighting the Communists. Father Symeon is in charge of the vineyards and wine cellars. He took us down to his cellars and plied us with his good wine.
He hopes it will be stronger next year, but already it is strong enough
and very clear—a good wine. He told us that one monk still smokes

and eats meat but that the rest have entered into the cenobitic way
of life. He asked Father Nicanor two days ago if he could buy a gun
for birding. When Chilandari was an idiorrhythmic monastery, the
monks had been given money each year to buy clothes, but Father
Symeon did not like to spend that much on clothes and so he had
been saving up. He would like to get a gun now so he can shoot the
birds who are eating his grapes and then roast and eat the birds. The
Father declined to give him this permission.

Friday, August 14

꿈 I sit on the pier at Esphigmenou awaiting the boat. My experiences here are, I think, somewhat illustrative of how much work
lies ahead in the ecumenical movement.

This morning, at Chilandari, I arose at four and prayed the Mass
for all on the Holy Mountain and all who have made it possible for
me to be here. I went to the katholikon then, for part of the Service.
As soon as Father opened the gates I set out by the light of a full
moon down to Esphigmenou. It was an easy fifty-minute walk. As I
arrived at the monastery the semantron and bells were announcing
the Liturgy. I went into the katholikon, venerated the icons, and settled quietly in a stall in the corner to pray. Several monks eyed me
suspiciously and finally the guestmaster came up to me and asked
where I was from. Then, if I was Orthodox. When I said I was a
Catholic, he politely invited me to the guesthouse for coffee. First,
however, he found an English-speaking monk who explained that I
could not be in the katholikon during Liturgy but that after two
hours I could come in and they would show me everything. I explained that I had hoped to get the early boat to Vatopedi. I was
told that I could go into the porch and see the katholikon from
there. We then went up to the guesthouse. The guestmaster served
coffee with the traditional sweets and ouzo. He told me the boat
time and indicated the pier, saying I was welcome to wait for the
boat in the guesthouse.

Later Father Michael came in; he is a law student who has been
here only three months but is already tonsured. He spoke English
quite well. He took me over to see the katholikon. The narthex is

separated from the nave only by two columns so that the church seems like a very large one. It was frescoed two centuries ago and is very bright. The iconostasis, carved by Russian monks, is very elaborate, with miniature biblical scenes worked in among vines.

I went down to the pier, picking some grapes from the trellis over the path. The sun was rising over the rocks that jutted into the sea, pinking the clouds in the east, and the dark thunderheads that had dampened the night receded to the west.

The sea is calm so the boat should have no difficulty picking me up. It is very cool. I have two shirts and a jacket on. As I sit here, I keep one eye, all the time it seems, on the headland around which the boat is due to come. That is the way life should be. Sharing in the unfolding of creation, for he made us to be part of it—its groaning for salvation and its joy in reflecting his love, joy, and beauty—yet always with an eye for the coming of the Lord. The sun is topping the watery horizon, a dull orb of fire through the haze, and the boat is rounding the cape and heading into the pier.

The passage to Vatopedi was a pleasant one on a rolling sea. Vatopedi is said to be the most beautiful monastery on the Mountain. It is large in area, second only to Megisti Lavra. The katholikon is very rich, with marble, ivory inlays in the wood, excellent icons, and many chapels. It is a wealthy monastery and the port is busy with ships loading lumber. There are about thirty-five monks in the community. It is idiorrhythmic and one of the more relaxed houses on the Mountain. The guesthouse has been redone very tastefully—quite modern. Vatopedi has the only functioning electrical system on the Mountain and its generator can be heard at night for great distances.

It is amazing to watch the workers loading lumber. After weighing each log, they carry them, one by one, to a rowboat. When about twenty are laid across it, it is rowed out to a ship and the wood is hoisted by hand with pulleys into the hold.

After a few hours of quiet prayer at Vatopedi, I took the afternoon boat back to the arsenas of Chilandari, passing en route the port of

Esphigmenou. A black flag flies from the tower of the monastery there, and on the wall is a large sign:

ΟΡΘΟΔΟΞΙΑ Η ΘΑΝΑΤΟΣ

"Orthodoxy or death." For the monks of Esphigmenou have joined the schismatic church of Greece, the Old Calendarists. Actually, all the Holy Mountain uses the old calendar and it is not a cause of schism. But this community is radically zealot and broke communion with the present Patriarch of Constantinople and the other monasteries when Demetrios addressed Rome, acknowledging the See of Peter as "first among equals."

Chilandari is certainly very different from Esphigmenou. Many pilgrims come here from Yugoslavia, bypassing the regular port of entry. There is a certain spirit here of openness to the rest of the world.

As I walked along the pleasant road from the arsenas up to the monastery, I passed into the woods and came upon a monk having a quiet smoke. There is a good bit of smoking in the idiorrhythmic houses, I am told. But even in the most fervent cenobia there are individual monks who smoke more or less on the quiet. Tobacco seems to be able to get a hold everywhere.

Saturday, August 15 / 28

꙳ Rain returned during the night. After Liturgy and coffee I started back down toward the arsenas with three Serbian Yugoslavs. As it was still raining hard, a monk asked a lay helper to drive us down. We waited over an hour for the boat to take us to Ierissos. The sea was so rough that the monk at the arsenas did not expect it to come. Afterward I was wishing it had not come. The tiny cabin was filled with diesel fumes and wet humans. I soon felt very ill and had to go up on deck. There, in the pelting rain and salty spray which sometimes became full waves over the deck, hanging on desperately to the very low guardrail, I felt my stomach churn as wildly as the sea as the little boat plunged over the mounting waves! An hour or more of this left us at Ierissos, feeling, at least myself, like drowned rats. I kind of got an idea of the feeling Pope Paul was expressing when he said he felt as if Peter's bark was again in the midst of the storm at sea. It is an experience I do not think I would care to repeat.

The bus ride to Thessaloniki—when I finally managed to get a bus —had its adventures, too. As the bus climbed into the mountains, we found ourselves in clouds as well as in driving rain. Soon we came upon a large trailer truck full of sand that had slipped off the road and toppled over. On most of the road there was no shoulder or guardrail along the edge—only a sheer drop. This truck was lucky in that it slipped over where the incline was not too steep and the front hung on to the road. Of course, the bus stopped and everybody got out to see. About an hour later, on a steep upgrade, we came upon a car that had gone off the road on the uphill side and was wedged in a water gully. Two bewildered women sat in the front seat. Our good Samaritan driver stopped and ordered all the able-bodied men out. Soon the ladies were back on the road pointed toward Thessaloniki.

We finally arrived ourselves. At the bus terminal a young English-Greek—Stephanos Phillips—introduced himself. He had come all the way from Athens, only to learn at Ouranoupolis that because he was an English citizen he could not go right out onto the Mountain like the Greeks. In response to a request from the Holy Community, the civil government in Thessaloniki is now giving only ten aliens a day permission to go out to the Mountain, each for only four days. Those with good reasons can easily get this time extended once they get there. Many foreigners arriving in Thessaloniki are informed that they will have to wait some days before they can go out. Last year there were very many young foreigners on the Mountain—many unfortunately merely as tourists and vacationers. This year the number of visitors has not lessened, but they are largely young Greeks who are finding new interest in the Holy Mountain. There are also young Orthodox converts from the West, especially from the Synod.

❈

The three Yugoslavians who were with me on the boat are brothers. One is a civil engineer, another a designer of metal-sculp-

ture water fountains, the third, Radomir Gajkobic, is a contractor
working for the Belgrade government in foreign-aid projects in Asia
and Africa. A fourth, older, brother (at home) is studying for his
doctorate, specializing in medieval arched bridges. Radomir had
studied English literature and planned to teach, but teachers are
poorly paid in Yugoslavia, so he went into economics. Most young
Slavs today, he says, learn and speak English.

Radomir tried to help me understand the situation in Yugoslavia.
The population is made up of six different peoples. Of the three
most important groups, the Serbs are mostly Orthodox, the Slovenes
and Croats mostly Catholic. There are also a couple of million
Moslems throughout the country, mostly descended from the converts made during five centuries of Islamic domination. There has
tended to be some rivalry among the different peoples.

During World War II the Chetniks, who identified with the King
and Orthodoxy, generally hid in the forest awaiting Allied help
against the Nazi occupiers. The Partisans, under Tito, were Com-
munist-led and gathered all the others in the resistance for all-out
war against the Germans. In the end, the Chetniks fought arm in
arm, according to Radomir, with the Germans against their brother
Yugoslavs, opposing the Partisans as Communists, though in fact the
Partisans were only a partially Communist group. The Germans
were finally expelled, the Chetniks were killed or went into exile
(some of them are monks now at Chilandari and dream of the return of the King), and the Partisans, and Tito, took over. The Communists maintain control of Yugoslavia, with a one-party system, and
all high governmental posts are reserved to party members. But on
the whole, the people are free to practice the religion of their choice
and pursue their desired way of life. For the first time in the region's
long history, the people have had thirty years of continuous peace.
The people are enjoying a new prosperity and identity as a nation.
The devout Orthodox Christians I met on the Mountain certainly
felt that Communism à la Tito was a benign dictatorship, good for
their people.

❈

This tour of mine around the Mountain has been a rather exhausting experience but on the whole a good one. I hope the conversations and contacts I've made have eased some prejudice. We have

reached the point where most of the monks on the Mountain (unfortunately not all) are courteous to Catholics. Some go further, much further, others not so far. Fluency in the native languages of the different monks, which I didn't have, would have been a great asset for me. But love, reverence, friendliness speak without words. For such moving about the Mountain I would certainly recommend as little baggage as possible and good strong shoes. There is no need to carry food with one, as was suggested to me by some other monks from the West who had visited the Mountain, especially this time of the year. And little money is needed; a few coins to buy candles and souvenirs.

This might be a good moment for me to take stock a bit of the experience as a whole. What have I learned? Certainly, a strong appreciation of tradition, especially monastic tradition; the need of involving the body and senses in prayer, both alone in the cell (the use of prostrations) and in the Liturgy (prostrations, kissing icons and relics, incense—incensing of each at the beginning of the Service is very good—the odor filling one helps to raise one to the new level of worship and prayer); a stronger resolve toward constant prayer; more use of the early monastic Fathers in *lectio*; what true monastic hospitality can be and can mean—the effects of this on all sorts of people; the value of joy and warm smiles; the great need of Spiritual Fathers; the importance of milieu, "climate," setting for monastic life; practical advice on prayer, *lectio*, monastic attitudes.

I thank you, Lord, for these days and all they have brought. May you be praised and blessed forever.

NOTE: At this time, with the blessing of Archimandrite Aimilianos, as mentioned above, I went south and visited the monastery on the Island of Patmos. This journal resumes at Ouranoupolis on the eve of my return to the Holy Mountain.

LAST DAYS ON THE MOUNTAIN

Dionysiou

Thursday, September 16 / 3

☙ I rose around 5:30, celebrated Mass in my room, and went over to Mrs. Loch's for breakfast. Then I got the 7:45 boat to Daphni. Father Amphilochios was there with the Land-Rover from Simonos Petras and we reached the monastery before eleven. And I am now settled back in the same old cell again. It feels good to be settled in. I hope to make the most of these remaining days, renewing my vows on the eighth and entering into the mystery of the Cross.

What does this retreat mean?

It means more time for reading Scripture, for *lectio*, for prayer, for limiting creative work; apart from that, it is the regular monastic life, with a certain freedom from the responsibilities in community which I usually have and a freedom for the most part from correspondence.

What do I hope to get?

Deeper, fuller conversion; more experience of Jesus in the Father and the Spirit; the insight I need to effectively love fasting; insight for other virtues, especially humility; better control over thoughts and imagination.

That is a lot of needs for a little time.

❈

How do I feel about the months gone by? I could have used some, maybe much, of the time better. It is difficult to know. The good seed grows imperceptibly. I have tried to be open and to pray constantly. I do not think I have consciously said "No" to anything I perceived being asked by the Lord. But I have not asked with enough insistence, I have not been a pesty widow (Luke 18).

I have not been getting any great lights or having particularly beautiful thoughts. But that is probably the way it should be. It is better to abide quietly with the Lord and enjoy his Presence than to be thinking beautiful thoughts about him. From this quiet love experience comes the desire and the strength to seek ever deeper union, greater purity, more oneness with God.

As I traveled I regretted that I had not taken past opportunities to learn Italian, Greek, and Spanish better. It is too late now. My time is committed to other things. The important thing is not to neglect the opportunity to become a saint. That is more the Lord's doings. But I tend to think up my own programs and get rather attached to them, rather than letting him work his way. This is the delicate area of freedom, purity, and discernment.

He . . . has put the timeless in their hearts . . .
— ECCLESIASTES 3:11

Avoid such godless chatter, for it will lead people into more and more ungodliness, and their talk will eat its way like gangrene.
— 2 TIMOTHY 2:16, 17

Abbot Thomas has written that my article on Centering Prayer was "warmly received." The editor of *Review for Religious* asked permission to reprint it as a separate brochure. I should feel good about that. And in a way I do. But there is no temptation to pride. Standing before God in prayer I get a glimpse of the reality. To speak of being a "vile" sinner sounds a bit pietistic, but it is hard to find any other expression of the reality that approaches adequacy. So when something good does emerge from my doing, I can only wonder at the goodness and humility of our God, that he deigns in some way to use, in his beautiful work of healing and saving the broken, such a disgusting sinner. His love is quite incomprehensible—his choices, his fidelity, his respect for the freedom and person he has given. He even allows us our degrading and shameful actions, which must be to him not only offensive but, anthropomorphically at least, painful, because he does love us and does not like to see us demeaning and frustrating ourselves so by our shortsighted, selfish grasping at passing satisfactions and pleasures.

❄

O Lord, our Lord . . .
What is man that you should be mindful of him,
    or the son of man that you should care for him?
You have made him little less than the angels,
    and crowned him with glory and honor.
You have given him rule over the works of your hands,
    putting all things under his feet . . .
                       — Psalm 8:1, 5

And yet see how he acts! Lord, be merciful to me a sinner.

Friday, September 4

☙ With this retreat has come the insight and will to act more effectively for the control of thoughts and purity of heart. Thank you, Lord. It seems strange now that the same "insight" and will was not previously present in me. It underlies the mystery of his grace and my weakness of mind and will coming from sin—original and personal. What before was perceived in a sort of vague way as not being all that it should be, but not clearly seen as something that should be effectively excluded, with the coming of grace is seen as wrong, contrary to what I really want, and is excluded with relative ease. Yet, with a clear consciousness that it is so by his grace, that without grace it would be as before, I would be letting these thoughts, this pesty swarm of flies, as William of Saint Thierry calls them, spoil the sweetness of the ointment, the devotion of mind and heart. How completely we are dependent on the coming and abiding presence of his grace.

Saturday, September 5

☙ At Vespers yesterday Father Kyrikos was deacon, at Apodeipnon Father Tikon was priest, and at Liturgy Father Serapion concelebrated with the Gerontas and gave Communion with the Elder watching over his shoulder. Fathers Kyrikos, Tikon, and Serapion were ordained last week, with Father Myron and Father Me-

trophanes, the deacon at Ormilia. It seems a bit strange to a Westerner how the Spiritual Father simply calls men to Orders without
any special preparation and sometimes without any more warning
than the few days necessary for the preparatory fast. For the most
part, their ministry will be restricted to liturgical duties. Their life,
apart from the time they are functioning in the Services, goes on exactly as before. Few of them will be called to be Confessors or Spiritual Fathers. For that ministry, they will depend more on what they
have learned from monastic living, *lectio divina*, and prayer. So, little
account is given to academic preparation for Orders. When I
discussed the question with the monks, they found it difficult to understand our courses in pastoral theology at Spencer. In practice, all
monks at this particular monastery who are capable of it and want to
can study theology at the university in Thessaloniki or Athens, and a
couple have studied abroad.

Last evening, when I was sitting on my favorite rock up on the
crest, looking at Athos' peak in the setting sun, I asked the Lord,
"What do you want to say to me this evening?" He seemed to say,
"You already have all the answers." And that is true in a very real
sense. For we have Christ. And he is the Way, the Truth, and the
Life. He gives us understanding of the Answer as we need it—
sufficient for the day, not overburdening us. And so we move quietly
on. What we do need is that kind of love experience that will trans-
form and motivate us to seek, to be attentive, to be receptive, and to
follow unhesitatingly. Love-knowledge, not brilliant concepts or
flashy ideas.

After supper I spoke with Father Dionysios and the Hegumen for
a while. The Hegumen spoke of his memories of Father Amphilochios, the Spiritual Father of Patmos, a man who deeply imbibed the
spirit of Saint John. Father Amphilochios was totally responsive to
whoever came, asserting that we all serve the one Lord Jesus in each
other and that each one works his own way out with Jesus.

The Hegumen and Father Dionysios have plane reservations to fly
to Constantinople on the twenty-ninth of September. Because
Greece and Turkey have suspended airplane operations between

their two countries, it is difficult to get any. They will take Air France to Belgrade and then to Constantinople. But they have not yet gotten visas.

❊

Acquire interior peace and a thousand souls around you will find their fulfillment. — SAINT SERAPHIM OF SAROV

❊

Isaiah says: "The idols will perish forever" (2:18). Lord, grant that all the idols in my life perish, and without delay, and forever. Especially idols of my own image before men. Let me simply be before you in all nakedness and simplicity, and let men see what they will, and say what they will, and think what they will. Help me to be myself, go my own way—the way you beckon. As Dom Déchanet has put it, "Accept then to be yourself, to be 'other' than the others." And he knowingly adds, "It is difficult."

Sunday, September 6

After Liturgy I met Dimitrius, a musicologist from the University of British Columbia, an old friend of the community here, who will be with us until Wednesday. He told me that Father John, the deacon, and two others had arrived on the Holy Mountain from Jordanville, to spend a year at the Skete of Propheti Iliou.

❊

While Bishop Gerasimos (who has retired to Athens from his see in Detroit) was here for the ordinations, the Hegumen tonsured Charalambos, the senior novice, giving him the name Gerasimos. Gerasimos then went off to Athens to see his family.

❊

It seems hard, and very tragic, to believe in this atmosphere that many, perhaps the majority of men and women go through the day without any thought at all of God, pursuing short-range goals, seeking ephemeral happiness, with no notion of where their true happiness and the meaning of their lives lie. Anyone who is close to Christ suffers from this realization and agonizes with him over their awakening and redemption. Even for those who, by his grace, do know, often the "fascination of trifles obscures the good." But at least, by his grace, we turn and turn again, albeit weakly, toward him and life's goal, and lite for us has some ultimate meaning—something we are eager to share with all our brothers and sisters, children of the one Father in heaven.

Lord, give me a very soft, warm, human heart that can gently and lovingly receive the impression of all who come and give them a place of secure rest, yet an exquisitely pure heart that, even in such an embrace, will not be tainted in any way that would make it unworthy of receiving you. For it is you I would receive in each. Not that I would in any way want a pharisaical purity—and I am painfully aware of my own real impurities and of my potential to make all impurities my own. But may I be an instrument of your great love to purify and uplift even as I receive and console.

I am impressed by the simple grace and dignity, the theological depth and poetry, of some of the monks I meet. Deep humanness and freedom are purchased at a price.

Whoever enters through me/will be safe./He will go in and out, and find pasture. — JOHN 10:9

We enter reality by Christ—see it as he sees it—have the Mind of Christ. Then we can attend to everything or withdraw from things for solitude, according to the grace of the moment, and in all we will be safe and find food for our spirits and be growing in Christ and God. Christ came that we may have life and have it to the full.

❀

I know my sheep and my sheep know me in the same way that the Father knows me and I know my Father—by the Holy Spirit—love-knowledge.

❀

Perhaps the beginning of Isaiah 5—the parable of the vineyard—applies to the Church today and some religious orders. The Lord did so much for us, yet we did not produce the fruit of true sanctity, so he has let his vineyard suffer.

❄

Christ promised a font of living water from within. But, as the Samaritan said, the well is deep. We must go deep with Christ so that the source can be set free. The Gospel must descend from the mind into the depths of the heart. Some things can only be learned by suffering and humiliation and contradiction. Then we can know how much Christ loves us, because he suffered these willingly for us. I have been afraid or unwilling to be open to suffering. I am now seeing the value of it more and beginning to want it, yet fearful of it and fearful about my being able to cope with it—not confident enough in Christ being with me to make me able. I tend still to want to be too much in control. That is why I am often in thoughts and plans for the future instead of being wholly present to the Now. Lord, help me.

❄

My Friend runs the world, so why should I worry about anything?

❄

Cast your cares upon the Lord, for he has care of you.

Monday, September 7

The Vigil of the Nativity of the Virgin. A day of quiet prayer and preparation. I am glad I will be able to celebrate this feast in a deeply contemplative way, thanking God for twenty years as a monk and asking pardon for all the unmonkish things I have done during that time. To be a monk is simply to be a wholehearted Christian in a special environment, one that fosters and gives space for the specifically Christian activity of prayer and praise to the Father in Christ, his Son, with whom we have become one. The monk has less excuse than most for not living the Christ life to the full. To

whom much has been given, from him much will be expected. And
we monks sure have received an awful lot!

> You are an enclosed garden . . .
>   an enclosed garden, a fountain sealed.
> You are a park that puts forth pomegranates,
>   with all choice fruits;
> Nard and saffron, calamus and cinnamon,
>   with all kinds of incense;
> Myrrh and aloes,
>   with all the finest spices.
> You are a garden fountain, a well of water
>   flowing fresh from Lebanon.
> Arise, north wind! Come, south wind!
>   blow upon my garden
>   that its perfumes may spread abroad.
> Let my lover come to his garden
>   and eat its choice fruits.
>   — SONG OF SONGS 4:12–16

We are meant to be hidden places which the Lord can make most
fruitful. We should have a desire that this will benefit all our
brothers and sisters, but it is not for us to be running out of our hidden place. Let him spread its perfumes abroad as he wills, by the
winds that obey his commands. We stay put, letting the garden grow
and develop, a garden of delights for him, and we long for him to
visit his garden. And he will.

> I have come to my garden . . .
>   I gather my myrrh and my spices,
> I eat my honey and my sweetmeats,
>   I drink my wine and my milk . . .
>   — SONG OF SONGS 5:1

We must be watchful for his coming, like the bride: "I was sleeping but my heart kept vigil; I heard my love knocking." But, unlike
the bride, we must not be slow in opening to him or, like her, we will
find,

> I opened to my lover—
>   but my lover had departed, gone.

I sought him but I did not find him;
  I called to him but he did not answer me.
                    — SONG OF SONGS 5:6

The monk is meant to be free, free from all that is, so as to be able at any moment to leap to the knock of the Lord and be wholly to him. That's what our poverty, our obedience, our celibacy are all about—freedom to be to him!

✻

To be quiet, to be still, to be silent long enough to know, to taste, to experience again the profound unity of my life.

Tuesday, September 8

Today is the Feast of the Nativity of the Blessed Virgin Mary. The bells started shortly after seven last night for the Vigil, which lasted until about twelve-thirty this morning. Father Eliseos and Father Justin were home from Karyes for it and Father Grigorios was here from Stavronikita. There was a large group of laymen. We got about four hours sleep, then had solemn Liturgy, followed by the festive meal. Having lunch at 6:30 A.M. in the morning makes for a rather strange day.

✻

This feast marks the twentieth anniversary of my consecration as a monk. To say the least, I never could have thought twenty years ago that I would spend an anniversary in an Orthodox monastery on Mount Athos. Moving with the Lord, our lives unfold in many wondrous ways.

During the Liturgy I realized for the first time how fitting was my Father Abbot's choice of this feast. By Providence I turned in pilgrimage to Saint Anne in the discernment of my vocation and made my preparatory vows on her feast. Then, three years later, on the birth of the Virgin, I made my solemn vows. It was as if Saint Anne watched over the gestation of my monastic life and brought it forth in the birth of what is essentially a Marian vocation—Mary's vocation of pondering in her heart and mothering Christ. The Church has often used that pericope of Mary in Bethany, at the Lord's Feet, choosing the best part, in the liturgy of Mary, the Virgin Mother of God. Our Lord has told us that in doing the will of the Father, we are his mother; we mother his growth among his people, the forming of the whole Christ. This is my vocation.

✳

What would I say I have gotten out of my four months on Athos?

— A period of almost total freedom for living the monastic life pure and simple.
— A rather intimate experience of Orthodox monasticism with its strengths and weaknesses.
— The experience of a community that does really run on love, leaving me with the conviction that it is not just an ideal to be striven for but something that can actually be done.
— A fuller understanding of what a Spiritual Father is supposed to be.
— The value of a sacramental living out of a reality to help it become a real interior value.

When one constantly bows to the Hegumen on meeting him, the faith reality of his being a Christ-Presence gradually roots itself, so there can be an easy loving relation without the danger of a descending to familiarity and losing that faith dimension that is an essential element of relationship.

The "how" is only an example—something the Orthodox retain and we Catholics had until recently. The important thing is that there be some sacraments which are able to function. We continue to use the title "Reverend Father." It is almost a nickname, yet it says to us, as we use it, that there is something special about this Father, as far as we are concerned—a special reverence is due here. He takes a special place in choir and refectory, sacramental of the special place he holds in our lives. Without our reflecting on this, it has its constant influence. Thus we are left free to enjoy a fully human, loving relation with this brother-father in Christ, while the important faith dimension is quietly kept alive and functioning. There will always be a question of proper balance here and of finding the right sacraments for our particular community at a particular time. But if we are aware of the values involved, we will make the necessary investment to do that.

— Personally, hopefully, a deeper life in Christ, a fuller commitment to him, along with a greater awareness of my weakness and dependence. But these are things that grow in us very subtly—the seed planted that grows night and day without our measuring it until it is harvesttime. All important, but more his business than ours. We can do little but want. His Spirit must work them in us. And he will in the willing heart.

For me I see the heart of Christianity in personal love of Jesus Christ. Until one gets to know him enough to be compelled by that knowledge to love him and want to do everything for him to please him, until, in a word, one has fallen in love with him, I fear one is centered on the one he knows best, himself and has love of self at the center. He knows enough *about* Christ to know it is important to love him and please him by doing what he wants, but it is a dutiful sort of thing, ultimately motivated by self-love, one's own good. I think the Lord accepts this, knowing it is a path, a way to true Christian life and love, but it falls short of it. And such a dutiful Christianity, while it brings a certain joy and peace from a sure knowledge that one is in the right way, yet lacks that fullness of joy and peace that makes the true Christian so attractive. Hence the practical importance of daily listening to the Gospels and spending time in listening prayer and using every other means we can to let Jesus reveal his most lovable Self to us.

— A fuller realization and a joyful one, of how Catholic and how Western I truly am. This is not to deny that I find immensely beautiful and attractive realities in Orthodoxy and Eastern Byzantine culture. I feel that the essence (a word that betrays my Westernness) of these realities are all present in Catholicism, but some of them we need to be more aware of and appreciative of and bring more effectively into act. I think there can be a truly Western Orthodoxy, but it is not yet. I might be able to enter fairly deeply into Byzantine Orthodoxy and very much enjoy it, but I doubt if it can reach to the most intimate part of my makeup. And we do want our Christianity to reach the deepest fabric of our being and totally to illumine and deify it with the Taboric Light.

✻

"Seek out instead his Kingship over you, and the rest will follow in turn." — LUKE 12:31

If we do really accept the Lord as our Lord and King and place ourselves under him, then he owes it to himself to have care of us and provide for all our needs. It is only when we decide to function independently that the burden of providing for ourselves falls upon our own quite incapable selves.

✻

A great number of wise men is the safety of the world.

— WISDOM 6:24

✻

What is the meaning of your life, Basil? Amen, Father, amen.

Wednesday, September 9

🙚 I went to bed early last night, before nine, because we had been up much of the previous night and I had not gotten a nap. I read Scripture a bit and thought I would soon be asleep, but in fact never got to sleep the whole night.

✻

"Be like men awaiting their Master's return from a wedding."

— LUKE 12:36

I read and heard that many times, but never really have I taken it too seriously. I suppose, to put it in a context more alive for me, I might think of a son awaiting his father's coming with his new step-mother or maybe just a group of us waiting for a very close friend bringing his bride. We might be sitting about, chatting, having a cocktail or some coffee, but all the time an ear would be attentive to the front walk or the door for the least sound of approach. And there would be frequent trips to the window to peek out and see if there was any sign of them on the horizon. It is with this kind of constant attentiveness the Lord wants us and even commands: "Be like . . ." We ought to be always awaiting his coming. I do not think this necessarily refers to the last coming—general or particular—but the daily visits of grace and Presence, many of which we probably miss because we are not attentive, do not hear the knock: "Be . . . so that when he arrives and knocks, you will open for him *without delay.*" Otherwise, we will have the experience of the bride in the Song— when we finally do open, he will be nowhere in sight. Such constant attentiveness as the underlying attitude to all we do as we go about the daily tasks or even as we sleep—"I sleep, but my heart watches" —can only come from very real love and the desire it engenders to see the Beloved and not to miss his least visit. A woman who is deeply in love has her husband present constantly as she goes about her daily tasks and especially as she prepares supper and expects him soon to arrive. A mother has an attentive ear to the least sound of her baby in his crib even as she gossips over tea or vacuums the rug. Love is attentive. But the Lord sets before us a moment of heightened attentiveness, a moment sharpened by special expectation, and commands us to live at this level: *"Be* like men waiting . . ."

Thursday, September 10

   We were greeted with a magnificent spectacle early this morning. The stars were bright and close, yet successive flashes of lightning illumined the sea and the Mountain. There was no roar of thunder. All was quiet, almost unnaturally so, except for the murmur of the sea and the breeze in the cypresses. Yet again and again the Mountain was bathed in something of a Taboric Light. I stood long on the balcony before going up to the Service.

. . . the lightning, when it flashes, is a goodly sight; and the same wind blows over all the land. The clouds, too, when commanded by God to proceed across the whole world, fulfill the order; and fire, sent from on high to burn up the mountains and the forest, does what has been commanded . . . —BARUCH 6:60–62

Father Aimilianos will be leaving tonight or tomorrow for Belgrade, so we spent a few hours together this afternoon. He explained what extraordinary times these are for the Mountain. We monks go apart, to be in a desert before the Lord. It is in the desert that the Church best knows herself. But the world comes after us into our desert. At this time Greece is discovering the Mountain in a new way, he continued, and it is necessary to respond to this interest in a way that the world can understand. So it makes great demands on the Gerontas and on some of his monks. It is important to preserve this place apart and this way of life for the Church. The man who stands before God, drawing his presence into the world, letting it reflect and dance in our midst as sun upon water, letting it enter in, such a man is more important than all the ecclesiastical programs and activities. Men in the West now, in a special way, seek this. Behind such lives, at the heart of the community, there must be one—he must remain behind, be hidden. If he stands out it is not good. It is the beginning of a fall.

Father went on to share with me some of his joy as a Spiritual Father. Most precious to him are those quiet hours of the night, alone in his cell or in the chapel of Saint Mary Magdalen in the hegumenate, when the Lord opens things to him and he is aware of his sons watching in the night in their cells or making their way to the katholikon for the Midnight Service or to join in the prayers of the brothers in the early morning. Or again at the nunnery at Ormilia, when, after the long hours of confession, he goes down into the courtyard to let the cold night air freshen his face and he perceives little lights in the cell windows where the sisters watch in prayer, or comes across solitary sisters seated quietly in odd corners (for the sisters are short of space, with three or four in a cell, and so have to go out for solitary prayer) with komvoschinions in hand. In the morning when he sees their radiant faces he knows he is sharing something of their mystic graces.

As I thanked Father Aimilianos and expressed my joy for all I had received, I spoke of my coming visit to Rome. And he shared something of his own love for Rome that went back to his boyhood, his love for the City of the Martyrs. As he well expressed it, these months we have been together not as members of different Churches in ecumenical dialogue but as brothers together before the Lord, both called to be abundantly fruitful in bearing sons to mystic life. This was his parting blessing and prayer.

❊

I have trusted in the Eternal God for your welfare,/and joy has come to me from the Holy One/because of the mercy that will swiftly reach you/from your eternal Savior. — BARUCH 4:22

❊

Tonight Father Dionysios fixes supper—boils the rice for the community. Tomorrow he goes to Belgrade on a sensitive diplomatic mission. Typical of the monk's life. And in between he will pray in the night because he was busy in the day.

❊

After supper I took a walk and picked ripe, sweet, green figs and walnuts along the way. Athos is a bit of Eden in September—grapes, figs, apples, all kinds of nuts, and springs of delicious water.

Friday, September 11

❧ Today is the Feast of Saint Theodora. One of the practices I like here is that on the feast of a Saint, if there is a relic of the Saint in the monastery, it is brought into the church at Orthros and venerated by all. It is a sort of welcoming of the Saint on his or her feast day. We had this today for Saint Theodora and last Wednesday for Saint Anne.

❊

The Byzantine tradition of the monastic charnelhouse—ossuary (kostnitsa)—a semi-submerged sepulchral crypt for the storage of bones and an upper-story chapel: The practice, in Christian times, of exhuming the body after several years [three years at Simonos Petras, longer in other monasteries] and a separate storage for bones, is first encountered in Palestine and Syria. Later it became widespread in the Byzantine empire including Greece, Georgia, Armenia and Mount Athos. — BEATA KITSIKI-PANAGOPOULOS, *Medieval Architecture in Greece: Western Monastic Orders in the Latin*

States Formed on Byzantine Territory (San Jose State University, unpublished manuscript)

❊

Pope Innocent III encouraged the Cistercians to establish monasteries in Greece in the hope of influencing the coming together of Orthodox and Catholics. There were twelve original foundations in Byzantine territory. Three are extant on mainland Greece: Zaraka, Isbova, Daphni.

❊

It strikes me, at first brush, that the succession of statements from the Lord in Luke 14:25ff. is rather strange: the call to discipleship meaning renouncing ties and taking the Cross, then the parables about building the tower and meeting an opposing army, then salt losing its savor. Jesus seems to be saying that this is what being a Christian means: before plunging in, stop, reckon the long-range cost. It is better never to join up than to join up and then not go all the way—if you do that, you are not even fit for the manure heap (the Lord certainly did not shy away from realistic imagery!). If that goes for Christians in general, how much more so for monks. That's what novitiate is all about. But how many of us really get the point! "Let him who hears this, heed it" (Luke 14:35). Lord, give us ears to hear and hearts to heed.

Saturday, September 12

꙳ Last evening I had supper with the guests. Each day still brings a dozen or two. English is certainly the universal language. Frenchmen spoke to Germans in English, Finns to Greeks in English, and, of course, the Dutch were completely at home in English. The Hegumen once said I have an apostolic heart. And I suppose it is so. I certainly wanted to reach out to each of these young men. It seems to me it is an especially tender time of grace for them—the few days they spend on the Holy Mountain. Many of them seem to be aware of it. Yet, in fact, the monks for the most part have little contact with the guests. A number of times young men have told me that in the course of their days on the Mountain they never had an opportunity to speak with a monk seriously at any length, nor had they attended any Services in the churches because they did not know if they were allowed.

It is true that in some monasteries there is no one readily available who speaks other than Greek. And some houses do not allow non-Orthodox to attend Services. But most houses do, although they do not tend to inform the guests when the Services will take place or the fact that they are welcome. Too, if mere "tourists" come to the katholikon out of curiosity, they would be distracted and distracting. I think the monks presume that serious pilgrims or guests will know or find out for themselves when the Services will take place, and they would just as soon let the others rest quietly in the guesthouse.

It seems to me that more of a spiritual outreach in the midst of all their hospitality would be very fruitful. But I see with the eyes of an energetic Western Church traditionally full of missionary zeal—something that has apparently been almost wholly absent from the Orthodox Churches. Maybe it is because Orthodoxy has been so "monastic"—content to be where it should be, before the Lord, as leaven in the lump, leaving the increase to him. That is a good position for a monk—but for a whole Church?

❊

The Scriptures are sometimes quite shockingly graphic in their imagery: "Like a eunuch lusting for intimacy with a maiden [what an image of utter frustration!]/is he who does right under compulsion" (Sirach 20:3). And yet the psychologists tell us how much we are all subject to our compulsions, how lacking in true interior freedom, acting from truly interiorized values. I agree wholeheartedly with the Gerontas here when he says that we should receive into the monastic life only men who are psychologically free and that the whole task of monasticism is to lead the monk to true and full spiritual freedom. As old Dom Edmund often quoted to us: "*Ubi Spiritus ibi liberatas*" (Where the Spirit is, there is freedom). To live completely under the compulsion of the Spirit, under his grace—that might sound like a paradox—but it is he and his grace that move us so that we can freely do what we really want to do and not be subject to the alien law that resides in us and so often compels us to do that which we do not wish to do. The mystery of grace and free will—only by grace can we have free will.

When I thanked the Elder for making my visit to Patmos possible he replied: "You have your own will to thank." That could be taken wrongly. In the context of a spiritual climate, that zeroes in on self-will as the arch enemy, to do "your own will" is the height of willfulness, selfishness, evil. But the Elder was simply pointing out the reality. Hearing I expressed some desire to visit Patmos, he had offered me the opportunity to do so. I decided to go, and so I did. If I decided not to, that would have been that. It illustrates in practice the role of the Superior in developing the freedom of his men—to facilitate their doing what they want to do. If we do believe in the basic good will of our brothers, then we will readily believe that what they really want to do is the best for them and for us the community and for God's people. Sure, we all remain fallible sinners. Mistakes will be made. But for those who love God, all things work together unto good—even sin, to quote Saint Augustine—and he should know! Men will grow in true freedom and really be able to function out of love—and that is what Christianity is all about.

❊

I just received a letter from Abbot Thomas telling me of Brother Walter's death:

We had news that Brother Walter of Snowmass* passed away in his sleep during the night of September sixth (Monday). Chris Wieban, a long-time friend and neighbor, died in the same way the night before. Perhaps there was some collusion since they had chatted together the Sunday afternoon before Chris died . . . Father Michael seems to be very much at peace since Brother Walter had been very happy these past few months, spending more time in prayer—although, when asked about this his only remark was: "The only thing that counts is the mercy of God."

The night before he died he gave one of those funny cards to Brother Bernard to have mailed in Denver. Someone was going over on a trip. He used to like to send this kind of card to Father Michael as a prank when he was over in Denver seeing the doctor. The idea was to keep Father Michael guessing as to where it came from. When Father Michael received this card the next day, after discovering Brother Walter's body, there was a message on the back which read: "Having a fine time—wish you were here. Your favorite Brother."

I suspect Michael said "Amen" to that!

❈

The will is no good unless it does its proper work, which is love.

❈

At Apodeipnon today I received this text from Matthew 6:32, 34:

". . . Your heavenly Father knows all that you need. . . . Enough, then, of worrying about tomorrow."

A good text, as my time on the Holy Mountain draws toward a close. One of my greatest faults is wasting time planning in my imagination—a lack of trust and, more, pride—thinking I have the best solutions, and wanting to impose my ideas on people and things. God is in the "now." Abide—in his silence—listening—being with him.

❈

The wisdom of a learned man is the fruit of leisure; he must starve himself of doing if he is to come by it.
                              — SIRACH (ECCLESIASTICUS) 38:24

❈

If we want to go somewhere and there are two people we can follow—one who knows the way definitely (he's been there and in fact built the road that leads there) and the other who might or might not know the way—which one will we follow *if we really want to get there?* If we want to get to heaven, what folly to follow anyone but Christ, and yet what do I do in practice? Perhaps the more basic question is, Do I really want to go to heaven *now*, or am I more interested in getting a few things done along the way, before I get there?

❈

Woe is me, because my exile is prolonged. — PSALM 119:5

When will I go and contemplate the Face of the Lord?
                                            — PSALM 41:3

I wish to be dissolved and be with Christ. — PHILIPPIANS 1:23

My soul thirsts for the Lord. — PSALM 41:3

Now, Lord, deliver your servant. . . . — LUKE 2:29

These are the cries of the holy ones in Scripture, taken up by Saint Basil in his first Long Rule.

❊

Eeternity means being present to every "now." Jesus and Mary and the saints are fully present to us and are present *now* (in their eternity). Am I present to them? Or in the make-believe land of the past and future? Man has a very basic desire to reproduce himself, to share in some way in God's creativity, in whose image he is made. When he foregoes the creativity of sexuality by choosing celibacy for the Kingdom and foregoes creative activity for the path of obedience (though obedience does not necessarily exclude creative work, it sometimes does), then he is tempted to compensate by a great deal of creative activity in thought and imagination. This is especially true of the contemplative. He needs to learn two things:

1. *A way to guide his thoughts and imagination to creative activity that is in line with his Christian quest.*

    He can use his mind and imagination to search into the Revelation to perceive it more fully and be more enlightened by it.

    Imagination can have a role here because our Lord taught very much by images. For example, the monk can with his imagination explore the scene of the sower, looking at the hill behind the crowd to which our Lord is speaking. The bare path that winds its way up among the green. The hard ground. The tumbling wall of stones along the side of the field. Because of the added warmth from the rocks catching and holding the heat of the sun, the seed grew quickly but now the stalks stand tall and dry, virtually straw for the fire. And the outcropping of thorns along the rocky piles—only stray stalks of wheat break through the tangled mass. But across the field the waving grain, some patches taller, thicker, greener—where the flow of ground waters are better (grace) and the field is free from the shade of overhanging trees (attachments that hinder complete openness to the radiance of Divine Love). Clouds sail by and shadow a patch for a bit (thoughts and imaginings), but if they are let pass on and not held, they interfere little with the fructifying Divine Radiance.

It is good for the monk to know how to use thoughts and images a bit—so that his creative need will not be wholly frustrated but have satisfying experiences in a well-channeled activity. But this can be overdone, and keep him ever on the surface and not immediately in contact with the present Reality.

2. *So he needs also to learn simple methods*—like Centering Prayer—*to quiet the mind and imagination and let the spirit rest in the depths* while the clouds go by.

There is a question here of being attentive to the call of God and discerning his will. Ordinarily, the monk and everyone called to a deeper life of prayer and union with him is summoned to enter more and more into the sterility of the desert, into the Emptiness that is Fullness, that is God, to the No-thing that is All, to a Silence that is all Word.

Sunday, September 13

🌊 After Vespers last night a few of us from Simonos Petras took a small motor launch with the consul general from Constantinople to Dionysiou for the enthronement of the new Hegumen, Father Ephraim. The ceremony, which took place between Orthros and Liturgy this morning, making it a seven hour Service, was quite simple. A neighboring Hegumen vested the new Hegumen in cross and cope while the Secretary of the Holy Community read the proclamation of the enthronement. Then the Hegumen of the Megisti Lavra gave the new Hegumen his pastoral staff and pastoral charge. Then the new Hegumen went to his throne where he stood, crosier in hand, through the Liturgy, neither concelebrating nor communicating. The ceremony was followed with the usual reception and feast.

※

As we arrived last night Father Eliseos was at the gate to meet us with his usual wonderful warmth. After we got settled, all the Simonos Petras' group sat together on a balcony. They wanted my impressions as I was completing my stay. I remarked on how similar I found the monks at Simonos Petras with those of my own monastery. There was a bit of happy laughter at this. Then Father Eliseos told me that the saying is going around that Simonos Petras is "the Catholic monastery." I am not sure whether that should be "catholic" with a capital or a small *c*. It certainly is catholic in its outlook, yet it is very solidly Orthodox in its faith and practice. The similarities rise from one common monastic tradition which we have the joy to share.

❊

I leave Mount Athos as it steps into a new era. The first glimmers of it came some years ago when Father Ephraim re-established cenobitic life at Philotheou with a group of young monks and Father Vasileios was named Hegumen of Stavronikita. It really dawned when Father Aimilianos and his monks came to Simonos Petras. It has been solidified with Father Georgios and his youngsters at Grigoriou, with the new group at Konstamonitou, and with Father Joseph at Koutloumousiou.

Through all the dark years, those concerned pointed to Father Gabriel at Dionysiou as a ray of light and hope. For forty years he had served as Hegumen and Father. Now at ninety, on the Mountain since 1908, he has passed on the crosier. Many new things have come to be integrated with the old: roads, telephones, showers. The generator is now turning at Simonos Petras, illuminating the first light bulbs there, and poles are going up to spread the power. More important, monks are studying, especially theology, at universities and the Spiritual Fathers' scope of activity among the laity of Greece and elsewhere is becoming broader and broader. Athos, always the heart of Orthodoxy, is sending life through the Church with a wonderful new vitality. For this, let us praise the Lord!

❊

I wish to know Christ
     And the power flowing from his resurrection;
Likewise to know how to share in his sufferings
     By being formed into the pattern of his death.
                              — PHILIPPIANS 3:10

❊

When it gets down to it, while I would like to think I am essentially a son, obeying God's law because I love him and see his and its goodness, in fact I am hardly even a mercenary working for the reward (that means that at least one's faith is sufficiently alive for his scale of values to set heaven first) but more the slave, obeying out of fear of hell. Even that is a gift and more than I deserve—the faith to realize there is a hell and I could very well go there. But how much I need that experience of God that engenders deep love from knowing him and how good he is and that evokes that desire for him and that desire to please him in all and to be fully united with him in all. This is the only way, by his mercy, I can become a loving son.

Election Day in America is less than two months away. I do not know if I will be able to vote, but certainly I am able to pray. Whether we like it or not and whether others like it or not, the President of the United States has a real influence on the lives of just about everyone in the world, especially everyone in the free world. If a true man of God and his Peace can lead the world from the White House, it should be a time of renewed hope for all mankind. Lord, you know our need, our unworthiness, our hope in you.

He who puts his value in the mouths of others appears now great, now little, now nothing at all.

Monday, September 14 / 27

The Agripnia began around seven-thirty last evening and finished with the exultation of the Relic of the Holy Cross somewhat after one this morning, my last on the Mountain. We got about four hours sleep, then had the First Hour and Liturgy. After warm goodbyes, I hurried down to the port. On the boat to Daphni I met a very friendly Orthodox monk who is doing a doctoral study in Canon Law, comparing the canons with the writings of the Fathers, beginning in the area of Penance. We had coffee together at Daphni and then went on together by boat to Ouranoupolis. The bus to Thessaloniki was very crowded. I reached John Kanonides' house around five in the afternoon.

John and I visited Dimitrios and his father to again thank them.

Then we went to the Kaimakis apartment but no one was at home.
At Father Theonas' home we found Father Metrophanes and Father
Germanos. They are staying with Father Germanos' family, returning to the Holy Mountain on Wednesday. Father Theonas is to take
his driver's test tomorrow and theology exams on the fifteenth.

❉

Father Georgios and I spoke together briefly at Dionysiou before I
left. He believes it has become so difficult for young men to live integrated Christian lives in today's society in Greece that more and
more will come to the Holy Mountain, and in a few years all the
monasteries will be full again. (Simonos Petras is now full.) When I
related this to John, he agreed. He felt that in Greece because of the
closeness of the people one to another and openness of the social
contacts, the environment has more impact than in the West, and so
those desiring to lead a Christian life have to get away or face a great
struggle. He, himself, is actually a very dynamic and active Christian
in his parish and there are many young men like him developing new
approaches to true Christian parochial living in the parishes in the
cities in Greece today. They, too, are a real hope for tomorrow.

❉

"If any one wishes to rank first, he must remain the last one of all
and the servant of all" (Mark 9:35). Ranking first in this text refers
to being first in the Kingdom—being first in love, being the most loving. Serving all is a joy because he said: "I assure you, as often as you
did it for one of my least brothers, you did it for me" (Matthew
25:40).

—A clear call to a life of serving—his kind of serving.

❉

What do I want?
Above all, before all, and in all things: "Thy Will be done." Dependent upon this:

—to see the Face of God—not the human face of God in Christ,
   for I have in a way seen that and do see it, but the very Face
   of God.
—to humbly, lovingly, and sincerely serve, as friend, father, brother,
   every person who comes into my life.

Lord, help me!

ROME

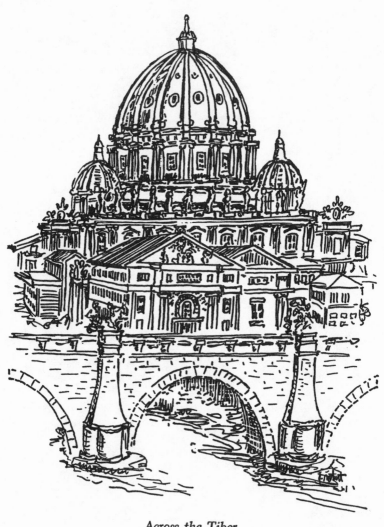

Across the Tiber

Tuesday, September 28

❧ I rose about six, and all John's family got up to fix breakfast for me and see me off. John went with me all the way to the airport. There we met Konstantin Paravantsos. He had seen me at Ormilia. We shared the flight together and he told me of his experiences visiting the monks at Simonos Petras. At Athens another gentleman greeted me in the airport saying that he had heard of my visit to the Holy Mountain. It has evidently been spread abroad.

❈

TWA put me on an earlier flight to Rome than the one for which I had been booked. In the Rome airport I met Sister Maria Regina, a sister of the Blessed Virgin of Nazareth. She had been born in Jerusalem of expatriated Polish parents, baptized in Bethlehem, grew up in England, did her novitiate in Rome and nurse's training in the United States. She has been working as a nurse in Rome in very adverse conditions. At the present time the people here are often verbally abusive to the religious. So most of the latter do not wear the habit outside their houses now. At the same time, her own community which is quite conservative, does not understand her working along what they consider secular lines. The sister and the Polish priest she was meeting at the airport drove me to Tre Fontane. This priest, Father Andrew, said that there had been workers' revolutions in June in Poland and that the situation there is very bad. There is a great scarcity of staples: meat, sugar, etc. Only about one half of the people continue to practice their faith seriously. The Churches are the only opponents to the one-party system.

❈

We arrived at Tre Fontane near eleven. As we drove up the alley leading to the monastery, with its age-old eucalyptus trees, I was very struck by the beauty and the peace and the prayerfulness of the site. I then realized that this had been a sanctuary of prayer for more than a thousand years before the founding of the monastery I just left on the Holy Mountain, Simonos Petras. Monks first came here in the fifth century and have not ceased, night and day, offering the Divine Services. The site, of course, was already sacred because it is the place where Saint Paul was martyred. And it was later made more sacred by the visits of Bernard of Clairvaux. This was where he had his great vision of souls being released from purgatory and ascending to heaven as he offered the Holy Sacrifice of the Mass. The beautiful Romanesque basilica dates back to almost the time of the foundation.

❋

Father Ansgar, the subprior, an American, and indeed all the monks welcomed me with great warmth and were most helpful and kind. I offered Mass in the basilica for my brother Dale as it is his birthday today.

After lunch I went up to Monte Cistello to see the Abbot General. He will be leaving early tomorrow for the United States for the meeting of the General Council. I was very happy to learn that arrangements have been made for me to see the Holy Father tomorrow.

❋

My retreat on Mount Athos is now over—but really it was a beginning. I see more clearly the selfishness, the lust, gluttony, and sloth in me. How little the love of inner silence and prayer has grown in these twenty-odd years. I can only try by God's help to keep my schedule and trust that by sitting day by day, waiting, I will learn my helplessness, my need, my unworthiness. And coming to know I have no claim, perhaps then he will come and I will really know that it is pure mercy, immense goodness, and be able to humbly accept it for that. Lord, have mercy and help. May I again give myself wholly to you. In spite of all my uncleanness and sin, please do not reject me, but take me and care for me and help me to be made worthy of the promises of Christ.

I sit before the Lord—my Master—very conscious that I am not worthy to be here. At least, I should be prostrate before him. I am surely not worthy to unbuckle his sandals. Yet he has said to me: "Come to me, you who are weary and heavily burdened." And I am weary—of chasing after illusions. I am burdened with my sins, my evil tendencies and inclinations, my terrible darkness. If only I could really see something of his true goodness—how attentive I would then be. How loving, by his grace. And I would leave behind all my illusions, totally taken by the beauty of his Face. Lord, show me your Face, and I shall live—truly live. I do not mean your human Face—beautiful and adorable though it be—but the Face of your Divinity. Because it is for this I thirst. And this alone can satisfy my desire and my need.

❋

This realization came to me today. If I have given myself to Mary, I belong to her. Then, to use myself body or soul in any way other than the way which she wants, is unjust because it is using what belongs to another contrary to her wishes. I have often been unjust. I must reform. Mary, help me.

❋

Prayer and sacrifice work together. Where there is no sacrifice, there will eventually turn out to be no prayer, and vice versa.

— THOMAS MERTON

❋

Everything can be taken up again and recast in God, even one's faults.

❋

It is coming clearer what course I must follow when I return to my community. First of all—I have been reading Henri Nouwen's *Pray to Live* and I think he expressed well what I have been going through at times during this retreat: "As often as a man ventures to a deeper, more fundamental level of life in trying to give form to his life, he exposes himself to a crisis which is more painful and heart-rending. In this sense, a man has just as many adolescences as he takes risks to fathom his life." It has been a sort of an adolescent experience—wanting in some way to get away from it all. But this is one of the areas where I am now getting some insight. This morning in my *lectio* I opened to Deuteronomy 6, the *Schema Israel*:

Hear, O Israel! The LORD is our God, the LORD alone! Therefore, you shall love the LORD, your God, with all your heart, and with all your soul, and with all your strength. — DEUTERONOMY 6:4, 5

But we ought to do this in *one another*—a total kind of love—effective feeling, not just intellectual willing—at least as best we can—all our strength. As I go back to community this is what I think the Lord wants me to try to do. Love these wonderful men in a full, feeling way. It is going to mean going out of myself more, especially with some, a real dying to self. It's going to be hard, and to keep the ideal and vision clear, it is going to demand greater fidelity to prayer and *lectio*. Just dropping everything, as I have these months, shows I can let things ride and do the important things.

Wednesday, September 29

⤳ We rose a little after three this morning. Vigils began at three-thirty and lasted for about an hour and twenty minutes. There was some time for quiet prayer and then Lauds and Concelebration at six.

✻

After Tierce I went to the Vatican. First, I visited the Secretariat for Christian Unity. Then I went to the new audience hall to see our Holy Father. On the way I met the Primate of the Benedictines, Archabbot Rembert, with a group of Benedictine Abbesses and our own Cistercian Abbess from Vitorchiano.

The new audience hall is absolutely magnificent, artistically, acoustically, visually, and physically. Because there were so many pilgrims in Rome at this time, the Holy Father actually was conducting two general audiences this morning. First, one in the Basilica of Saint Peter's for those who spoke German, Spanish, and Portuguese, and then a second in the new audience hall for those who spoke Italian, French, and English. Near the back entryway of the hall where the Holy Father first comes in there are some smaller rooms where he receives in small groups those whom he especially wants to speak with before entering the main hall.

As the Holy Father entered the room I had an experience which I was wholly unprepared for. After spending some beautiful hours with some of the truly celestial Fathers on the Holy Mountain, I did not expect this meeting with the Holy Father to be of that same order. Yet as he entered the room and his smiling eyes looked into mine I felt the immense love and compassion of Christ descending upon me, totally engulfing me. It is an experience that remains, and will remain, a moment that belongs to another order of time. There is no doubt that the Holy Father is a very holy man. He must walk very slowly as his knees are painfully stiffened by arthritis. But apart from that, there is a liveliness and vitality about him which is certainly filled with warmth and true humanness, even as divine love radiates from him. He spoke with deep personal conviction on the importance of the contemplative life for the Church. He also spoke of the importance of a deepening life of faith to walk hand in hand with the great march of progress that is taking place in our times.

After the audience I went into the great Basilica of Saint Peter. It is always an overwhelming experience to enter this vast church. But today I was drawn very directly and immediately to the heart-center of it, to the tomb of the Prince of the Apostles. Certainly one of the fruits of my time on the Holy Mountain has been to make the Saints much more present and to appreciate their presence in their relics and in their sacred places. As I knelt there, close to the Prince of the Apostles, having just received the paternal blessing of his two hundred and sixty-third successor as Bishop of Rome, hearing about me the languages of many nations as pilgrims went to and fro, I felt very much at the Heart of the Church. But this is truly where the monk always is or should be—at the Heart of the Church, the Heart of Christ, feeling, loving as he feels and loves, one with him in his saving mission to uplift all mankind under his headship to the praise and glory of the Father in the oneness and love that is the Holy Spirit.

GLOSSARY

ACATHIST HYMN A Service of praise in honor of the Holy Mother of God, which was probably composed in 532 and is prayed daily in the monasteries on the Holy Mountain before Apodeipnon or Vespers.

AGHIA ANNA A skete dedicated to Saint Anne, the mother of the Mother of God. It is located on the southern side of the Holy Mountain, near the end of the peninsula.

AGHIOS PANTELEIMONOS One of the twenty autonomous, or ruling, monasteries of the Holy Mountain and the only one of the Russian Orthodox Church. It is dedicated to Saint Panteleimon, a fourth-century martyr who is very popular in Orthodoxy because of his many miraculous interventions. It is sometimes popularly called "Russiko."

AGHIOU ANDREOU A Russian skete, dedicated to Saint Andrew, which has now fallen empty. Part of the immense buildings now houses the Theological Academy. It is located on the outskirts of Karyes.

AGHIOU PAVLOU One of the twenty ruling monasteries and dedicated to Saint Paul. It is located on the southern side of the Mountain near the end of the peninsula.

AGRIPNIA The All-Night Vigil, celebrated on the great feasts and Sundays. It includes Great Vespers and Orthros, and usually concludes with Liturgy. It may last from six to fourteen hours, depending on the solemnity with which it is sung. Sometimes there is a break before Liturgy. Sometimes other Services are included, such as the blessing of water.

ANALAVOS Part of the Great Schema.

ANGELIC SCHEMA See the Great Schema.

ANTIDORON Specially blessed bread. When the priest prepares the bread for the Liturgy he also prepares a tray of small pieces of bread, usually from the loaf out of which he has cut the Lamb, the large square he is going to consecrate and change into the Body of Christ. Before the Communion, these pieces are brought to the altar and blessed. Those who receive Communion eat also a bit of this blessed bread, to insure that the Divine

Bread is properly consumed. Those who do not receive Communion receive a bit of this blessed bread from the priest at the end of the Liturgy as a sort of lesser communion or participation in the Sacred Sacrificial Meal.

APODEIPNON What is called in the West "Compline," the last Service of the day, celebrated at sunset.

APOTHEGMATA Short stories recounting the doings and sayings of the early monastic Fathers which convey a spiritual lesson.

ARSENAS The fortlike storehouse built at the port of an Athonite monastery.

BELLEFONTAINE A Cistercian monastery southwest of Paris near Angers.

BEURON A Benedictine monastery not far from Bonn, West Germany.

CANON Rule. It may also refer to one of the provisions in the Code of Canon Law or to collections of laws, either ecclesiastical or civil.

CENOBITIC Pertaining to cenobitism.

CENOBITISM That form of monastic life which involves living in common in obedience to a Superior.

CENOBIUM A monastery in which the monks live a cenobitic life.

CENTERING PRAYER The currently popular name given to a very simple method of entering into and abiding in contemplative prayer that comes from our Western monastic tradition. A full description of it with an indication of sources can be found in my book, *Daily We Touch Him* (Garden City, N.Y.: Doubleday, 1977).

CHANDELIER See Corona.

CHEVTOGNE A monastery in Belgium which is shared by a community of traditional Western Benedictines and a community of Byzantine monks.

CHILANDARI One of the twenty ruling monasteries of the Holy Mountain. It is the one nearest the mainland, about eighteen miles from Karyes, in an area that is quite level and open to cultivation. It is Serbian and celebrates the Services in Slavonic.

CONYERS The Abbey of Our Lady of the Holy Spirit, a Cistercian monastery in Conyers, Georgia. (In the Cistercian tradition, a monastery is usually referred to by the name of its geographic location.)

CORONA A large, hinged, brass rim in the middle of the nave of the church, suspended from the dome. It usually has twelve or six-teen sections; in the middle of each there is hung a double-faced icon, and mounted on each are many candles. These are lit only at the more solemn Services, and at climactic moments the ecclesiastikos, by means of a rod, sets the whole massive thing gyrating. The chandelier hanging in the middle of the corona is set rotating at the same time. The result is a fantasy of moving lights, which causes the Saints and Angels in the icons to begin quite literally to dance in their gilded heavens. This "heavenly dance" expresses the participation of the heavenly hosts in the celebration.

CUCULLA An ample robe reaching to the ground, with long, wide sleeves and a hood. This is the distinctive garment of the monk in the West.

DAPHNI The port of entry for the Holy Mountain, on the southern coast of the peninsula. It can hardly be called a village, as there are very few residents. There are a couple of eating places, several shops which sell souvenirs and provisions, a post office, a warehouse, and a Greek military post. The dirt road to the southern coast from Karyes ends here.

DIAMONITIRION A permit given by the Iera Kinotis allowing the visitor to travel on the Holy Mountain and seek the hospitality of the various communities. A photograph of one can be found on page 47 of C. Dahm, *Athos: Mountain of Light* (Offenburg, Germany: Burda, 1959), an excellent pictorial presentation of the Holy Mountain.

DIONYSIOU One of the twenty ruling monasteries of the Holy Mountain, located on the southern coast about five miles east of Simonos Petras.

DISKOS A paten or gilded plate used at the Liturgy for carrying and holding the bread that will be changed into the Body of Christ. It usually has an attached stand of two or three inches height.

DOCHEIARIOU One of the twenty ruling monasteries of the Holy Mountain.

DOXA The first word of the doxology most frequently used: "Glory be to the Father and to the Son and to the Holy Spirit, now and forever, and unto the ages of ages, Amen." *Doxa si* (Glory to you).

ECCLESIASTIKOS   The monk charged with the well-ordering and general functioning of things in the katholikon. His most time-consuming tasks would be the ringing bells, sounding semantrons, and lighting lamps and candles, all of which call for oft-repeated attention through the unfolding of the liturgical day. Some of his tasks call for the help of the whole community: the cleaning and polishing to get ready for a feast or making the annual supply of candles.

ECONOME   The procurator, the monk responsible for the temporal needs of the monastery or a metokion.

ECONOMIA   A provision made which is contrary to the requirements of the Sacred Canons but is in accord with and even demanded by the mercy of God.

ELEISON   "Have mercy"—a petition frequently used in the Services.

ENDOKIA   A chapel or shrine, usually in a city, which depends on a monastery.

EPICLESIS   A solemn invocation calling down the Holy Spirit.

ESCHATON   The ultimate realization of God's plan for the created universe.

ESPHIGMENOU   One of the twenty ruling monasteries of the Holy Mountain, on the northern side of the peninsula. This monastery has broken communion with the rest of the Holy Community and the Patriarchate of Constantinople and has joined the Old Calendarists, the schismatic church of Greece.

FILIOQUE   "And the Son"—a Latin word added to the Creed or Symbol of Faith that was formulated by the first two Ecumenical Councils, those of Nicaea (325) and Constantinople (381). It was first added in Spain, but gradually came into common usage in the whole of the West and became a focal point for controversy between Eastern and Western Christianity. It expresses the doctrine that the Third Person of the Blessed Trinity, the Holy Spirit, proceeds from both the First and Second Persons of the Trinity, the Father *and the Son*, as a common principle, and not just from the Father as does the Son. The West finds this doctrine in the New Testament and the writings of the Fathers. The Orthodox deny this and hold that this doctrine is the fabrication of some Western Fathers and theologians. Orthodox teaching maintains that the true teaching is that there is but one principle in the Trinity, the Father, who is exclusively the principle of both the Son and the Holy Spirit.

GERONTAS "Elder" is perhaps the best English equivalent (and the one most commonly used by Orthodox) for Gerontas (literally, old man), the title of honor usually accorded to the Spiritual Father. He may or may not be the Superior of a community. The fact that Archimandrite Aimilianos of Simonos Petras (q.v.) used this title when speaking to me, a Catholic monk, was considered an extraordinary mark of esteem.

GERONTISSA The feminine equivalent of Gerontas.

GETHSEMANE The garden in Jersualem where Jesus prayed prior to his arrest. The reference in the text is to the Abbey of Our Lady of Gethsemane, a Cistercian monastery not far from Louisville, Kentucky.

GOLDEN EPISTLE The *Letter to the Brothers of Mont Dieu,* written by William of Saint Thierry, a twelfth-century Cistercian Father; usually called the *Golden Epistle* because it contains such a fine synthetic presentation of basic monastic spirituality. An English translation by Theodore Berkeley was published by Cistercian Publications, Kalamazoo, Michigan, in 1971.

GREAT SCHEMA The fullest form of the monastic habit. Originally there was only one monastic profession and one monastic habit, but in time a variation of grades developed in the Orthodox Church and hence the distinction between the Little and the Great Schema. In the Russian tradition, taking the Great Schema means committing oneself to a more exclusively contemplative life; in the Greek tradition, this is not necessarily so and some of the monasteries on the Holy Mountain do not observe the distinction, but immediately give the Great Schema to all monks. The habit includes the robe or tunic, leather belt, rason, skouphos, veil, mandyas, and analavos, which is the part which distinguishes the Great Schema from the Little Schema. This last resembles in its form the scapular worn by Western monks, but probably has no connection with it in its origins. It is of black cloth or soft leather and has embroidered on it, usually in red, the Cross of Calvary, with spear, reed, and sponge, the skull and crossbones of Adam, and certain monograms. It is usually worn only when the monk or nun is going to receive Holy Communion. The Great Schema is also known as the Angelic Schema.

GRIGORIOU One of the twenty ruling monasteries of the Holy Mountain, on the southern shore between Simonos Petras and Dionysiou.

HEGUMEN The head of an autonomous monastery, somewhat similar to an Abbot in the West, although he need not be the Spiritual Father of the community. He is usually elected by the community.

HEGUMENA The Superior of a convent of nuns.

HEGUMENATE That part of the monastery reserved to the use of the Hegumen.

HESYCHASM A quality of stillness or silence. This term can be interpreted at many different levels: exteriorly, meaning solitude or withdrawal into a cell; interiorly, a certain return to oneself, inner silence, spiritual poverty, a listening to God.

HESYCHAST One who practices or has entered into a life of hesychasm.

HIEROMONK A monk who is a priest.

HOLY COMMUNITY See Iera Kinotis.

ICONOSTASIS A partition, usually covered with icons and having three openings, which separates the sanctuary from the nave of the church or chapel.

IDIORRHYTHMIC A style of life, adopted in some of the monasteries of Orthodoxy in the fourteenth century because of historical circumstances and still prevailing in some, by which the monks receive an allowance from the common income, retain their own property, and do not have a common Superior or lead a common life.

IERA KINOTIS The Holy Government, or Holy Community, a synod of representatives from the twenty autonomous monasteries, which through an annually elected council of four, one of which is named Protos, guides the internal affairs of the monastic republic.

IERISSOS A town on the northern coast of Chalkidiki, just west of the Athonite peninsula. The bus line used to end here and it is still possible to take a boat from here to enter the Holy Mountain from the north.

IVIRON One of the ruling monasteries of the Holy Mountain. It is idiorrhythmic. It is located on the northern coast, at the end of one of the bus lines running from Daphni via Karyes. It has a good pier and so serves as a center of communication.

JORDANVILLE The Orthodox Monastery of the Holy Trinity near Jordanville, New York.

JOSEPHITE MONASTICISM A ritual monasticism inspired by the Rules written by Joseph Volotskii (1440–1515). It might be compared in some ways with the monasticism that prevailed in the West under the Cluniac reform or that found in the Solesmes Congregation, a monasticism which places a great emphasis on the Services and is content to allow the monks to live off endowments and lands in order that they might be free for such Services. In Russia there was a clash between this ideal and that of Saint Nilos of Sora (1433–1508) who had brought back to Russia from the Holy Mountain the teaching of Saint Gregory Palamas. Saint Nilos believed monks should live by their own labor. When Saint Joseph of Volokalamsk prevailed, Saint Nilos retired to his monastery and died in relative obscurity. Saint Joseph's Rules show a dependency on the Rule of Saint Benedict. An English translation of the last Russian monastic rules, with an extensive introduction, has been prepared by David Goldfrank as a doctoral dissertation at the University of Washington (1970) and is available from University Microfilm (No. 71–08492), Ann Arbor, Michigan 48104.

KARAKALLOU One of the twenty ruling monasteries of the Holy Mountain, on the northern coast, a bit east of Iviron.

KARYES The civil capital of the Holy Mountain, the seat of Iera Kinotis, located in the center of the republic high up in the hills, just over the crest. The main street and the squares are lined with shops, eating places, and a couple of small hotels. Surrounding the village are the residences of the representatives of the twenty ruling monasteries who meet regularly to conduct the affairs of the Mountain. The Greek governor also resides here.

KATHOLIKON The principal church of a monastery.

KAVSOKALYVIA A skete of about forty houses hidden away at the eastern end of the Holy Mountain.

KELLION A household of monks under a Gerontas, or Spiritual Father, which has relative autonomy.

KILROSI   The traditionally octagonal, flat-topped lectern used in choir in the monasteries of Orthodoxy.

KOLIVA   A special confection or cake made of whole grain and various nuts and spices, which is blessed on the feasts of the Saints and in commemoration of the faithful departed to celebrate their victory in Christ. It is sometimes shared at the door of the katholikon immediately after the Service; other times it is served in the refectory.

KOMVOSCHINION   The prayer cord—the Russians call it *tchotki*—used by the monks, and by lay people also, in their prayers, especially when they are praying the Jesus Prayer, not so much to keep count, although that is part of it, as to facilitate attention. It is usually made of black wool, although sometimes strands of other colors or colored beads are added for decoration. In a properly made cord, each knot is very carefully and prayerfully made, with much symbolism going into its construction. The usual cord has one hundred knots separated into sections of twenty-five by beads, having an appendage of a woven cross. A full cord of three hundred knots might be used in the cell and a smaller one of fifty in the pocket.

KONSTAMONITOU   One of the twenty ruling monasteries of the Holy Mountain and the most hidden, lying in the center of the peninsula, toward the north.

KOUTLOUMOUSIOU   One of the twenty ruling monasteries of the Holy Mountain, lying just a few minutes outside of the capital, Karyes.

KYRIAKON   The principal church of a skete where the monks usually gather on Saturday evening and on the eves of great feasts for the celebration of the Agripnia.

KYRIE   The Greek word for "Lord," heard constantly in the litanies *Kyrie eleison* (Lord, have mercy).

LATROUN   A Cistercian monastery in Israel, midway between Jerusalem and Tel Aviv.

LECTIO   A Latin expression commonly used by Western monks, either alone or in combination as *lectio divina* (divine reading) to refer to that kind of prayerful reading undertaken to lead the monk into contemplative prayer.

LENT OF THE VIRGIN   Fifteen days of fasting preceding the Feast of the Dormition (August 15).

LITI The outermost part of the monastic church. Besides an enclosed porch, the church has three distinct sections: the liti, or
esonarthex, where the Little Hours are celebrated, primarily a
place of preparation; the nave with its choirs, the Kingdom of
Heaven presided over by the Pantokrator in the dome, and the
angels and saints frescoed on the walls; and the sanctuary, or
holy place, separated from the nave by the icon screen. The liti
is usually separated from the nave by a full wall, with a central
door called the "royal door" and one or two small side doors.
The royal door is closed for the Little Hours and opened only
when it is time for the community to enter into the nave for
Orthros, or Vespers.

LITTLE HOURS The minor prayer Services which belong to the daily
Services. In the West they are called Prime, Tierce, Sext, and
None. Among the Orthodox these are referred to simply as the
First, Third, Sixth, and Ninth Hours. (Compline is also con-
sidered a Little Hour; see Apodeipnon.)

LITTLE SCHEMA See Great Schema.

LITURGY A term used in the West to refer to the whole of the public worship of the Church, but among the Orthodox, and in this
journal, it refers to the Eucharistic Sacrifice only.

MANDYAS The very ample outer cloak that makes up part of the
Great Schema. It is worn by the monks when performing certain services in the katholikon. There is also a mandyas worn by
both Bishops and Archimandrites, not unlike the copes familiar
in the West. It is usually made of violet silk with gold banding
and little bells attached to the bottom.

MARIAWALD A Cistercian abbey in West Germany.

MEGISTI LAVRA The senior of the twenty ruling monasteries of the
Holy Mountain, the founding of the monastic republic being
computed from the establishment of this monastery by Saint
Athanasios in 963. While its frescoes, icons, and library are
among the best on the Holy Mountain, it is today a dwindling,
idiorrhythmic community, far overburdened by tourists, with little hope for the future apart from a small procenobitic group.

MESONYKTIKON See Midnight Services.

METANIA A ceremonial act of reverence. Among the Orthodox the
different kinds of ceremonial reverences are distinguished as follows: (1) proskynesis—bowing down and touching the ground

with one hand; (2) gonyklisia—going down on both hands and both knees; (3) metania. There are two kinds of metanias: great —going down on hands and knees and touching the ground with the forehead—and little—a low bow of the body.

METEORA   A medieval monastic center in the middle of Greece, near Trikala, where twenty-four monasteries were built on extraordinary granite outcroppings. Today it is largely uninhabited by monks and is chiefly a tourist attraction. There seems to be some revival of monastic life in the largest monastery, in spite of the fact that most of the monks transferred to Simonos Petras in 1973.

METOKION   Any monastery or convent outside the Holy Mountain that has some relationship of dependency with an autonomous monastery on the Mountain.

MIDNIGHT SERVICES   The first Service celebrated by the monks when they arise, actually sometime after the middle of the night. It is a relatively brief Service celebrated in the liti.

NEW SKETE   A skete dependent on Aghiou Pavlou and located just to the south of it. There is also a Catholic New Skete in New York State.

OCTAVE   The seven days following a great feast, during which the feast is continuously celebrated.

OFFICES   A Western expression indicating the complexus of prayer services that mark out the hours of the day and night for monks and others who join in this official prayer of the Church.

ORMILIA   A village in south-central Chalkidiki. In this book, the reference is to the Convent of the Annunciation, which is a metokion of Simonos Petras and is located in the region of this town.

ORTHROS   One of the principal Services prayed by Orthodox, usually at dawn.

OURANOUPOLIS   A small village, formerly called Prosphori, now something of a tourist center, which grew up around an old tower that belonged to the Monastery of Vatopedi. It is about a mile from the Athonite boundary. When Greece was celebrating the millennium of the founding of the monastic republic of Mount Athos in 1963, the national highway was extended to this village. Since that time, the normal way to approach the

Holy Mountain is to drive to this point and then take a boat to Daphni.

PALAMITE Referring to Saint Gregory Palamas (1296–1360), the monk who has perhaps the greatest influence on modern Greek Orthodox spirituality and theology. He came to the Holy Mountain in 1316 and lived successively at Vatopedi, Megisti Lavra, in a cave near Simonos Petras, and then as Hegumen of Esphigmenou. He came to fame in his debates with a Western monk, Barlaam, concerning the doctrine of the Uncreated Light and the hesychast practice of the Jesus Prayer. Saint Gregory was subsequently appointed Archbishop of Thessaloniki. The best study of him available in English is George Lawrence's translation of John Meyendorff, *A Study of Gregory Palamas* (London: Faith Press, 1964).

PANAGHIA Mary, the Mother of God, the All Holy One, who never knew the stain of any sin.

PANTOKRATOR The majestic image of Christ as the creator of all.

PANTOKRATOROS One of the twenty ruling monasteries of the Holy Mountain, on the northern side of the peninsula. It is idiorrhythmic.

PARAKLISIS The Office of Comfort, or Strengthening, usually celebrated in the monasteries on the Holy Mountain on fast days before the meal. On Mondays and Wednesdays and during the Lent of the Virgin (the two weeks preceding the Feast of the Dormition), it is directed to the Holy Virgin; on Fridays, to the patron of the particular monastery.

PATMOS A small island belonging to Greece, a short distance off the west coast of Turkey. It was here that Saint John the Evangelist was exiled and wrote his Book of Revelation.

PENDELI An Orthodox monastery on the northeast outskirts of Athens, well known for its conference center.

PHILOKALIA A collection of ascetical and mystical writings from the monastic Fathers, put together in five volumes by Macarios of Corinth and Saint Nikodimos of the Holy Mountain in the eighteenth century.

PHILOTHEOU One of the twenty ruling monasteries of the Holy Mountain, high up in the hills on the northern side of the peninsula, with a road down to the port of Iviron. It is noted for the strictness of its life and its fidelity to Palamite spirituality.

POLYELOS   The "all-merciful," that portion of Agripnia which comprises singing of Psalms 134 and 135.

PORTATISSA   The "door keeper," the title of a famous icon of the Holy Virgin kept in a special chapel by the gate of Iviron.

PRODROMOU   The only Romanian skete on the Mountain, located in the northeastern corner of the peninsula. It is dedicated to Saint John the Baptist.

PRO-HEGUMEN   A resigned Hegumen. In an idiorrhythmic monastery he often plays an important role in the affairs of the house.

PROPHETI ILIOU   The Prophet Elijah's, a former Russian skete dependent on the Greek monastery Pantokratoros. The skete's kyriakon is the second largest church on the Holy Mountain. Today the skete is inhabited by a small group of American monks who, however, celebrate the Services in Slavonic, according to the typicon of their Russian predecessors.

PROSPHORA   Small loaves of bread, marked with a seal, specially baked for use at the Liturgy.

PROTATON   A church in the center of Karyes, the oldest on the Holy Mountain, having served the Holy Community and its predecessor, the original Synaxis, for nearly ten centuries. The frescoes that cover the walls of the Protaton were painted in the fourteenth century by a celebrated artist from Thessaloniki, Panselinos.

PROTHESIS   A ceremony performed by a priest before the celebration of the Liturgy at a table on the left side of the sanctuary, during which he prepares the bread and wine that is to be used at the Liturgy. Part of the Prothesis involves cutting small pieces of bread and placing them on the diskos while asking the Lord to remember particular intentions. In this way the priest brings the particular intentions of the faithful to the Liturgy.

PROTOS   The monk chosen each year to head the Holy Government.

RASON   An outer garment, reaching to the ankles and having wide sleeves, which is worn by the married clergy as well as the monks. For the monks and for the Greek clergy it is always black. Its origins are traced back to the garment worn by Turkish officials in court in the High Middle Ages.

RASOPHORE   A novice who has received the rason but has not made his vows. The extent to which he is really a monk is interpreted differently by different traditions. Most monasteries do not have rasophores but immediately admit novices to full monastic profession.

ROPE   A popular way of referring to the komvoschinion.

RUSSIKO   See Aghios Panteleimonos.

SEMANTRON   A board, usually about eight feet long and six to ten inches wide, which a monk carries about the monastery, striking it with a wooden mallet to announce the Services. A very particular rhythmic stroke is employed, which engraves itself in the memory of any visitor to the Holy Mountain. Tradition says this is the way Noah called the animals into the ark. There are larger semantrons of wood and small ones of metal, usually hung near the entrance of the katholikon, which are also used.

SERVICES   This is the word usually employed by the Orthodox to refer to those prayer services laid out by the typicon. Its usage is similar to the Western expression "Offices."

SIMONOS PETRAS   One of the twenty ruling monasteries of the Holy Mountain and in its number of monks probably the largest. It is situated about seven miles by road southeast of Daphni, perched on an immense granite crag, a thousand feet above the sea.

SKETE   A monastic household or community, usually quite small, dependent on a monastery, or a grouping of such households.

SKOUPHOS   The black, cylindrical head covering that is worn constantly by Orthodox monks of Greece and some other countries.

SNOWMASS   A small Cistercian monastery in the Colorado Rockies, not far from the peak of the same name. It is a daughter house of Spencer.

SOSTIKON   The robe of the Orthodox monk, not unlike the Western cassock.

STARCHESTVO   A practice whereby the monk reveals to his Spiritual Father all his inner thoughts, intentions, and temptations and receives his counsel. It is usually done daily, at least at the beginning of monastic life, and is a most effective means to move toward inner quiet and purity of heart.

STARETZ   The name the Russians give their Spiritual Father.

STAVRONIKITA   One of the twenty ruling monasteries on the Holy Mountain, a few miles north of Karyes, on the northern coast of the peninsula.

THE SYNOD   The common expression used to refer to the Russian Orthodox Church-Outside-of-Russia, which is headed by Metropolitan Philaret and ruled by a synod of Bishops in communion with him. This Church does not accept the authority of the Patriarch of Moscow, nor accept communion with him nor with most other Orthodox Churches.

SYNODIKON The room in an Orthodox monastery where the monks gather for meetings.

THESSALONIKI Salonica, the second largest city in Greece and capital of northern Greece.

TRAPEDZA The refectory of the monastery, often very elaborately frescoed.

TRE FONTANE A Cistercian abbey on the outskirts of Rome.

TROPARIUM An antiphon or text sung at the Liturgy or Services commemorating a particular feast or saint.

TYPICON The rule of the particular monastery which spells out the details of the daily life and especially the way in which the Services will be conducted. There is also a common typicon for the whole Mountain.

UNIAT CHURCHES Those Churches of the Eastern or Byzantine rite which are in union with the Pope, the Bishop of Rome, as the Vicar of Christ on Earth and Head of the Church.

VATOPEDI One of the twenty ruling monasteries of the Holy Mountain. An idiorrhythmic community, it is reputed to be one of the richest and, in discipline, one of the most relaxed. It is on the northern coast of the peninsula.

VESPERS One of the principal Services of the day, celebrated usually a couple of hours before sundown.

VLATADON An Orthodox monastery, situated on the top of the hill overlooking Thessaloniki, which now houses an Institute for Patristic Studies.

XENOPHONTOU One of the twenty ruling monasteries of the Holy Mountain, on the southern coast of the peninsula.

XEROPOTAMOU One of the twenty ruling monasteries of the Holy Mountain, located on the road from Daphni to Karyes.

ZEALOTS The name given to those Orthodox who have severed relations with the Patriarch of Constantinople and those in communion with him because of his alleged heresies, especially in the area of ecumenism. At the present time there is only one zealot monastery on the Holy Mountain, Esphigmenou. Although it is technically one of the ruling monasteries, it has broken off relations with the others and generally ignores the Iera Kinotis and has joined the Greek schismatic church, the Old Calendarists. There are also many zealots in the sketes. In principle, zealots close themselves off from any contact with non-Orthodox, save perhaps a certain amount of polemical debate, but in practice they show a kind and gracious if firm hospitality toward such visitors.

ZOGRAPHOU One of the twenty ruling monasteries of the Holy Mountain, rather remotely situated in the hills. It is inhabited largely by monks from Bulgaria and the Services are conducted in Slavonic.